Ghislaine Thesmar in Pierre Lacotte's production of the celebrated Taglioni ballet, *La Sylphide*.

The Paris Opéra Ballet

Ivor Guest

ALSO BY IVOR GUEST

Napoleon III in England
The Ballet of the Second Empire
The Romantic Ballet in England
Fanny Cerrito
Victorian Ballet Girl
Adeline Genée
The Alhambra Ballet
La Fille mal gardée (editor)
The Dancer's Heritage
The Empire Ballet
A Gallery of Romantic Ballet
The Romantic Ballet in Paris
Dandies and Dancers
Carlotta Zambelli
Two *Coppélias*
Fanny Elssler
The *Pas de Quatre*
Le Ballet de l'Opéra de Paris
The Divine Virginia
Letters from a Ballet-master
Adeline Genée: a pictorial record
Adventures of a Ballet Historian
Designing for the Dancer (contributor)
Jules Perrot
Gautier on Dance (ed. and trans.)
Gautier on Spanish Dance (ed. and trans.)
Dr John Radcliffe and his Trust
Ballet in Leicester Square
The Ballet of the Enlightenment
Ballet under Napoleon

The Paris Opéra Ballet

Ivor Guest

DANCE
BOOKS
Alton

First published in 2006 by Dance Books Ltd
The Old Bakery
4 Lenten Street
Alton
Hampshire GU34 1HG

Copyright © Ivor Guest 2006
ISBN: 1 85273 109 5

A CIP catalogue record for this book is available from the British Library

Printed and bound in Great Britain by Latimer Trend and Company Ltd, Plymouth, Devon

Contents

Preface		1
Chapter 1.	The Cradle of the Classical Dance	5
Chapter 2.	The Virtuosi of Rococo	13
Chapter 3.	Noverre	23
Chapter 4.	The Dominance of the Gardels	31
Chapter 5.	The Romantic Heyday	41
Chapter 6.	Romanticism in Decline	53
Chapter 7.	The Decadence	61
Chapter 8.	A Time of Transition	69
Chapter 9.	The Lifar Years	81
Chapter 10.	A New Strategy Emerges	95
Chapter 11.	Nureyev and After	105
Appendix		
List of Ballets produced at the Paris Opéra		117
Principal dancers (étoiles) of the Opéra		136
Guest Artistes with the Ballet of the Opéra		140
Ballets performed at the Opéra more than 100 times		143
Index		145

Illustrations

Frontispiece: Ghislaine Thesmar in *La Sylphide*.

Between pages 58 and 59

1. Jean-Baptiste Lully.
2. Pierre Beauchamp.
3. Louis Pécour.
4. Marie-Thérèse Subligny.
5. Françoise Prévost.
6. Marie-Anne Cupis de Camargo.
7. Marie Sallé.
8. Anne Heinel.
9. Louise Madeleine Lany.
10. Jean-Georges Noverre.
11. Maximilien Gardel.
12. Pierre Gardel.
13. Marie Gardel.
14. Emilie Bigottini.
15. Geneviève Gosselin.
16. Marie and Paul Taglioni in *La Sylphide*.
17. Fanny Elssler dancing the *cachucha*.
18. Carlotta Grisi as Giselle.
19. *Giselle*, Act I.
20. Arthur Saint-Léon and Fanny Cerrito in *Le Violon du Diable*.
21. Carolina Rosati in *Le Corsaire*.
22. Emma Livry and Louis Mérante in *La Sylphide*.
23. Marfa Muravieva in Act II of *Giselle*.
24. Adèle Grantzow.
25. Giuseppina Bozzacchi as Swanilda in *Coppélia*.
26. Eugénie Fiocre as Frantz in *Coppélia*.
27. Scenes from the first production of *Sylvia*.
28. Rita Sangalli in *Yedda*.
29. Rosita Mauri.
30. Carlotta Zambelli.

Between pages 90 and 91

31. Lycette Darsonval with Paulette Dynalix and M. Blanc in Albert Aveline's *La Tragédie de Salomé*.
32. Alexandre Kalioujny and Tamara Toumanova in *Le Baiser de la fée*.
33. Balanchine's *Palais de crystal*.
34. Lifar's *Les Mirages* with Michel Renault, Yvette Chauviré and Paulette Dynalix.
35. Nina Vyroubova and Serge Lifar as Arzigogola and Scapin in *Les Fourberies*.
36. *La Belle Hélène*, John Cranko, Yvette Chauviré and Michel Renault.
37. Cyril Atanasoff in *La Damnation de Faust*.
38. Claude Bessy with Gene Kelly during the rehearsals of the latter's *Pas de dieux*.
39. Wilfride Piollet in Maurice Béjart's *Les Noces*.
40. Jacqueline Rayet and Jean-Pierre Franchetti in Maurice Béjart's *Webern Opus V*.
41. Rudolf Nureyev and Carolyn Carlson in Glen Tetley's *Tristan*.
42. Jacqueline Rayet, Christiane Vlassi, Georges Piletta, Nanon Thibon and Claire Motte in Roland Petit's *Turangalila* to Messiaen's symphony of that name.
43. Zizi Jeanmaire and Michaël Denard in Roland Petit's *La Symphonie fantastique*.
44. Michaël Denard in Maurice Béjart's *L'Oiseau de feu*.
45. Jean Guizerix and Dominique Khalfouni in Yuri Grigorovich's *Ivan le terrible*.
46. Ghislaine Thesmar and Pierre Lacotte in the latter's reconstruction of *Coppélia*.
47. Maurice Béjart rehearsing *La IXe Symphonie*, with Élisabeth Maurin.
48. Roland Petit during a rehearsal of *Clavigo*.
49. *Raymonda*, choreography by Rudolf Nureyev, after Marius Petipa. Aurélie Dupont, Jean-Guillaume Bart.

Illustration credits

1 - 30 Collection of the author, Bibliothèque-musée de l'Opéra, Bibliothèque Nationale de France
31, 32, 33, 35 Roger Viollet/Lipnitzki
34, 36, 38 Sipa Press/S. Lido

Cover & frontispiece, 37, 39, 40, 43, 44, 46 Colette Masson
41, 42, 45 Daniel Cande
47, 48, 49 Jacques Moatti

PREFACE

The Ballet of the Paris Opéra is a company of legend. As with every other legend, it has had its brilliant chapters and its sombre chapters. When I came to the Opéra in 1969, its ballet was just emerging from one of its less brilliant periods. Heir to a brilliant past, it had passed through many phases since the beginning of the twentieth century, and in the wake of Serge Lifar's departure was then in a period of stagnation.

But, under the direction of Raymond Franchetti, a revival was soon under way. Based on a healthy artistic policy of open programming, and strengthened by a modernisation of the training made possible by the appointment, in 1972, of Claude Bessy as head of the School of Dance, the ballet was successfully undergoing a rapid transformation. Rolf Liebermann had infused it with a breath of rigour and modernisation.

Nevertheless, public opinion in the wider world remained negative. Both a glorious past, which few seemed prepared or desirous to recall, and a revitalising present were buried in a similar scorn. Even the period of revival that had been initiated by Serge Lifar and Jacques Rouché was the object of hostile judgements.

No longer was Paris regarded as the Mecca of the dance. Now New York, London and Leningrad were contending for supremacy. The Anglo-Saxon centres had eyes only for their own ballets, and their leading choreographers declined every invitation to come and work with our company.

Rolf Liebermann, who had been Administrator of the Opéra since 1973, was accused of having no liking for the ballet. Again, rumour was refuted by fact. In a single season, Merce Cunningham, invited by Michel Guy to take part in the Autumn Festival, worked for the company for the first time; George Balanchine returned to the Opéra after many years of sulking; and Jerome Robbins staged his first ballet at the Palais Garnier for the pupils of the School in a memorable programme in honour of Stravinsky. And Carolyn Carlson made a shattering entrance upon the scene, opening with her Groupe de Recherche Théâtrale de l'Opéra de Paris (GRTOP), the first creative workshop of avant-garde choreography in the heart of the great '*Maison*'.

It was necessary to give the lie to those detractors who, suffering from a typically French disease, spread the word that the grass was greener in other fields. All this was undermining the work of the dancers and their environment, and isolating them. Moreover, this was the time when Maurice Béjart accused the Opéra of being 'the tomb of the unknown dancer'! I was then Rolf Liebermann's assistant, and the ballet fell under my jurisdiction. Every day I was given the opportunity of working with Raymond Franchetti and Gérard Mulys, who was then the ballet administrator, and to follow the work of the dancers. The injustice seemed to me all the more insulting as I watched their efforts. It then struck me that the story needed to be told so that, by recalling the past, pride in the present and confidence in the future would be restored. But at that time no book existed that traced the three centuries of the Paris Opéra's existence.

Once the decision to publish a book had been made, the question arose of seeking an author. For me the answer was clear, for Ivor Guest was already recognised as one of the great specialists on the history of the classical dance. He had to his credit an abundant bibliography, concentrated particularly on the French ballet, which he had studied in great detail, spanning a very long period from the eighteenth to the twentieth century. The fact that he was a British subject merely confirmed me in this choice, for he would place us beyond the reach of any accusation of *parti pris* or chauvinism.

Ivor Guest's first visit to the Bibliothèque-Musée de l'Opéra goes back to the end of the Second World War, when he entered its portals in the uniform of the Allied Forces. For more than half a century now he has been at home there, completing his research in all the great institutions of French conservation, with whose holdings he is admirably conversant – in particular the Bibliothèque Nationale, the Archives Nationales and the Bibliothèque de l'Arsenal. Ivor Guest's passion extends to the dance of the present day, and he follows closely the most recent choreographic developments both in Europe and in the United States.

He was good enough to accept my offer on the spot, and carried out his task with enthusiasm and dedication, producing a history of the Ballet de l'Opéra with broad brush-strokes yet without major omissions, in some 300 pages. The French publishers, Editions Flammarion, were pleased to undertake the publication and distribution of this work, even though it did not then fall within the boundaries of any of their collections. Furthermore, they acceded to my request to publish the book at a very low price so that it would be accessible to the greatest number of readers. This little book has now become a classic. Soon out of print, it was reprinted, and that reissue in turn was soon exhausted. Then, at the beginning of the third millennium, Flammarion again agreed to work with the Opéra to have the book brought up to date. And now, the specialist English publisher, Dance Books, has produced the first edition in the author's native language.

Ivor Guest was delighted to bring his original text up to date, revising it and adding two new chapters to bring the narrative as far as the dawn of the twenty-first century. In it he pays tribute to the activity of the *maîtres de ballet* who have succeeded Serge Lifar, and particularly to that of Rudolf Nureyev, in all areas that relate to the company – both in the development of the repertory and in the construction and renovation of the buildings in which the dancers have to work.

Preface

The development of the ballet branched into a new field of activity when the Opéra Bastille was opened. Numerous series of performances given in this building, which had originally been conceived for operatic performances but which has proved to be a perfect frame for choreographic works, have enabled the ballet to broaden its audience to a remarkable degree.

Without frills or hyperbole, but by setting forth the facts with professional rigour, this book pays homage to the long chain of generations of dancers, choreographers, ballet-masters, teachers and directors who, down the centuries, have fashioned the history of the Ballet de l'Opéra de Paris, and frequently the very history of dance itself. They are too numerous for all their names to be recorded in the text, but an appendix lists all the choreographic works presented at the Opéra since 1669. In their factual dryness – a title, a few names (of composer, choreographer, and scenery and costume designers) and the date of the first performance – the tables in this appendix constitute a monument erected against oblivion. Nor are these lists final, for they will expand as the programmes of future seasons add further stones to the edifice. The present work may have been completed and published, but already the next chapter is in course of preparation in the children's classes of the School of Dance, where the stars of tomorrow are being formed.

To conclude, it is my privilege to pay tribute to the work of Brigitte Lefèvre, Director of Dance, Claude Bessy, Director of the School of Dance, Patrice Bart, *Maître de ballet* attached to the Direction of Dance, and to the *étoiles* of today – Aurélie Dupont, Marie-Agnès Gillot, Agnès Letestu, Elisabeth Maurin, Clairemarie Osta, Laëtitia Pujol, Jean-Guillaume Bart, Kader Belarbi, Laurent Hilaire, Manuel Legris, Nicolas Le Riche, José Martinez – the *premiers danseurs* and the *corps de ballet* of the Opéra, to all of whom these lines are dedicated.

Hugues R. Gall
Director of the Opéra National de Paris
Paris, March 2004

I

The Cradle of the Classical Dance

The Paris Opéra is, in a true sense, the cradle of the classical dance. For it was there, in its early years, that the technique introduced from Italy in the sixteenth century was moulded and refined into the *noble* style that was to add a new elegance and distinction to theatrical dancing and be recognised universally as a predominantly French accomplishment. No other dance company can boast a tradition as long as that of the Opéra. Its ballet has roots that stretch back to the court ballets of Louis XIV and, earlier, of Catherine de Medici and the last Valois kings, and that have grown and spread in an unbroken development, which continues today with undiminished vigour. Unlike some other opera houses, the Paris Opéra, as these pages will show, is as much a centre of ballet as it is of opera.

It was from the august patronage of Louis XIV, *le roi soleil,* that dance first acquired the dignity and respect that has surrounded the art of ballet ever since. The formation of the Académie Royale de Danse in 1661 was the first overt expression of royal concern for the standards of dance teaching. While this institution was to have little influence on the development of theatrical dancing, the very fact of its establishment announced the importance that dancing had acquired in the entertainments of the court and the capital. Much more significant was the creation by letters patent in 1669 of the Académie d'Opéra – the seed from which the Paris Opéra has sprung. This second royal initiative was to bring about the transference of the hybrid form of spectacle that then went under the name of ballet from the court to the wider arena of the public stage. It was also to establish theatrical dancing as a profession in its own right.

For nearly a century the French court had been an active centre of the dance, which had been a dominant feature of its diversions ever since Catherine de Medici had sponsored the celebrated *Balet Comique de la Royne* in 1581. Successive kings had developed the genre of court ballet according to their own tastes or those of their advisors until it attained its apogee during the youth and early manhood of Louis XIV. The glorification of the prince was the *raison d'être* of the Renaissance court festivity, of which the French *ballet de cour* became a supreme example in the years following the rebellions of the Fronde. As Louis XIV consolidated his political mastery by establishing a court of unparalleled brilliance, the court ballets took on a heightened meaning and a new splendour. In these productions, in which operatic and dance elements existed side by side, a steady improvement in the standard of dancing became evident with the increasing use of professional performers. The focal figure, however, remained the king, who moved with superb elegance and, by personifying some allegorical character such as Apollo or the Sun King, conveyed the political message of his absolute authority.

The king took his dancing very seriously, returning to his chamber after his morning ride to take a lesson from his teacher, Maître Beauchamp. With this royal example, dancing was considered as essential an accomplishment for a gentleman as fencing. This attitude was to be a powerful stimulus to the development of ballet as a typically French art in the seventeenth and eighteenth centuries.

In time, what had been fitting in a youthful king became, inevitably, slightly ridiculous in a monarch who was losing his figure and growing increasingly preoccupied with affairs of state, and in 1670 Louis XIV made his final bow in a court ballet. His retirement deprived the court ballet of its main purpose and reduced it to an emasculated divertissement. However, it did not diminish the prestige that the dance had gained through royal support and the coming together, in the glorious final phase of the court ballet, of five remarkable men, all geniuses in their respective spheres: the composer Jean-Baptiste Lully, the ballet-master Pierre Beauchamp, the stage designers Giacomo Torelli and Carlo Vigarani, and Molière, actor and author of imperishable comedies.

The key figure in this development was Lully, a miller's son who had come to Paris as a boy from his native Florence to enter the service of the *'Grande Mademoiselle'*, the king's cousin. A few years later he was engaged as a dancer for the court ballets. The famous *Ballet de la Nuit*, in which the fourteen-year-old Louis XIV was to appear as the Sun King, was then in preparation. In no time the newcomer impressed the king with his gifts as a performer and a musician, and with royal favour he advanced rapidly from being a mere *baladin* to composing for the 'Twenty-four Violins', the select band that played at court balls, dinners and concerts. No one could have been more adroit at consolidating his position, and by the time he was thirty Lully was in sole command of all musical activities at the French court.

Lully's dance background enabled him to appreciate the gifts of another rising star in the firmament of the court ballet – Pierre Beauchamp, the son of one of the Twenty-four Violins, and an extraordinarily skilful arranger of dances. Born in 1631, and thus a year older than Lully, Beauchamp had grown up in a household that lived and breathed music and dancing. He acquired, possibly from his father Louis Beauchamp, an exceptional facility for the violin and the dance, and in 1648 appeared in a ballet at the Palais Royal in the presence of the king. His rise to eminence was swift; within a few years he was the king's personal dancing master, and his supremacy as a composer of dances was undisputed. In collaboration with Lully, the poet Benserade and the stage designers Torelli and Vigarani, Beauchamp was involved in the creation of most of the court ballets of the later 1650s and the 1660s. His services were also in demand for another type of work that was becoming popular at the court, the *comédie-ballet*.

The *comédie-ballet* was the creation of Molière, whose accession to the group of artists working for the court entertainments was a matter for no surprise, considering the varied nature of these spectacles. Unrivalled as a writer of comedies, Molière understood the effect that music and dance could add to his productions, and devised this new theatrical form in 1661, when he was invited by the minister of finances, Fouquet, to produce a comedy for a festival he was preparing at his château of Vaux-le-Vicomte in honour of the king. Aware of the royal passion for the dance, Molière conceived *Les Fâcheux*, a work that was part play and part ballet, the small number of dancers at his disposal making it necessary to interpolate the dance scenes as separate interludes in order to give them time to change costumes and rest. The king was as pleased with Molière's skill as he was offended by Fouquet's ostentation; the luckless minister found himself disgraced, while the playwright was commanded to present his work at Fontainebleau. More royal commissions followed, and for a few years a brilliant sequence of *comédie-ballets* were performed at court, culminating with the supreme example of the genre, *Le Bourgeois Gentilhomme*. For these works, Molière enjoyed the collaboration of Lully and Beauchamp; but he had no imitators, and the *comédie-ballet* was to die with him.

In the summer of 1669, when these court entertainments had reached their peak, Louis XIV granted a *privilège* to Pierre Perrin, authorising him to form an 'Académie d'Opéra en Musique et Verbe François' and giving him a virtual monopoly for a period of twelve years. The king had been impressed by Perrin's conception of fusing music and poetry to form a French school of opera; but in spite of royal support, nearly two years were to pass before the new institution was to present its first production to the public. This was *Pomone,* with a libretto by Perrin himself and music by Robert Cambert. The dances were arranged by Des Brosses, but two months before the run of performances ended, he was replaced by Beauchamp, who devised the dances for the next work, *Les Peines et les Plaisirs de l'Amour*.

Lully was meanwhile astutely biding his time. He observed the tensions and the financial wrangles that soon forced Perrin to sell shares in the enterprise, and, skilfully choosing the moment when Perrin had become thoroughly disenchanted, he purchased the *privilège* from him. The king, who did not establish academies light-heartedly, was anxious to bring order to the ensuing confusion, and in 1672 appended his signature at Versailles to a new *privilège*, authorising Lully to establish an 'Académie Royale de Musique'.

Installed in a hastily converted tennis court in the Rue de Vaugirard, the reconstituted Opéra was inaugurated in November 1672 with *Les Fêtes de l'Amour et de Bacchus,* a selection of extracts from works that Lully had composed for the court. The structure of the makeshift theatre was in a highly dangerous condition, but it lasted long enough for Lully, who a few months later was able to take advantage of Molière's death to manoeuvre the Opéra into the latter's theatre in the Palais Royal.

Throughout his administration of the Opéra, Lully monopolised its artistic activity to the extent of allowing no other composer's work to be heard there and working mainly with one librettist, Philippe Quinault. The content of the libretti, which included long passages of recitative, relegated the dance to a less important role than it had played in the court ballets. To a certain extent this development was dictated by necessity. There was no professional company available when the Opéra was formed, and while singers of professional standard, even virtuosi, could be found without much difficulty from those who sang in cathedrals and elsewhere, there was a dearth of passable dancers. A large proportion of the participants in the court ballets had been courtiers, who were not interested in adopting a theatrical career, even though the *privilèges* specifically permitted them to appear in operas without prejudice to their rank. To strengthen the nucleus of professional dancers who had been used for the court ballets, the Opéra had to seek reinforcements among the pupils of the dancing masters of Paris, whose main business was the teaching of amateurs. As a result, the small corps de ballet originally had to be composed of men. Although a few professional *danseuses* had appeared at court, none was taken into the ranks of the Opéra, and for ten years female parts were danced by boys *en travesti* – a subterfuge made less noticeable by the wearing of masks.

The mask was an almost obligatory accessory in a dancer's costume, a convention that was well established and accepted, and at this time by no means as absurd as it became a century later, when Noverre demanded its abolition. A dancer was not required to mime the narrative, for this was conveyed in song by others. As the Abbé de Pure had explained in his *Idées des spectacles anciens et nouveaux*, a dancer had to concentrate on physical transformation, which was achieved by adopting the carriage and attitudes of the god, nymph, shepherd or other character he was representing. The mask was supposed to assist in this transformation by indicating the character and, through its immobility, avoiding any distraction occasioned by the dancer's features. Not only was it obligatory in burlesque roles, where it augmented the effect of caricature, and in roles played *en travesti*, but it was worn also for *noble*, or serious, dancing. However, its use was apparently restricted to men, as it was in the *commedia dell'arte*, where acting with the mask had been brought to a high pitch of perfection. Indeed, the example of the Italian comedians, who were then a popular feature of the Parisian theatrical scene, reinforced this convention.

Lully's experience as a dancer stood him in good stead when composing dances for his operas. His minuets were written with a tautness that showed his understanding of the dance form, and some of his meditative dances had a grace and dignity that were in advance of their time. He and Beauchamp collaborated closely in the production of the dances, for both were dancers and both were musicians. Beauchamp was given a free hand in arranging dances for shepherds, nymphs and the like, but Lully considered himself more qualified to produce the mimed *entrées* essential to the action. He would demonstrate what he wanted with an energy and suppleness that revealed a profound understanding of Italian pantomime. It was thus in a very real sense that Beauchamp completed, with Lully and Quinault, the triumvirate which, over the next fifteen years, firmly established the foundations of the French school of opera, in which ballet was from the outset, and would remain, an essential element.

Under Beauchamp's direction the corps de ballet became steadily more proficient until, in 1681, it was possible to introduce professional *danseuses* to the stage of the Opéra for the first time. For this historic occasion Lully wrote the ballet *Le Triomphe de l'Amour*, in which the dance was considerably more prominent than in his earlier operas, or *tragédies lyriques* as they were generally described. The four ladies who stepped on to the stage in this work were led by Mlle de Lafontaine, the first ballerina of the Opéra, who became known as the 'Queen of the Dance'. The historian Castil-Blaze listed the others as Mlles Roland, Lepeintre and Fernon.

Pierre Beauchamp, who remained as composer of ballets until the year of Lully's death, 1687, was the architect of the Opéra Ballet. His claim to fame is not only as an exceptional arranger of dances, but equally as the teacher who trained and built up the original company of dancers. It was he who laid the foundations of the *noble* style that was to be the hallmark and glory of French ballet until the early nineteenth century. His clear, incisive mind enabled him to analyse the technique of dancing as it had developed in his day and to reduce the classroom exercises to a well-defined method. He was credited with establishing the five positions of the feet, and he laid down other rules that were to be universally accepted in the instruction of classical dancing.

He also invented an ingenious system of notating dances. In this he was encouraged by Louis XIV himself, who, recognising perhaps that the dance must be recorded if it was to merit the prestige of an academy, suggested the idea at Chambord in about 1674. To Beauchamp this was tantamount to a command, and he dutifully set to work devising a table of symbols and words to record dance movements. This was to provide the basis for the system that Raoul Feuillet developed and published in 1700, which was widely used throughout Europe in the eighteenth century. Beauchamp was incensed by what he regarded as a theft of his creative work, and tried unsuccessfully to prevent the publication.

Of Beauchamp the man, little is known. Saint-Léon, writing long afterwards but possibly relying on verbal tradition, described him as 'small, but lively and witty' and 'concise and sarcastic in repartee'. To his specialised knowledge of dancing and music he brought a wide understanding and appreciation of art, being the possessor of a remarkable private collection that included objects from Japan and paintings by Raphael, Veronese and Poussin. His acute sense of observation was remarked by the *Mercure Galant*:

To those who complimented him on the variety of his entrées, Beauchamp said that he had learned to compose the patterns for his ballets from the pigeons in his loft. He would go up there himself to give them their grain, and throw it to them. As the pigeons ran to the grain, the different patterns and the varied groupings they formed gave him ideas for his dances. It was said that as a dancer Beauchamp did not have much allure, but was full of vigour and fire; no one danced better *en tourbillon*, and no one has been able to make people dance better than he.

Lully's death in 1687, from blood poisoning resulting from a quack's treatment of an infected toe, unexpectedly deprived the Opéra of its presiding genius. In the same year, Beauchamp retired as composer of ballets, being succeeded by his pupil Louis Pécour, who retained the post until his death in 1729 – a tenure of forty-two years that has never been surpassed.

The Opéra under Lully had been a private and self-supporting enterprise, enjoying a royal monopoly but receiving no subsidy. After Lully's death it passed into the hands of his son-in-law Nicolas de Francine, who directed it with associates until 1714. Throughout this period, Lully's operas continued to form the foundation of the repertory, but now works by other composers were admitted. It was established that song and dance were both essential elements in an opera, but the proportions of these ingredients varied with the type of work: a ballet or an opera-ballet would contain a generous amount of dancing, while in the *tragédie lyrique* or the *pastorale héroique* emphasis was laid more on the singing. The day when opera and ballet were to become separate forms still lay in the future. The most successful composer working for the Opéra at the close of the seventeenth century was André Campra, whose *L'Europe galante* (1697) and *Le Carnaval de Venise* (1698) initiated the new form of opera-ballet. As the term implies, the dance element assumed added importance, but the most distinctive feature was that each act was an independent scene linked with the others only by a broad common idea. For the management, such a structure had the attraction of enabling programmes to be made up of successful fragments from different works without making nonsense of a dramatic narrative. Campra repeated this formula in his opera-ballets *Les Muses* (1703), *Les Fêtes vénitiennes* (1710), *Les Amours de Mars et de Vénus* (1713) and *Les Âges* (1718).

This growing prestige of the ballet could not have been achieved without a corresponding rise in the standards of performance. Although lacking Beauchamp's flair, Louis Pécour proved a worthy successor. He had established his superiority as a dancer early in Lully's time, when he and Louis L'Étang had been the leading dancers of the Opéra. Both excelled in the *noble* style, but Pécour was the more versatile, being proficient in other styles with equal grace, precision and lightness. At the time of Lully's death he had had some experience in composing dances for the court, but a much sterner test awaited him at the Opéra. In the judgement of an early historian, 'he had to exert all his powers to be a worthy successor to the master who had preceded him, but he accomplished this by the infinite variety and additional graces he gave to the ballets already composed by Beauchamp'. Like his predecessor, he became the dominant figure in the dancing world of Paris, not only fulfilling the task of composing ballets for the Opéra, but also arranging dances for the ballroom. It was said that his services were in such demand in high society, and the material rewards so great, that he somewhat neglected his theatrical duties. Indeed, he was regarded with such respect that he was able to mix with the great on terms of equality – to the extent, it was said, of sharing the favours of the elderly but seemingly immortal Ninon de l'Enclos with the Marshal de Choiseul. The two men passed one another in the lady's house one day, and the Marshal, mistaking the elegantly attired dancer for a fellow officer, enquired what corps he commanded. Pécour's reply was to pass into legend: '*Monseigneur, je commande un corps où vous servez depuis longtemps*' (Your honour, I command a body with whom you have served for a long time).

A selection from Pécour's choreography for the Opéra was recorded for one of the *Receuils*, which Feuillet periodically published using his system of notation. Here are preserved, in beautifully engraved track drawings, solo dances for Mlle Subligny, *pas de deux* for her and Balon, and dances for other members of the Opéra ballet that Pécour had arranged for *L'Europe galante*, *Le Carnaval de Venise* and other operas produced around the turn of the century – a unique treasure-trove of the theatrical dancing of that period.

Under Beauchamp and Pécour, a succession of talented dancers appeared to beguile the public. Both Beauchamp and Pécour were pre-eminent among the men in their youth, and they were in turn succeeded by two no less remarkable performers: Nicolas Blondy, the pupil and nephew of Beauchamp, and Claude Balon. Almost exact contemporaries, these two men entered the Opéra in the same year, 1691, and stimulated the public to a high pitch of enthusiasm by their rivalry. Blondy was praised as 'one of the finest dancers who has ever appeared' and 'the greatest dancer in Europe for the *danse haute*, the *entrées* of furies and characters', while Balon was admired for his 'infinite taste and prodigious lightness' and an expressive quality that had no equal. In particular, connoisseurs remarked on 'a certain air of tenderness which Balon put into his attitudes, particularly in *pas de deux*'.

These were days of unquestioned male supremacy. Encumbered by the heavy costumes of the time, the *danseuse* was still the lesser partner. Nonetheless, the acclaimed 'Queen of the Dance', Mlle de Lafontaine, a tall, well-proportioned woman who may have been the daughter of one of the king's violinists, established her supremacy by the nobility of her style, and enjoyed the privilege, shared only with Pécour, of composing her own *entrées*. Her successor was Marie-Thérèse de Subligny, who made her debut in 1688 and retired in 1708. An expressive dancer, she was partnered by both Blondy and Balon. Then, in 1699, there appeared a new star – Françoise Prévost, Blondy's pupil, who after her retirement as a dancer was to give valuable services as a teacher.

Meanwhile, in the corridors of the administration, a sorry farce of intrigue and insolvency was being played, as the heirs and successors of Lully manoeuvred incessantly for control of the theatre. Finally, in January 1713, the old king, in an attempt to bring order to this chaos, imposed regulations for running the Opéra which, if they did not cure the administrative ills, recognised the Opéra as an institution of state and an official expression of French culture. In particular, they laid down an establishment of performers that included twenty dancers, ten from each sex. The salaries of the men were somewhat higher than those of the women, the four principal male dancers being paid 1000 livres a year each and the two principal danseuses 900 livres. Pécour's salary as composer of ballets was fixed at 1500 livres, and 500 livres was to be paid to the *maître de salle de danse*. But the most significant innovation for the future of ballet was the formal establishment of the School of Dance, at which the pupils would receive free tuition. By regularising what previously had no doubt been haphazard arrangements for training the dancers, Louis XIV created the indispensable condition for maintaining a ballet company of the highest professional standard. It was his final legacy to the dance, crowning the efforts of those two illustrious teachers, Beauchamp and Pécour.

II

The Virtuosi of Rococo

The bells that tolled for the soul of the old king in 1715 were also ringing in a new age. Louis XIV was succeeded by his infant great-grandson, Louis XV, and society, taking its lead from the regent, the Duc d'Orléans, shrugged off the austerity of the previous reign and threw itself into a frenzied round of licence and pleasure. There was an immediate change of style that left no corner of life untouched, and the stately art-forms of baroque began to yield to the delicate tracery of rococo.

The cry of 'Long live the Regent who goes to the Opéra rather than to mass' expressed the relief of a war-worn society. The Opéra now found itself at the brilliant centre of Parisian social life. With its complement of desirable women who for the most part were willing to accept the protection of the highest bidder, it was found necessary to post sentries in the corridors leading to the dressing rooms to give the artists some protection from young noblemen and *abbés* in search of amorous adventure. Many of the audience had little respect for art. Often men would arrive in the theatre besotted with wine and bent on creating a disturbance – behaviour that was all too readily tolerated as fashionable high spirits. The Opéra was the playground of young bloods, who flocked there not only for the performances, but also for the masked balls which, from 1716, took place three nights a week from November to the end of Carnival. These balls proved an immediate success, offering opportunities for intrigue that were made even more enticing when the dancers of the Opéra began to feature in the *mascarades* and take part in the contredanses and minuets.

In tune with the style of the age, a lighter touch was to be observed in many of the new productions that were added to the repertory. While lyric tragedies with solemn mythological themes still made their appearance, it was the less substantial opera-ballet, with settings that often evoked distant lands – Italy, Spain, the Orient, even America – and with an increased content of dancing, that found the greatest favour with the public and the management. The opera-ballet form was to maintain its popularity until the second half of the century, as also was the custom of extracting individual acts and making up programmes of 'fragments'.

It was the composer Jean-Philippe Rameau who brought the genre of the opera-ballet to its highest pitch. His masterpiece, and the greatest work of this kind, was *Les Indes galantes* (1735). Its structure was typical. The linking idea was expressed in the prologue, in which the God of Love decides to abandon the war-obsessed youth of Europe for remoter lands. The acts that followed were individual love scenes set respectively in the Indies, Peru and Persia, each complete in itself and each introducing a spectacular effect – a shipwreck, the eruption of a volcano, a festival of flowers. A year after the first production a fourth act was added – 'The Savages', set in North America. That the dance was conceived as a prominent element in this and other opera-ballets by Rameau was evident from the care he devoted to the dances. Composing for dancers whose technique was becoming increasingly brilliant, he used a wide variety of dance forms, which he infused with a rich vitality and many subtle touches: gavottes and minuets with nostalgic undercurrents, solemn *loures* and *gigues* tempered with elegance, mingled in his scores with the more popular forms of *rigaudon*, *bourrée*, *tambourin*, *musette* and *contredanse*. His operas also included a number of movements composed for scenes calling for stage action rather than formal dancing, such as the *'entrée et combat figuré d'athlètes'* in *Castor et Pollux*.

The productions at the Opéra were still composed of song and dance in varying proportions, and the use of the term *ballet* in describing a work did not denote a conscious striving towards the *ballet d'action*, but rather evoked the form of the *ballet à entrée* once popular at the court. The dancers never played dramatic roles, but were introduced in slight dance scenes that all too often interrupted the emotional effect that was being been built up by the sung drama. It was the rule that ballets should be inserted in an opera, but their purpose never went beyond illustrating or reinforcing the action, which was expressed primarily in song or recitative. *'Faire entrer les danses'* was the requirement made of the librettist, and the term *entrées* was given to these interpolated dance passages.

There was little real collaboration between the composer or the librettist and the *maître de ballet*, the dance being considered as an adjunct to the piece rather than an integral part of the action. The *maître de ballet* was not treated as an equal. According to Noverre, he was usually handed a specification that gave no indication of the plot, and was required to compose his dances to airs composed without regard to the dramatic situation. Perhaps exaggerating a little to prove his point, Noverre imagined the following scenario as typical:

> Prologue – *passepied* for dancers representing Games and Pleasures, *gavotte* for the Laughs, and *rigaudon* for the Pleasant Dreams. First Act – march for the Warriors, second air for the same, *musette* for the Priestesses. Second Act – *loure* for the People, *tambourin* and *rigaudon* for the Sailors. Third Act – march for the Demons, lively air for the same. Fourth Act – *entrée* of Greeks and *chaconne*, not to mention Winds, Tritons, Naiads, Hours, Signs of the Zodiac, Bacchantes, Zephyrs, Shades and Fatal Dreams – for there is no end to them.

The delineation of character and the expression of strong passions had not yet entered the dancer's domain. He was still a long way from being presented as a true interpretative artist. Masks were still accepted without question, the audience finding their pleasure in the movement and style of the performer.

The first half of the eighteenth century was the age of the performer, as the second half was to be that of the choreographer. Under a succession of able ballet-masters – Pécour until 1729, Blondy until 1739, Antoine Bandieri de Laval until 1748 and Jean-Barthélemy Lany until 1769 – the *noble* style of French theatrical dancing was elaborated and skills developed in other genres that went far beyond the capabilities of the amateur in the ballroom. Inexorably, the theatrical dance was separating from the social form, and moving towards what it was to become well before the century's end – a discipline apart and exclusive to the professional theatre.

Spearheading this development, a series of brilliant stars succeeded one another on the Opéra stage. In 1714, the last year of Louis XIV's reign, a young male dancer faced his first audience. His elegant figure, the length of his limbs, and the astonishing harmony and nobility of his movements at once set him apart as an exceptional performer, and in time were to earn him the accolade of *'Le Dieu de la Danse'*. His name was Louis Dupré, but on account of his commanding stature and majestic style, he was more often called *'le grand Dupré'*. The poet Dorat described him in these eloquent lines:

> *Lorsque le grand Dupré, d'une démarche hautaine,*
> *Orné de son panache avançait sur le scène,*
> *On croyait voir un dieu demander des autels,*
> *Et venir se mêler aux danses des mortels.*[1]

Noverre appraised him more dispassionately as 'a beautiful machine in perfect order, but lacking a soul... His rare qualities gave him the air of a god. But he was always the same: he never varied his style; he was always Dupré.' The Paris public remained faithful to him throughout his long career. With his polished execution and majestic style, he was regarded as the very embodiment of the *danse noble*.

Casanova saw him in 1750, when he was well into his fifties, and left a vivid account of his charismatic presence:

> Suddenly, I heard the pit applaud the appearance of a tall, handsome dancer, wearing a mask and an enormous black wig that fell way down his back, and dressed in a robe, open in front and reaching to his heels. Patu *[Casanova's companion]* said to me almost reverently, 'It is the inimitable Dupré.' I had heard of him before, and became attentive. I saw that fine figure advance with measured steps and, reaching the front of the stage, slowly

---

[1] When the great Dupré, with haughty mien / and crowning plumes, advanced upon the stage, / it was as if one were seeing a god claiming worship, / and coming to take part in the dances of mortals.

raise his rounded arms, move them with grace, extend them, draw them in, shake his feet with precision and lightness, take a few small steps, perform a few *battements à mi-jambe* and a pirouette, and then disappear like a breath of wind. All this did not last half a minute. Applause and bravos broke out from every part of the house. I was astounded and asked my friend what it was all about.

'We are applauding the grace of Dupré and the divine harmony of his movements. He is now sixty *[sic]*, and those who saw him forty years ago say he is always the same.'

'What, has he never danced differently?'

'He cannot have danced better, for the *développement* you have seen is perfect, and what can there be above perfection?'

'Nothing, unless perfection is relative.'

'Here it is absolute. Dupré always does the same thing, and every day we think we are seeing it for the first time. Such is the power of beauty and excellence, sublimity and truth, that speaks to the soul. Dancing such as this is harmony itself; it is true dancing, of which you have no conception in Italy.'

At the end of the second act Dupré came on again, his face concealed by a mask, and danced to a different melody, but to my eyes doing the same as before. He immediately advanced to the front of the stage and stopped for a moment in a perfectly designed position. Patu wanted me to admire him, and I complied. Suddenly I heard a hundred voices from the pit crying, 'Oh, *mon Dieu, mon Dieu*, he is extending'. And in very truth he appeared to have an elastic body which, as he extended, grew longer.

For the first fifty years of the Opéra's history the male dancers exercised an uncontested supremacy, but in the 1720s they were challenged by two extraordinary young ballerinas who in style, temperament and the very approach to their art were so different that, although they were regarded as rivals, each was in fact supreme in her own sphere. As the brilliant exponent of technique, with all its new-found ornamentation, Camargo was the rococo ballerina *par excellence*, while Sallé, with her expressive graces, foreshadowed the rational attitude of the new school of thinkers known as the Philosophes.

Marie-Anne Cupis de Camargo caught the public's imagination on the very day of her Paris debut in May 1726. A raven-haired beauty of sixteen, and reputedly of noble birth, she had come from Brussels to study under Françoise Prévost, who presented her to the public in *Les Caractères de la danse*. Composed by Jean-Ferry Rebel, one of the king's Twenty-four Violins, this was a suite of contrasting dances, which Mlle Prévost may have herself arranged to show off her versatility. Having danced it many times with conspicuous success, she was unprepared for the extraordinary sensation that her young pupil caused. The more ardent enthusiasts in the audience could not be restrained from invading the stage to pay homage to the débutante. For sheer virtuosity, nothing like Camargo's dancing had been seen before: her *cabrioles* and *entrechats* were performed without the slightest effort. More impressive still was an indefinable artistry: a lightness of touch that concealed her strength, and a sensitive ear attuned to the slightest nuances in the music.

The adulation paid to her young pupil was very galling to Mlle Prévost, who insisted that the girl be relegated to the anonymous ranks of the *corps de ballet*. There Camargo had to bide her time, but another opportunity was not long in coming. One evening David Dumoulin was to perform a solo in a dance of demons, but when the orchestra struck up the air for his *entrée*, he was nowhere to be seen. On an impulse Camargo darted forward and improvised a brilliant solo to his music. The audience was enraptured; her triumph was complete. As might have been expected, Mlle Prévost was far from pleased, and to vent her spleen she refused to teach the girl an *entrée* that had been requested by the Duchesse de Bourbon. Happily, Nicolas Blondy was at hand to tell her to wipe away her tears and study under him instead.

Camargo reaped an obvious benefit from the acquisition of a male teacher, developing, under the counsels of Blondy, and later Pécour and Dupré, an attack and a nobility that enhanced her innate grace and lightness and her infectious gaiety. She soon eclipsed Mlle Prévost, from whom she had acquired, and was never to lose, a touch of piquancy that had been the older dancer's most appealing characteristic. As a contemporary recalled, 'she performed *gavottes, rigaudons, tambourines, loures,* all that were known as *"les grands airs"*, in their correct manner, with all the range of steps proper to them, for she had it all in her legs, and if she eschewed the *gargouillade*, it was only because she considered it unsuitable for a woman'. And no one else could dance the steps of the minuet as she did. There was, in this dance, one moment that her admirers could not savour too often – a mere crossing of the stage, from one side to the other and then back again, but performed with a deftness and grace of magical perfection.

The first true virtuoso ballerina to appear at the Opéra, Camargo inspired such enthusiasm as only male dancers had aroused previously. Her name became a household word: ladies shod themselves *à la* Camargo, and a *contredanse* called '*La Camargo*' became so popular as to be danced at society balls for the rest of the century.

The early years of her career coincided not only with progress in the technical accomplishment of the ballerina, but also with a significant development in costume. Fashion had recently introduced the pannier and lighter materials for the skirt, which the professional danseuse was to adopt, with the important variation from her society counterpart that the skirt was raised a few inches from the floor. Provocative though this may have seemed at a superficial glance, its consequences were to be much more fundamental, for it enabled the beaten steps that Camargo and her successors introduced to be admired and perfected, while the lighter costumes encouraged the *danseuses* to emulate their male companions and jump.

Casanova saw Camargo too when he was in Paris in 1750, and his friend Patu explained that she had been the first *danseuse* to dare to jump on the stage of the Opéra. He went on to add the intimate detail that she never wore knickers, but this was a misconception, for in her retirement Camargo stated unequivocally that she had always worn this necessary article of clothing, which had already been introduced at the time of her most brilliant successes. Camargo left the stage in 1751, the year after Casanova saw her, and died at the age of sixty in 1770.

Her great contemporary, Marie Sallé, came of very different stock and background, with gifts of quite another order. The daughter of a humble travelling player, she had begun her stage career at the fairground theatres in Paris, and in 1716, at the age of nine, had appeared in London, being billed as a pupil of Balon. During her second London season in 1717, she may well have been taken to see John Weaver's *Loves of Mars and Venus* at Drury Lane, one of the first attempts at conveying a complex, serious narrative in gesture and mime. If so, it conceivably had a significant influence on her artistic development, young though she was. From her experiences in London and the fairground theatres she acquired a style that, while being founded firmly on orthodox technique, was free from virtuosity and, most importantly, distinguished by a strongly developed gift for expression. Her unique talent was not lost on the Opéra, and in 1721, still no more than fourteen, she made an isolated appearance there, replacing an indisposed Mlle Prévost in an *entrée* in *Les Fêtes vénitiennes*. But as yet there was no opening for her, and 1725 found her in London again, now fully grown, dancing – unusually, with a male partner – in *Les Caractères de la danse* at Lincoln's Inn Fields Theatre and appearing in pantomime with John Rich. Not until 1727 was she formally engaged at the Opéra, where her successes coincided with some of the early triumphs of Camargo.

The extraordinary contrast between the styles of these two young dancers stirred strong passions in the audiences of the time, which split into two opposing factions. Even the highest in the land were affected by their rivalry; the King and Queen and the older members of the court preferred the graceful and modest dancing of Sallé, while the majority of the public were carried away by the virtuosity of Camargo. Poets addressed verses to the ballerinas, and even Voltaire deigned to speak of their individual talents in lines that may be hackneyed but describe their contrasting styles with illuminating brevity:

Ah, Camargo, que vous êtes brillante,
Mais que Sallé, grands Dieux, est ravissante!
Que vos pas sont légers, et que les siens sont doux!
Elle est inimitable et vous êtes nouvelle:
Les nymphes sautent comme vous,
Mais les Grâces dansent comme elle.[2]

But while Camargo's position was secure, Marie Sallé could not accustom herself to the intrigues of the Opéra, and more than once escaped to the freer atmosphere of London. At the Opéra she felt artistically stifled, for her desire to make theatrical dancing more expressive was only dimly understood there. In London, on the other hand, this aspect of her talent was well appreciated. There, at the new theatre in Covent Garden in 1734, she produced *Pigmalion*, a pantomime ballet in which the entire action was conveyed in movement and dance. She was even able to dispense with the pannier, and to appear 'without even skirt or corset, with her hair all flowing and in disarray, and without any headdress'. It was in this ballet, and the dramatic *Bacchus and Ariadne* that followed it, that she fulfilled her artistic aims most completely. While in London, she also danced in several operas by Handel, who recognised genius when he saw it and added a new prologue, *Terpsichore*, to *Il Pastor Fido* specially to bring out her expressive qualities.

On her return to Paris, Sallé found that Camargo had retired – temporarily, as it turned out – and Rameau's new opera-ballet, *Les Indes galantes*, was in preparation at the Opéra. In this she took the part of the Rose in the act of *Les Fleurs*, a 'graphic portrayal of the life and fate of flowers in a garden', in which 'the Rose, Queen of Flowers, dances in solitary state' and, after resisting the fury of the winds, finally receives the homage of the other flowers.

In later years, when Noverre was fulminating against the lack of intelligent themes in the dance productions at the Opéra, he cited as rare exceptions this act and two others in which Sallé appeared: the Turkish *entrée* in *L'Europe galante* and the *entrée*, *La Danse*, in Rameau's *Les Fêtes d'Hébé* (1739). In these works a new force was to be discerned that some decades later was to break through the conservatism of the Opéra and lead to the establishment of the independent *ballet d'action*.

Louis de Cahusac wrote a vivid description of Sallé's interpretative qualities in the *passecaille* in *L'Europe galante*:

We see her portraying a young odalisque or concubine. She is surrounded by her companions and rivals and displays all the grace and passion ex-

---

[2] Oh Camargo, how brilliant you are, / But Sallé, my goodness, is ravishing! / How light are your steps, but how gentle are hers! / She is inimitable, while you are novel. / The Nymphs leap like you, / but the Graces dance like her.

pected of a girl who has designs on her master's heart. Her dance is composed of all the pretty attitudes that can portray such desires. Gradually it grows livelier, and a whole range of feelings can be read in her expressions. She hovers between fear and hope, but at the moment when the Sultan gives the handkerchief to the favourite sultana, her face, her features, her whole bearing at once assume a different aspect. She rushes off the stage in that utter despair that is felt only by the most sensitive folk… This scene, full of art and passion, was devised entirely by the dancer. She had improved upon the framework of the librettist, and with this she rose above the level of ordinary performers and entered the select class of creative talents.

On a more restrained level, Rameau's new opera-ballet, *Les Fêtes d'Hébé*, presented her with another opportunity of displaying her gift for expression. The *entrée, La Danse,* was constructed on the theme of peasants vying with the gods for the favours of a shepherdess, and Sallé took the part of Terpsichore, who yields gradually to Mercury's request to take the shepherdess into her company of mortals. For her it was another triumph, yet surprisingly, only a few weeks after its first performance in 1739, she announced her intention to retire.

The reason for this resolve was believed to be the appearance of the Italian virtuoso Barbarina Campanini, a dancer of Camargo's school, but with a technique that was even more extraordinary. According to the *Mercure de France,* 'she performed *entrechats huit* with amazing speed', and a caricature by Hogarth revealed her exceptional elevation more vividly than any words could describe. Sallé had a gentle and sensitive nature, and this triumph of virtuosity on a stage where she had striven against odds for greater expression may have disheartened her. After retiring from the Opéra in 1740, Sallé accepted the occasional royal command to dance at Versailles or Fontainebleau, and for one season, in 1743, assisted in the production of ballets at the Opéra-Comique. That theatre's small company of dancers included an impressionable boy of sixteen who even then appreciated her artistic philosophy and never forgot this early contact: his name was Jean-Georges Noverre.

After the retirement of Camargo and Sallé, a younger generation of ballerinas rose to prominence, though none of them stirred the same enthusiasm. Mlle Puvignée *fille,* so known because her mother was also a dancer, entered the Opéra in 1743 and was a remarkable interpretative performer in the style of Sallé. It was an appropriate gesture when Louis XV awarded the '*pension baladine*', which Sallé had received until her death in 1756, to Puvignée, who retired to everyone's regret four years later. More in the tradition set by Camargo were Marie-Françoise Lyonnois and Louise-Madeleine Lany: they had entered the Opéra respectively in 1744 and 1748, and retired in the same year, 1767. Mlle Lany, sister of the *maître de ballet,* was a woman of great beauty who for many years was the mistress of the director of the Opéra. As a dancer she extended the limits of technical virtuosity with a precision and boldness that her predecessors had lacked. She performed *entrechats six* with great ease, and her only shortcoming was a lack of expressiveness, which Noverre attributed to nervousness resulting from the excessively harsh training to which her brother had subjected her.

At the half-century mark, in 1750, two main trends were developing within the ballet at the Opéra: an ever-increasing virtuosity and a growing awareness of the need for expression. The changes were there for all to see, and they did not please everyone. 'I have heard murmurs of discontent at the agility of modern dancing,' reported Cahusac. 'It is not right, people say, that women should dance in this manner. What is decency coming to? Oh for the good old days, oh for Mlle Prévost! She had turned-in feet and long skirts which we would still consider too short today.'

But time would not stand still, and by the mid-century Dupré had become an anachronism. When he retired at last, in 1751, his mantle was assumed by Gaétan Vestris, a Florentine dancer who had been trained as a burlesque dancer before adopting the *noble* style on being engaged at the Opéra, at the age of twenty, in 1749. Almost insufferably vain and arrogant, Vestris was a continual thorn in Lany's side. In 1754, after a scandalous incident when he drew his sword on the long-suffering ballet-master, he was arrested and incarcerated in the comfortable prison of Fort-L'Évêque, and then dismissed from the Opéra. But within a few months he was back, the indispensable favourite of the public… and also of scores of ladies in both high society and the world of gallantry, whose favours he accepted as of right. Anecdotes of his overweening vanity were legion. Coming off the stage one evening with the cheers still ringing in his ears, he offered his leg to an admiring pupil to kiss. Another day, when a lady inadvertently stepped on his foot in the gardens of the Palais Royal and enquired apologetically if she had hurt him, he replied: 'No, madame, but you have almost put the whole of Paris into a fortnight's mourning'. His view of his own importance was summed up in another superb remark: 'There are only three great men in Europe – the King of Prussia, Voltaire and myself'.

Gaétan Vestris, however, was much more than a strutting peacock, for with his Italian origins, and particularly his early experience in the burlesque style, he gave the *danse noble* a different flavour when he succeeded the stately Dupré. Dupré had performed his *entrées* with an emphasis on the purity of the movement, but Vestris added a sensual quality and an expressiveness that made the style much more acceptable to his generation. He was universally acclaimed as a worthy successor to the former '*Dieu de la Danse*', a title that was bestowed on him too after his brother, in a transport of enthusiasm, had cried out from the crowded pit in his thick Florentine accent: '*C'est le diou de la danse*'. The accolade was justly earned, for, on the evidence of Noverre, Vestris 'equalled his mentor in perfection and surpassed him in versatility and discrimination'. Behind his vain exterior a keen intelligence was at work. He stood at the threshold of a new era. By developing a powerful dramatic skill he was to play an important part in gaining acceptance for the *ballet d'action*, while at the same time maintaining the essential purity of the *danse noble*. Noverre was to be grateful for his support in promoting his ideas, but he recognised also that his retirement was 'a fatal blow to fine dancing which, deprived of that beautiful model, fell into extravagance'.

The Opéra was by now a venerable institution approaching its centenary, but the theatre that had been its home since 1673 had become a disgrace to the arts that were practised within its walls. Its entrance, reached by a dark cul-de-sac, was more appropriate for a prison than for an opera house. Inside, the aspect that met the spectator was no more edifying: the auditorium was low and narrow, its only apparent merit being that it was so ill-lit that much of the grime that virtually concealed the decorations could not be seen. During the Easter recess of 1763, 'the justice of God', as Voltaire expressed it, was visited upon the Opéra. At a time when happily the building was deserted, it caught fire from an exploding boiler in an adjoining apartment, and, despite all attempts to quench the flames, was reduced in a matter of hours to a smouldering heap of ashes. Early the following year the Opéra was temporarily established in the vast Salle des Machines of the Palace of the Tuileries, where it was to remain until the spacious new theatre in the Palais Royal was inaugurated in 1770.

III

Noverre

In 1760 there appeared a book that was to have a most profound effect on the development of ballet: *Les Lettres sur la danse et sur les ballets* by Jean-Georges Noverre. It was to become enshrined as the most celebrated classic in the literature of theatrical dancing, for in it Noverre proclaimed the message that dancing must become truly expressive if it was to gain acceptance as a serious art. He recognised that what he called a *ballet d'action* – a dance work that unfolded solely through dramatic movement expressing the relationship between the characters – could become a major theatrical form only if a number of essential reforms were carried out. The most important of these was the development of pantomime to express the theme intelligibly and, above all, to stir the emotions of the spectators. Furthermore, not only the dancing and the mime, but also the music, the scenery and the costumes had to be treated as component parts of the production. A *ballet d'action* had to be convincing in all its parts, and it was the task of the *maître de ballet* to coordinate all these components so as to create a work that could merit serious attention no less than a poem or a drama. For this, the ideal choreographer needed an array of gifts: taste, a fertile imagination, an acute power of observation, and a sound knowledge of music, geometrical forms and the techniques of stage machinery. In short, Noverre was advocating the emergence of the choreographer as a creative artist in his own right. It was a significant indication of the impact of his ideas that the term *choreography*, which previously had been taken to mean the notation of dance, began now to be used to embrace the process of creating a dance work for the stage.

Many of Noverre's criticisms were levelled specifically at the Paris Opéra, where the ballet was still what it had always been: seldom more than a fanciful ornament to an opera, having no real connection with the main theme. Connoisseurs and directors alike were firmly rooted in the traditions of the past, and seemed blind to the progress that had been made elsewhere in the development of the dance as an expressive theatre art. As an example, Noverre pointed to the retention of so many old works in the repertory, particularly the operas of Lully, whose dance music, once regarded as so charming, now seemed 'cold, tedious and devoid of character'. Noverre conceded that:

> It was, of course, composed at a time when dancing was restrained and the performers paid no attention to expression. Then it was all wonderful, the music was composed for the dance, and vice versa. But what was suitable then is no longer so: the steps have been multiplied, the movements are

quick and follow one another in rapid succession, there is an infinite number of *enchaînements* and variations of timing; the difficulties, the sparkle, the speed, the hesitations, the attitudes, the various positions – all this, I say, cannot be harmonised with the grave music and uniform intonation that characterise the works of the composers of old.

Here was the dilemma of the Opéra ballet in 1760: the dance was admired for its technical merit, but, as Diderot, one of the most advanced thinkers of his time, recognised, what ought to have been its essential purpose – the reflection of human passions – was disregarded.

In Noverre's eyes the most meaningless convention of all was the use of masks. To this he devoted the whole of his Ninth Letter. If ballet was to develop into the dramatic form he envisaged, the mask was all too obviously restrictive. 'Destroy the masks,' he argued, 'and we shall gain a soul, and be the best dancers in the world.' The costumes, too, cried out for reform: the panniers of the women needed to be drastically reduced to reveal the body more effectively, and the custom of dressing the *danseur noble* in a stiff *tonnelet* and Roman cuirass was clearly absurd if any regard was to be had for illusion.

Noverre could have pointed to other conventions at the Opéra that were no less ridiculous. There was, for example, the *défilé*. When the moment arrived for the ballet to begin, it was customary for the dancers to enter in procession and parade three times round the stage, the men with their arms crossed and the women fluttering their fans. Then again, the stage was not the exclusive preserve of the performers. Many of the spectators had their view obstructed by two rows of gentlemen seated in the '*balcons*' on either side of the forestage. Understandably, these men were frequently the butt of ribald and obscene remarks from the unruly mob that stood, tightly packed, jostling one another in the pit, but it was not until 1772 that the stage was finally cleared.

However, the Opéra had not been entirely untouched by the trend towards greater expression in the dance, although for many years this influence had penetrated only through the experience that some of its dancers acquired outside. Balon and Françoise Prévost, for instance, were never able to repeat at the Opéra their interesting experiment, carried out at one of the Duchesse du Maine's '*Grandes Nuits de Sceaux*' in 1714, of miming a scene from Corneille's tragedy, *Horace*. Louis Dupré may have been impressed when he went to London in 1717 to play Mars in Weaver's *Loves of Mars and Venus*, but he was given no opportunity to develop a dramatic side to his talent at the Opéra. By Sallé's time, it was possible for her to introduce some expression into her roles at the Opéra, but it was again in London that she fulfilled her aspirations most completely, in her ballet *Pigmalion* in 1734. Paris was intrigued by the reports of this novel work, but was to see it only at second-hand in a version by Sallé's friend, François Riccoboni, at the Comédie Italienne. This theatre, the home of the

Italian comedians, proved a natural nursery for the development of the dance divertissement with an injection of simple, and at times rollicking, pantomime. Its ballet-master, Jean-Baptiste De Hesse, produced a whole series of ballets in which he made use of the expressive body movements of the *commedia dell'arte*. At the same time, significant developments were taking place in Vienna, where in the 1740s Franz Hilverding produced a number of substantial dance dramas, and later, in 1761, his pupil Gasparo Angiolini collaborated with Gluck in the production of the ballet *Don Juan*. These were only some of the landmarks in a development that was taking place all over Europe, and that had now found a most persuasive spokesman in Noverre.

In 1760 the name of Noverre was little known in Paris. Apart from a brief spell at the Opéra Comique, where some years before he had produced several excellent, but hardly revolutionary, ballets, his experience had mostly been gained in London and the French provinces. Taking nothing for granted, he had reflected long and deeply on the problems of his art, and in the formation of his personal philosophy on the dance one of the strongest influences had been his friendship with David Garrick. Noverre was not alone among Frenchmen to be overwhelmed by the great English actor. The dramatist Charles Collé had been so amazed by Garrick's power of facial expression in the dagger scene from *Macbeth*, which he had seen the actor perform impromptu at a private dinner party, that he called it 'a kind of tragic pantomime'. This remark perhaps gives a clue to the source of Noverre's vision of transforming ballet into an independent dramatic form. In 1760, with his book just published, Noverre went to Stuttgart, where the opportunity awaited him of realising his ideas to the full. The reigning Duke of Württemberg, Charles-Eugene, was prepared to spend on the theatre a large part of the immense fortune that poured into his treasury for the hiring of troops to France. The dance owed much to his extravagant folly, because the six years that Noverre spent in Stuttgart gained him international fame and brought many celebrated dancers under his influence. Among these was Gaétan Vestris, who spent several months in Stuttgart each year, and was intelligent enough to absorb the new ideas that Noverre was putting into practice.

Gaétan Vestris succeeded Lany as *compositeur et maître de ballets* at the Opéra in 1770. He was not an inspired choreographer, but he had learnt valuable lessons during his summers in Stuttgart, and at the outset of his term he tentatively offered the Paris public a glimpse of Noverre's great dramatic ballet, *Médée et Jason*, discreetly interpolated into an opera by La Borde. It was no more than an impression of the original, for it had to be given with music by La Borde, but it was memorable for giving Vestris the opportunity of breaking with tradition and appearing as Jason without a mask.

At the end of his term, during the last days of 1775, Vestris was able to present this ballet in its entirety to the score that Rodolphe had written for

Noverre. This second version, featuring Vestris as Jason, Anne Heinel as Medea and Madeleine Guimard as Creusa, created a profound impression. Nothing like it had been seen at the Opéra before. Far removed from the rococo ballets that were the general rule, it conveyed, in bold and direct mime, a narrative charged with powerful emotions. The *Mercure de France* catalogued these in great detail:

> The fickleness of Jason who abandons Medea to marry Creusa, his new love, the rancour of Medea, her attempt to reawaken her faithless husband's affection by presenting his children to him; the rage of this jealous woman and her wiles, Creusa's marriage festival, the deceitful reconciliation that Medea offers her rival and the poisoned gifts she bears; the agony and death of Creusa; Jason's despair and the fury that consumes him, the abusive rage of Medea as she is carried away in a chariot drawn by dragons; the murder of her children whom she stabbed in full view of their father; the rain of fire and the burning of the palace – all this action and spectacle was most effective. But the highlight of it all was the energetic acting of Mlle Heinel in expressing the most contrasting passions and feelings; her dancing, her gestures, the play of her features form a rapid and impressive picture which moves and transports the audience, so powerful is the art of pantomime when the performance is clear and natural.

A fresh breeze was blowing through the corridors of the Opéra. Even the mask had now been relegated to oblivion. In 1772 Maximilien Gardel had been called upon to replace the elder Vestris in a performance of *Castor et Pollux*, and had insisted on dancing without the customary black wig and mask. The public was more than ready for the change, and from that moment the mask was an accessory of the past, being used only occasionally for a few years more, in certain ensemble dances.

If the Opéra had shown itself excessively conservative in its artistic policy, the technical strength of its ballet company had not been neglected. Among the men who had risen to the rank of *danseurs seuls* alongside Gaétan Vestris were Maximilien Gardel and Jean Dauberval, who had entered the company in 1759 and 1761 respectively. Following them were two no less brilliant younger men: Pierre Gardel, Maximilien's brother, and Auguste Vestris, the son of Gaétan Vestris and Marie Allard, described by Noverre as 'the most astonishing dancer in Europe'.

The debut in 1772 of Vestr'Allard, as the wits called him, was presented as an occasion of special circumstance. Although not yet thirteen, he was even then recognised as 'a prodigy of talent that had to be seen to be believed', possessing a combination of strength, precision, brilliance and grace astonishing in one so young. When he was formally engaged a few years later, he soon established a new model for the male dancer. The individual styles of the great male dancers before him – Dupré, his father, the elder Gardel – had played a notable part in the development of the *noble* style of dancing. Young Vestris, however, possessed a brilliance of attack and an ebullience that distinguished him from his predecessors as the protagonist of the intermediate genre between the *noble* and the *comique* – the *demi-caractère*. The facility of his execution was incredible: there seemed little that he could not perform with consummate ease. He was in no way a copy of his father, for he was essentially a dancer of his own generation with a mastery of all the latest innovations in technique and style. It was he, for example, who more than anyone else stimulated the development of the pirouette at the Opéra: in Noverre's opinion, his pirouettes could have been performed more smoothly, but he turned with extraordinary rapidity and possessed an uncanny control.

Among the women, young Vestris's mother, the petite and vivacious Marie Allard, delighted the Parisians from 1761 until her retirement in 1774, but she was far outshone by Madeleine Guimard and Anne Heinel.

Guimard, who was able to appear almost eternally youthful through her skill at make-up, reigned for many years at the Opéra virtually unchallenged. She made her debut in 1762 and did not retire until she was forty-six years old, in 1789. In physique she was small, and so unfashionably thin that her enemies called her 'the Skeleton of the Graces'. She gave the lead in discarding the panniers and the mountainous coiffures of her youth, a reform that echoed the general simplification in women's dress that was coming into fashion some years before the Revolution, and was hastened by the introduction of ballets-pantomimes, which demanded a natural style of presentation. As an artist, her most notable quality was her affecting acting, which was a great asset for the new type of ballet bring produced by Noverre and the Gardel brothers. Her dancing, too, was expressive and was marked by a dignified simplicity and impeccable taste. In his appreciation of her, Noverre explained that 'after dancing for a long time in the serious style, she abandoned it in order to devote herself to the mixed style' – or, as it was now being called, the *'genre de demi-caractère'*.

In her private life, she cut a flamboyant figure. Worshipped by a host of admirers, and supported in princely fashion by powerful protectors, she lived luxuriously in a splendid mansion on the Chaussée d'Antin, which in the end she was forced to sell in order to pay her debts. In her years of affluence, she presented erotic comedies at her private theatre and gave three supper parties a week – one for the nobility, another for artists and intellectuals, and a third for the most sought-after courtesans of the town. She was a personality to be reckoned with, and at the Opéra her influence was at one time virtually limitless.

Anne Heinel, who was ten years younger than Guimard, came from Vienna to make her debut at the Opéra in 1768. She was a large woman, and according to Grimm possessed 'precision, assurance, aplomb and a nobility that could be compared with the qualities of the great Vestris'. This proud man was at first very much put out by the success of the young German ballerina, and for some time their relationship was decidedly strained. But gradually they warmed to one another, and eventually married. Heinel retired from the stage in 1781.

These were the dancers heading the company in 1776, when Noverre was appointed as *maître de ballet* in succession to Gaétan Vestris. The appointment was a departure from normal precedent, for the principal ballet-master had always risen to that post from within the ranks of the company. Noverre owed his advancement to the Empress Maria Theresa, who had admired his work in Vienna. On hearing of Vestris's resignation, she had recommended him to her daughter, the young Queen of France, Marie Antoinette. Faced with a royal wish, the Controller of the King's Pleasures, who was responsible for the Opéra, had no alternative but to comply; but he very carefully specified the conditions under which Noverre was to work. Significantly, he drew a distinction between *ballets d'action* and ordinary ballets, or the ballets customarily interpolated in operas. Great care was to be observed in experimenting in what was regarded as a very novel genre, and the direction reserved to itself absolute discretion in deciding when a *ballet d'action* was to be produced, the right to approve the plan of any such ballet and the music in advance, and rigid control over the expenditure.

Almost at once Noverre found himself isolated by various factions that formed within the theatre. The Gardels were particularly hostile, and their mother made a spiteful complaint that Maximilien had been unjustly passed over in favour of a foreigner, 'le petit Noverre' as she called him, and deprived of his rightful succession.

Ignoring these difficulties as best he could, he staged, in rapid succession, two *ballets d'action* that he had successfully produced elsewhere: *Apelles et Campaspe* (1776) and *Les Caprices de Galathée* (1776). In mood and theme they were very different: the first was based on a story from antiquity, the love of an artist for the favourite of Alexander the Great and the Emperor's magnanimity in pardoning the lovers, while the second was a happy pastorale about the caprices of a pretty shepherdess, which Grimm likened to 'a bouquet of flowers, a thought of Anacreon such as Boucher might have expressed on canvas'. These productions, however, were only the prelude for the important work that Noverre saw as his testing piece.

Les Horaces (1777) was a bold undertaking: a dramatic rendering of Corneille's classic tragedy 'in which stage action, mute declamation and pantomime compete with dancing and music to form a spectacle'. The Queen attended the first performance to encourage her *protégé*; and in the roles of the elder Horatius and Camilla, Gaétan Vestris and Anne Heinel gave performances of prodigious intensity. Nevertheless, the public was puzzled by the work's novel structure, and the general opinion was that it was too long, was difficult to follow, and contained too little dancing. It was, however, an impressive production, and though it was soon dropped from the repertory, it long remained in the memory of those who had seen it, and it conceivably supplied Jacques-Louis David with the inspiration for his famous painting, *Le Serment des Horaces*.

Not until nearly the end of his engagement, when he revived *Médée et Jason* (1779), was Noverre allowed to produce another tragic ballet. The butt of intrigues and jealousy, he had to content himself with divertissements in operas and with works such as *Les Petits Riens* (1778), a trifle that would have been forgotten had the composer not been Mozart. The twenty-two-year-old Mozart was then in Paris, composing for the *concerts spirituels*. He frequently lunched with Noverre, and no doubt they were discussing plans for future collaboration when their meetings were interrupted by the death of the composer's mother. Mozart left Paris to join his father, and their paths never crossed again.

Noverre's position was rapidly becoming unbearable. His enemies now included the all-powerful Guimard, who was the driving force behind the committee of artists that virtually ruled the Opéra. In 1779 Noverre accepted the inevitable and struck a bargain with Gardel and Dauberval whereby he would resign in their favour if they would obtain an academician's pension for him. Luck was to be against him to the end, for when he eventually resigned, in 1781, no such pension was forthcoming.

For Noverre it must have seemed an unhappy, even unsuccessful, engagement, but in fact his achievement was immeasurable. Although his major works had proved too serious for French taste, he had steered the ballet of the Opéra into new waters by shaking the theatrical dance free of rococo artificialities and gaining belated but unequivocal acceptance for the *ballet d'action* as a branch of dramatic art. His own fame was to rest, justly, on his ideas rather than on the productions in which he tried, often against odds, to put those ideas into practice. Viewed in broader perspective, his ideas echo the new thinking of the age: in them can be recognised the clear reasoning of Voltaire, Rousseau's call for simplicity and the release of emotions, and the psychological insight of the Abbé Prévost. Out of them came a concept of ballet that has remained essentially valid to this day. If he needed a crumb of satisfaction to allay his disappointment, it was to know himself esteemed by posterity – *pace* Mother Gardel – as 'the celebrated Noverre'.

IV

The Dominance of the Gardels

Towards the end of Noverre's time as ballet-master, the Opéra came under the control of a new director, de Vismes, who tried bravely to initiate a policy of great activity and change, but made many enemies in the process. Believing that the new director was making a disproportionate fortune, the artists formed themselves into a committee, which met in the mansion of Madeleine Guimard. It was an act of open revolt. Auguste Vestris hotheadedly announced himself as the Opéra's George Washington, and once, when de Vismes in a moment of exasperation asked who he thought he was talking to, retorted: 'To the exploiter of my talent'. Guimard held this committee together with great skill, and for a time its influence was felt in almost every department of the Opéra. It was a typical outburst in those dying years of the Old Regime, expressing not merely opposition to established authority but at the same time a genuine desire to remove abuses and introduce reform.

It was while the artists were imposing their authority, on 8 June 1781, that the sumptuous new opera house in the Palais Royal was burnt to the ground only eleven years after it was opened. A far more terrible tragedy was averted by the presence of mind of Dauberval, who first noticed the flames and ordered the curtain to be lowered. The performance was nearing its end, and the public left the theatre in ignorance of why the final ballet had ended rather abruptly. Even so, a number of lives were lost when the flames took hold, among them being two of the dancers. Paris nearly had to mourn Madeleine Guimard as well: she was trapped in her dressing room, and owed her life to a stagehand who heard her cries, broke open the door, wrapped the curtains round her half-clad body and carried her to safety through the flames.

Remembering the long delays that had hindered the building of the destroyed theatre, it was decided that a provisional theatre should be built immediately on the Boulevard de la Porte-Saint-Martin. 'I will give you until October 31,' the Queen was said to have told the architect Lenoir, 'and if the key of my box is handed to me on that day, I promise you the ribbon of the Order of St Michel in exchange.' The builders completed the work with several days to spare, but Lenoir apparently never received his decoration.

Noverre's departure had left Maximilien Gardel and Jean Dauberval in possession as joint *maîtres de ballet*. Their partnership seems to have been an uneasy one, for Dauberval's share of the creative activity shrank almost to extinction. He was at this time in love with Mlle Théodore, one of the Opéra's most brilliant dancers, who had such wonderful *ballon* that she seemed scarcely to touch the ground. But she was having difficulties with the management, and when she lost hope of resolving them, she persuaded Dauberval to resign with her. The Opéra thus lost a choreographer of rare genius, for Dauberval was never able to return. He ended his career at Bordeaux, where he created a repertory of masterpieces, including the greatest of all comedy ballets, *La Fille mal gardée,* which was produced there on the eve of the Revolution in 1789.

In 1783, with Dauberval conveniently out of the way, the Gardel brothers began their dominance of the Opéra ballet, which was to last, virtually unchallenged, for nearly forty years.

Maximilien, the elder brother, possessed several advantages over Noverre. With the powerful Madeleine Guimard he enjoyed an easy and even intimate relationship. He was also the more pleasant character, being endowed with a gentle nature and a charm that was in no way affected by the disfigurement he had suffered from smallpox as a young man. When he succeeded the irascible Noverre, the company must have breathed a sigh of relief, for he imposed his authority more by winning the dancers' affection than by instilling fear.

He had begun his choreographic career as assistant to Gaétan Vestris, revealing an unusual flair for arranging ballets in operas within the conventional limitations of the time. The arrival of Noverre to deprive him of what he assumed to be his rightful inheritance had dealt a bitter blow to his self-esteem, but in the long run it was to benefit him enormously. Maximilien Gardel was not an innovator, but he understood Noverre's message, and directed his talents, in a modest but effective way, to the new form of the *ballet d'action.* His own contribution was the discovery, or at least the exploitation, of a sure formula for success. Perceiving the great vogue for *opéra comique,* he became adept at translating a well-known work of this sort, with its simple story that invariably had a happy ending, with its catchy melodies, into a ballet-pantomime. Although artistically inferior, the ballets he produced to this formula – *La Chercheuse d'esprit* (1778), *Ninette à la cour* (1778) and *Le Déserteur* (Fountainebleau 1786, Opéra 1788) – had a more immediate appeal to the public than the weightier productions of Noverre.

In Madeleine Guimard, Gardel found an ideal interpreter. Discovering and developing her aptitude for miming, she brought his heroines to life with a touching sentiment that one imagines found an echo more than a century later in the early stars of another emerging art, the silent cinema. To a much more limited public, Guimard seems to have had the same sort of appeal, the same mixture of innocence and fun, and in particular a gift for portraying naïve and even rather gauche heroines without losing her natural grace.

Maximilien Gardel was allotted only a few years to enjoy his supremacy. In 1787 Paris was shocked to learn of his death, the result of an absurdly minor injury. In the beginning, it was no more than a cut on the toe; but in a world that knew nothing of antiseptics the wound became infected and gangrenous.

In a week he was dead. His post then devolved, as smoothly as if he had been a reigning monarch, on his younger brother Pierre, who had been his assistant since 1784. *'Gardel est mort, vive Gardel!'*

Guimard's retirement in 1789 marked the close of an era. In the wider world outside, events were gathering momentum: in a few months the storming of the Bastille sparked the Revolution that was to engulf France in strife, terror and war. In the grim but stirring years that followed, through all the phases of the Revolution, the Directory, the Consulate, the First Napoleonic Empire and into the Restoration, the Opéra continued to play its part in the entertainments of the capital. From time to time its name was officially changed to suit the regime of the day, but the activity within proceeded with a continuity that contrasted strongly with the violent changes in the political arena. In no other department was this state of calm more necessary than in the ballet, not merely because of the traditional foundation of its technique, but more immediately because it was in the course of consolidating the developments that had been initiated by Noverre. At this juncture a strong and consistent leadership was essential, and history, as it so often does, provided the man of the hour – Pierre Gardel.

Made of sterner stuff than his brother, Pierre Gardel became the virtual dictator of the ballet in France until he partially retired thirty-six years later, in 1820. Even after that he continued to work at the Opéra, and it was not until 1827 that he retired completely. Under his rule, the ballet at the Opéra was to acquire a prestige that it had never attained before, and this at a time when Paris was beset with the troubles of civil strife and war. By the end of the eighteenth century, when the excesses of the Revolution had spent themselves, the dance enjoyed a greater popularity than did opera. Appearing in a repertory that offered them plentiful opportunities, the dancers were inspired to a degree that would have been unthinkable had they not been directed by a man in whom they had faith. Although he seems to have been a remote and rather cold figure, Gardel shared their hardships, remaining at his post in the dark years and never yielding to the temptation to seek more lucrative triumphs elsewhere. In other times this would have been regarded as insularity, but in the country's hour of need it gained him a respect that he never lost. It also explained his reluctance to accept the return of dancers who had, to his way of thinking, been guilty of desertion.

As a choreographer Pierre Gardel was a perfectionist, sometimes devoting many months to the preparation of a ballet before he was satisfied. Once, when reproached by the director of the Opéra for the time he was taking, he retorted: 'Monsieur, I do not build dances as a builder builds houses. In that trade you can have as many hands as you want, but I have only my genius to help me.' Even so, in the early years of the Revolution he was able to produce three masterpieces, all based on mythological themes, which long formed the mainstay of the repertory: *Télémaque* (1790), *Psyché* (1790) and *Le*

Jugement de Pâris (1793).[1] Being, like his brother, a competent musician, Pierre Gardel not only devised the scenarios and the choreography of his ballets, but also selected melodies that he wished to be woven into the score. For *Télémaque* and *Psyché*, the original parts of the scores were written by Ernest Miller, the bibulous father of Marie Miller, an entrancing young dancer who was beginning to make her name. The music for *Pâris* was arranged and in part composed by Méhul, who also incorporated passages by Haydn and Pleyel. These three ballets revealed Pierre Gardel as a choreographer greatly superior to his brother, and even to be classed with Noverre and Dauberval.

His great merits were his development of pantomime to express the action, and the inclusion of a generous admixture of dancing for the *premiers sujets*. This balance between mime and dance was to distinguish the French school of ballet from the Italian. In France, Gardel recognised that Noverre's reforms should not be carried out at the expense of the dancing, while in Italy the emphasis was concentrated on mime and rhythmical gesture to such an extent that the action was sometimes given over entirely to mimes. Such an approach produced the great choreodramas staged by Viganò and Gioja at La Scala, Milan, but was detrimental to the standard of dancing, which took second place. Indeed, Italian companies at this time were often forced to import principal dancers from France, a practice that led to the prevalent use in Italy of the term *'coppia di rango francese'*.

Finding their talents given full play, the Parisian dancers responded with enthusiasm to their new master. In *Télémaque*, Victoire Saulnier as Calypso revealed 'a powerful and true expressiveness, giving herself up in turn to love, hatred, jealousy, revenge, yet never losing her nobility', while the young Marie Miller, soon to become Mme Gardel, had some delightful scenes as Eucharis. A year later, Marie Miller created the title role of Psyche, causing a sensation by the realism of her torment when cast into the flaming pit. In *Pâris* the heroine was again Victoire Saulnier, who was a natural Venus, and was particularly ravishing in a scene where the goddess, surrounded by her attendants, takes a bath to a voluptuous musical accompaniment on the lyres. In *Télémaque*, Gardel took the title role, but the leading parts in the other ballets – Cupid in *Psyché* and *Pâris* – were played by Auguste Vestris, who in his maturity was revealing himself as not merely an extraordinary dancer but also an expressive actor of a high order.

It was a sign of Gardel's artistic integrity and single-minded application that these works, so timeless in their flavour, could be produced when they were. While he was rehearsing *Pâris*, for example, Louis XVI was guillotined in the Place de la Concorde, and as France moved into the Reign of Terror these ballets

---

[1] For many years *Psyché* was the most-performed ballet in the history of the Opéra, being given 560 times during a period of nearly forty years: its record has been surpassed only by *Coppélia* and *Giselle*. *Télémaque* achieved 413 performances, and *Pâris* 188.

continued to feature on the playbills of the Opéra. In 1794, by order of the Committee of Public Safety, the Opéra left its provisional home by the Porte-Saint-Martin and moved into a new theatre in the Rue de la Loi, opposite the Bibliothèque Nationale. The Revolution was passing through its most violent phase, and for a time the repertory had to give place to politically inspired spectacles; it was not until the last years of the century that anything like normal activity could be resumed. During these years, Gardel skilfully avoided causing offence to the politicians, and in this way retained his control over the ballet. Luck was with him too, for everyone was at the mercy of some malicious denunciation that could lead to the guillotine, and under his direction the dancers of the Opéra seemed to steer a careful course and keep safely clear of entanglements. Indeed, the only dancer who found herself in danger was the golden-haired Clotilde Mafleuret, who unwisely brandished a royalist flag during an insurrection in the South and was brought to account before a military tribunal. For Gardel the choreographer this was a particularly frustrating period, for the grand ballet he was planning, *Guillaume Tell*, remained unproduced, and he had to bow to political expediency and arrange the sort of patriotic spectacle that the *sans-culottes* demanded: *L'Offrande à la Liberté*, for example, which featured the *Marseillaise*, a whole stableful of horses, and the singer Marie-Thérèse Maillard representing Liberty on a practicable mountain.

As employees of a state theatre, the dancers were occasionally obliged to take part in official festivities outside the Opéra, organised to propagate the new republican ideals. In one of these Mlle Maillard was forced, by a thinly veiled threat of the guillotine, to portray the Goddess of Reason, a role that was also taken by the dancer Julie Aubry in the cathedral of Notre-Dame. 'My eyes have seen,' remembered an old man long afterwards, 'Mlle Aubry of the Opéra – upon my word, a well-built girl – sitting on the high altar and taking the part of Liberty so literally that you could see through her dress as clearly as I can see the statue of St Peter on the wall of the choir – in short, absolute liberty!'

Marie Gardel, the former Mlle Miller, was spared such indignities, and was able to pursue her career at the Opéra without hindrance or serious rivalry. To Pierre Gardel she was both wife and muse, adorning his ballets with her unassuming presence and purity of style for many years. She proved to be a worthy successor to Madeleine Guimard, and remained the leading ballerina of the Opéra until her retirement in 1816. The elderly Noverre admired her without reservation. He wrote:

> In my desire to praise Mme Gardel, the pen slips from my hands, words fail me, and I seek new phrases to describe her rare talents. Her dancing is dazzling; diamonds seem to sparkle from her feet; her execution has a priceless finish; the most difficult movements, the most complicated *enchaînements* are performed by this rival of Terpsichore with equal ease

and perfection; she has a delicate touch and an impeccable ear which gives her dancing great precision and a novel charm. This astonishing dancer has aplomb, firmness. In admiring her, I am reconciled to the pirouette because she turns gently, finishes it with a good pause, and does not prepare the public for what she is about to do with a disagreeable effort. Her body is always well placed; it is relaxed and unaffected by the rapid, dazzling movements of her legs… She is to the dance what the Venus de Medici is to sculpture.

In contrast to many of her companions – particularly the ravishing Clotilde – Marie Gardel was delicate in build and had no obvious sensual appeal. She was therefore judged almost exclusively on her artistry and grace. Her versatility almost defied description: one writer, trying to do justice to her multiple resources, wrote that 'she acted like Innocence, turned like Coquetry, posed like Reverie, moved like Abandon, darted like Pleasure, and shimmered like Joy.'

When the nineteenth century dawned, Pierre Gardel was as firmly entrenched as ever. His rule was accepted without demur by the dancers, on whom he imposed a strict discipline. When he came onto the stage for a rehearsal, their chatter ceased at once and complete silence reigned. To Noverre the Opéra seemed like an absolute monarchy surviving in a land of liberty. It was indeed isolated from other centres, and this was both a strength and a weakness. Gardel had a sort of pre-Copernican view of the ballet, regarding Paris as the centre of the dance universe and paying little attention to what was happening elsewhere. Noverre recalled a revealing comment that Gardel had made during his only visit to London, in 1782: that what merits he saw in the ballet there 'inspired him not at all'.

In his later works, successful though many of them were, Gardel was never quite able to recapture the inspiration that shone through his three early masterpieces, but he did produce one other remarkable ballet, *La Dansomanie* (1800). This was a light and amusing piece about a wealthy *'dansomane'* who will only hear of his daughter marrying a man who shares his passion for dancing. Marie Gardel was, of course, the daughter, and as the young colonel who loves her, Auguste Vestris had an amusing role in which he nearly spoils his chances by admitting he does not know the Gavotte de Vestris but wins his heart's desire in the end. The subject provided opportunities for dancing in many styles; in it the waltz made its first appearance on the Opéra stage, but Noverre thought Gardel went a little too far in parodying the *danse noble*. With Méhul's charming music, this ballet remained popular for many years, never failing to arouse laughter and applause.

Gardel continued to replenish the repertory with skilfully constructed ballets that appealed to the taste of the public and often had moments of memorable originality. *Achille à Scyros* (1804), with music by Cherubini, featured the young male virtuoso Louis Duport in a highly original scene in which Achilles disguises himself as a woman to make advances to Deidamia and gives himself away by the masculine vigour of his dancing. The ballet ended with Achilles's departure for Troy, a denouement that was no doubt designed to please the newly crowned Napoleon, who attended the first performance. *Paul et Virginie* (1806), with a score by Kreutzer, was based on Bernardin de Saint-Pierre's sentimental novel about two lovers on the Île de France, and provided Vestris with the unusual role of a Negro servant. *Vénus et Adonis* (1808) was another ballet in the anacreontic manner, but not to be classed with Gardel's earlier masterpieces.

In 1800 Gardel acquired an assistant, Louis Milon, who was to serve the Opéra as a ballet-master and teacher until 1826. Milon owed his engagement to the success of an enchanting ballet, *Pygmalion*, which he had produced at the Théâtre de l'Ambigu-Comique and was to revive at the Opéra in 1800 with Marie Gardel in the part originally played by his young sister-in-law, Emilie Bigottini. He seems to have worked with Gardel in complete harmony, and one suspects that he had a compliant personality, being content to support his superior in matters of policy while he devoted himself to the more congenial task of choreography. Although he produced a number of ballets that enjoyed great success – notably *Nina* (1813), *Le Carnaval de Venise* (1816) and *Clari* (1820) – he never appeared to Gardel as a threat.

Milon's muse was Emilie Bigottini, who ascended the hierarchy of the Opéra steadily but, owing to the presence of Marie Gardel, somewhat slowly, being appointed a principal dancer only in 1812. She inherited from her father, who was a celebrated Harlequin, a natural understanding of mime and owed her success as much to her sensitive acting as to her graceful and modest style of dancing. The roles of Nina and Clari – those innocent, ill-used heroines of sentimental romance, enduring injustice and suffering before achieving the happiness that ultimately rewarded them – suited her to perfection. She often moved people to tears by the pathos of her portrayals, and when she retired it was said of her that she had revealed to many the great range of emotions that could be conveyed through mime.

Gardel was to be criticised for keeping other choreographers away from the Opéra, an attitude that he defended on the ground of precedent. He maintained that the *maîtres de ballet*, by reason of their knowledge of the dancers, were alone competent to produce works there. This was a normal reaction from a man in an established position; but now that ballet had become a flourishing independent art, the Opéra, with its great reservoir of personnel and material, appeared as the ultimate goal to aspiring choreographers. Although Gardel and Milon had to accept a certain amount of erosion to the exclusivity they considered to be their right, they nevertheless produced twenty-seven out of the thirty-three ballets added to the repertory between 1800 and 1820.

Gardel saw the first threat to his position when Louis Duport asked to be allowed to produce a ballet. Duport had returned to the Opéra, where he had received his early training, with Milon, and quickly came into prominence as a dancer with an incredible technique, great lightness and a self-satisfied presence. His pirouettes were dazzling and he bounded like a rubber ball, but he often overstepped the bounds of good taste and shocked the purists by seeming to adopt the 'grotesque' style of Italian dancers. Not content with out-dancing the ageing Vestris, he advanced claims to be considered as a choreographer with such persistence that eventually the Opéra disregarded the objections of Gardel and Milon and granted him his wish. Duport produced three ballets at the Opéra, including an uninteresting anacreontic ballet called *Acis et Galathée* (1805) and *Figaro* (1806). His ambitions soared; he made further demands, and when the Opéra demurred, became increasingly dissatisfied and difficult. Finally, receiving an offer from St Petersburg, he slipped out of Paris disguised as a woman. Gardel was no doubt glad to see him go.

Two other young choreographers managed to have ballets performed at the Opéra during the heyday of the First Empire. The first was Louis Henry, whose *L'Amour à Cythère* (1805) was a work of immaturity that hardly revealed the gifts he was later to develop in Italy. The other was Jean Aumer, a man of much greater experience, who had already acquired a considerable reputation at the Théâtre de la Porte-Saint-Martin. This was the same theatre that the Opéra had occupied from 1781 to 1794. After lying empty for some years, it had reopened under private management to present a fare of popular melodrama, pantomime and ballet. Although still under contract to the Opéra as a dancer, Aumer had accepted an engagement as ballet-master there; after reviving several ballets by his teacher, Dauberval, he began to produce works of his own invention, including a version of *Paul et Virginie* entitled *Les Deux Créoles*, which followed Gardel's ballet on the same subject by only a few days. The Opéra became alarmed, and Aumer was threatened with dismissal. However, he had influential friends, and not only was he kept on the establishment, but his proposal to produce *Les Amours d'Antoine et de Cléopâtre* (1808) was made at the opportune moment when Napoleon had given orders for a new ballet and neither Gardel nor Milon had anything ready. With Vestris and Clotilde in the title roles and a score by Kreutzer, it was an impressive work; but for the moment there was no permanent place for Aumer at the Opéra, and he left Paris to take up an appointment in Vienna.

In 1815, when the fate of Napoleon was finally decided, a much more dangerous competitor to Gardel appeared in the person of Charles Didelot, who formerly applied for the post of ballet-master. Didelot came with very substantial qualifications: he had been ballet-master for nearly ten years in Russia, and later in London, but he was a Frenchman and had studied as a child at the Opéra's School of Dance. His request for a permanent appointment was rejected, but his persistence, aided by powerful support from Russian friends when the allied armies occupied Paris after Waterloo, countered the objections of Gardel and Milon and he was granted permission to produce his *Flore et Zéphire* (1815). Didelot had polished and perfected this work over a period of nearly twenty years, and it had been triumphantly received in London and St Petersburg. When it was first performed at the Opéra, the newly restored king, Louis XVIII, was so delighted with it that he summoned the choreographer to the royal box to compliment him. Although the anacreontic form of the ballet was conventional, the production was richly imaginative. For the public, its most striking feature was the flights, for which new machinery had been constructed that enabled Zephyr to soar effortlessly into the air as though he were really flying – and once, miraculously, bearing Flora in his arms. It was a sign of the times that the leading roles were taken by two of the younger dancers: Albert, now the leading *danseur noble,* was Zephyr, with the remarkable Geneviève Gosselin as Flora.

Despite Gardel's traditional outlook, the period of the Revolution and First Empire was one of radical change. Although he had been brought up in the *noble* style of the Old Regime, Gardel not only countenanced but even encouraged the developments in dance style and technique that were preparing ballet for its great flowering during the Romantic period. These developments included pirouettes of ever-increasing virtuosity, and a shift of the basic placing to the three-quarter point, which changed in a most fundamental way the whole style of the dancer's performance.

This change was effected surprisingly quickly, being stimulated no doubt by the great social upheaval of the time. Writing in 1816 and looking back to the days of his youth, Guimard's husband mourned the loss of the old style:

> Dancing today is nothing like what I myself saw from 1770 until 1790 or '92. The lower-class public with red bonnets who took over the pit, the boulevard dancers…who were introduced on to the stage of the Opéra, have caused us to forget the grace that gave the gloss to the moving tableaux at the Opéra. Talent in dancing does not consist of knowing how to perform all kinds of steps in time to some rhythm… Speed is only a minor advantage.

But dazzling *tours de force* were what the public increasingly wanted, and what Duport and later Paul, with their astonishing pirouettes and jumps, gave them. Their female counterparts were also drawn towards technical display. Guimard had danced in a *terre à terre* style that was always firmly founded on grace, and, as her husband declared, 'disapproved of the present custom of raising the foot to the height of the hip'. Movements such as that, he went on, dislocated the body, were ungraceful, and were done only to astonish the pit.

But time never stands still, and no one was more conscious of the currents of change than Gardel. Through his control of the School of Dance, he skilfully steered a middle course, managing to preserve much that might have been lost in those heady times, while keeping the door open for new developments. Continuity was maintained during the Revolution through Jean-François Deshayes, who directed the School from 1780 until 1798, and in 1807 Jean-François Coulon was appointed to take charge of the perfection class. Coulon was one of the greatest teachers of his time, and among his most celebrated pupils were Louis Duport and Geneviève Gosselin.

If there was a portent for the future among the dancers of the First Empire, it lay in the feet of Geneviève Gosselin, whose career was so short that she was to be virtually forgotten until a later dancer revived memories of her artistry. After dancing for a few years with no special recognition, she suddenly appeared as if completely transformed. Until then, ballerinas had momentarily risen on the tips of their toes, but those moments of weightlessness were so fleeting that they hardly attracted notice, and *pointe* work as such had not been thought of. In 1813, however, Mlle Gosselin revealed, albeit in a primitive form but nonetheless quite unmistakably, the possibility of an exciting new technical development. The public was overwhelmed, but there was more to her performance than just this technical accomplishment. There was beauty, a power of expression, qualities that evoked memories of Guimard and Dauberval – all in all, gifts that prompted one critic to acclaim her as 'the phoenix of the dance'. This expectation was tragically to be unfulfilled, for only a year or two of dancing were left to her and she died in 1818. But her style was not lost, for her teacher, Coulon, was even then giving classes to the child who in later years was to be acclaimed as her reincarnation. This child, who became a phoenix in her turn, was Marie Taglioni.

V

The Romantic Heyday

In 1820 the Opéra was forced to move once again. While leaving the theatre after a performance, the King's nephew, the Duc de Berry, was fatally stabbed, and the Archbishop of Paris made it a condition of administering the Last Sacrament that the building would never again serve as a place of public entertainment. So the following year the singers and dancers found themselves in a new opera house that had been hurriedly erected in the Rue Le Peletier. Like the theatre at the Porte-Saint-Martin, it was intended only as temporary quarters; but it was to endure for more than fifty years, to see Romanticism flower in both opera and ballet, and to become an important focus of social life in the Paris of Balzac and the Second Empire.

In 1820 the ideas of Romanticism were sweeping through the arts. Emerging in a world recovering from a quarter of a century of civil strife and war, and experiencing the first shocks of the Industrial Revolution, younger artists were rejecting the forms of their forbears as irrelevant to the modern age. Allowing their imaginations free rein, they sought more personal means of expression, probed new resources of inspiration, and created works that throbbed with emotional content. They were impetuous, enthusiastic and imbued with a sense of their mission. As Théophile Gautier, who was one of them, recalled, they were 'mad with lyricism and art' and were convinced that they had discovered the great lost secret of poetry. Within a few years their ideas triumphed in every branch of art, and it was clear that there could be no return to the formal classical styles of the past.

While Géricault and Delacroix, Lamartine and Victor Hugo were establishing new standards in painting and literature, the performing arts were beginning to undergo a similar liberation, which was first experienced on the more popular stages of the boulevard. Melodrama was not subject to the rigid conventions of tragedy. The productions at the Théâtre de la Porte-Saint-Martin disregarded the 'three unities' with impunity and were presented with lavish attention to scenic effect. Making full use of the theatre's resources, including the new gas lighting that made possible a whole range of new effects, Pierre Ciceri, the greatest stage designer of his day, created scenes that glowed with local colour and mystery and were essentially Romantic. The new drama that was about to take root was influenced strongly by the works of Shakespeare, who not long before had been considered *'un barbare et un fou'* for his lack of form. This was an entirely new approach, which was to be imposed in the legitimate theatre only against violent opposition from the champions of the classical school.

By its very nature as a department of the King's Household, the Opéra was a bastion of conservatism. The new ideas had hardly penetrated its walls in 1820, and for some years the ballet was to continue in its traditional fashion. There could be little doubt of its artistic decline. Although the company contained many fine dancers – Bigottini, Fanny Bias, the lovely Lise Noblet, and among the men the majestic Albert and the vigorous Paul – a definite lowering of standards was noticeable. Only Bigottini, who was approaching the end of her career, seemed to preserve something of the taste and purity of the past. There were still people living who had seen the old style of dancing, and they did not hide their concern. In their eyes, ballet had degenerated to the level of an acrobatic display and pandered too much to popular taste: there was 'no elegance, no taste; only frightful pirouettes, ghastly efforts of muscle and calf, legs ungracefully stretched, stiff and raised to the level of the eyes or the chin all evening long'.

In 1820 Pierre Gardel and Milon, although remaining the *maîtres de ballet* in name, had withdrawn into the background, concerning themselves with the School of Dance and producing divertissements for operas, but leaving the creation of major ballets mainly to Jean Aumer. Aumer was a man of humble origins who, while he had learnt much from his master, Dauberval, lacked the spark of genius and, a more serious shortcoming, taste. He never fully mastered the art of weaving the dance into the action of his ballets as Dauberval had done, and his years at the Porte-Saint-Martin, the home of popular melodrama, had not been a refining experience. Much of the work he produced for the Opéra in the 1820s consisted of revivals of ballets he had produced in Vienna, or of works by Dauberval. Of the Viennese ballets the most impressive was *Alfred le Grand* (Vienna 1820, Opéra 1822), a historical epic with a moving narrative enlivened by brilliant divertissements and stirring battle scenes. His two Dauberval revivals were *Le Page inconstant* (Bordeaux 1786, Opéra 1823), a version of Beaumarchais's *Le Mariage de Figaro* with Bigottini as an entrancing Cherubino, her last creation, and the immortal *La Fille mal gardée* (Bordeaux 1789, Opéra 1828). The extent to which these revivals were authentic, however, was open to question, for the scores of both were heavily re-worked: the former by the conductor Habeneck, who himself revised a score that Gyrowetz had arranged for a recent Viennese revival, and the latter by Ferdinand Herold, who in a manner of the time incorporated a number of passages from the operas of Rossini.

Aumer's greatest achievements came at the end of his career, when he was persuaded, against his better judgement, to accept the collaboration of a scenarist. This was a novel departure, for until then the choreographer had always been responsible for his own narrative. Aumer saw that this new policy of accepting a scenario and imposing it on the choreographer would reduce the latter's standing as a creative artist; but he was himself to be fortunate in his literary collaborator, for Eugène Scribe, the most versatile and prolific dramatist of his day, provided him with three skilfully constructed plots: *La Somnambule* (1827), *La Belle au bois dormant* (1829) and *Manon Lescaut* (1830).

Scribe's scenario for *La Somnambule* was later to serve for Bellini's opera of the same name. In the ballet, for which Herold wrote the music, Pauline Montessu created the role of the sleepwalking heroine in a sentimental story of wronged innocence. *La Belle au bois dormant*, which also had a score by Herold, was less interesting, but *Manon Lescaut* was an impressive ballet by any standard. If Aumer's ballets had not been discarded after his departure from the Opéra in 1831, it would have certainly lasted much longer than it did. Ciceri evoked the Paris of the Old Regime brilliantly in his scenery, and Pauline Montessu gave a moving rendering of the heroine of the Abbé Prévost's classic novel. The most distinguished element in this work was the score – the first work for the Opéra by Fromental Halévy, who was later to write one of the greatest Romantic operas, *La Juive*. Composed with unusual care for a ballet score, his music for *Manon Lescaut* contained some expressively scored pages to accompany the dramatic action, an excellent pastiche of eighteenth-century dance music for a divertissement, and perhaps the earliest example in ballet of leitmotiv in a recurring theme for Manon.

The first sign that something new and exciting was in the air came unexpectedly on a summer evening in 1827, when Marie Taglioni made her first appearance in Paris. 'Her debut,' prophesied *Le Figaro* afterwards, 'will open a new era. It is Romanticism applied to the dance.' What was so novel about her style was the sensitivity inherent in her every movement. Her whole body seemed imbued with a natural and gentle harmony; there was no apparent physical effort, no artificiality, nor even any sensual appeal. All was 'poetry and simplicity, grace and gentleness'.

Therein lay the secret of the revelation that led to the Romantic revival of ballet. Technique became subjugated to style again, but with Taglioni it was so completely mastered that it never obtruded to produce an effect. It has often been stated that she was the first ballerina to rise on her points, but this was not so. She was, however, the first to use this extension of technique to add expression and meaning to her interpretation. With her it never became an ungainly trick. In Vienna she had observed the skill of Amalia Brugnoli, one of the early pioneers of point work, and it was perhaps significant that she had studied under Coulon, the teacher of Geneviève Gosselin. Indeed, many memories of Gosselin were reawakened when Taglioni appeared in Paris, not so much by the mere mechanical feat of rising on the toes, but by the smooth and seemingly natural way in which she performed these novel difficulties.

Young Henri Duponchel, a future director of the Opéra, was so excited that he threw a bouquet on to the stage as she disappeared into the wings. Her effect on the company was infectious. In no time the other dancers were trying to emulate her, *'en taglionisant'*, but invariably they failed to perceive the secret of artistry that lay beyond the technical difficulty. Taglioni was engaged as a *premier sujet*, and for the first few years took her place on an equal level with Noblet, Legallois and Julia, appearing with success but in roles that were not particularly memorable, such as a naiad in *La belle au bois dormant* and the slave girl in the last act of *Manon Lescaut*. Her moment was still to come.

In the summer of 1830, the people of Paris rose in revolt against the growing oppression of the restored monarchy, and Louis-Philippe ascended the throne as a constitutional sovereign. The Opéra too underwent a radical change of regime, being transformed from a dependency of the Royal Household into a subsidised private enterprise with a degree of governmental control. Dr Louis Véron, a man of great energy and drive, was appointed as the new director in 1831 and immediately began to refurbish the whole institution.

Véron fully understood the issues that had precipitated the Revolution of 1830, and realised that his prime task was to draw to the Opéra the upper bourgeoisie whose influence was now paramount in the political arena. Ballet, he saw, was capable of becoming a powerful source of attraction for the new public. From a study of the box-office returns, he concluded that complex dramas and comedies of manners were not suitable subjects for ballets, and that the secret of success lay in simple and uncomplicated narratives in which the dance could evolve naturally out of the action. He also saw ballet as a composite form, recognising the importance of music and décor in achieving a fully effective production.

All these elements were now brought together, each touched by the pervading Romantic spirit of the time. The scenarists, being literary men, were already committed to the Romantic movement, but their collaborators were no less sympathetic: composers were writing in a much more expressive idiom; stage designers such as Ciceri were adept at translating mysterious and exotic scenes on to backcloths, flats and built pieces and making full use of gas lighting; and the Opéra's costume department, in which Paul Lormier was to be the dominant designer for some forty years, peopled the stage with colourful figures or fantastic spirits as the action demanded. With this wealth of collaboration, choreographers and dancers were able to transform ballet almost overnight from a routine spectacle into a vital art that was specially fitted to convey the 'lost poetry' that the Romantic artists claimed to have rediscovered.

In Véron's reorganisation, Aumer was replaced as *premier maître de ballet* by Jean Coralli, a man already in his fifties who had been a pupil at the Opéra's School of Dance but had gained most of his early experience in Vienna. From 1825 to 1829 he had been ballet-master at the Théâtre de la Porte-Saint-Martin, not only staging ballets but also being involved in the production of some of the plays that looked forward to the triumph of Romantic drama, culminating with Delavigne's *Marino Falieri*. Coralli was engaged by Véron in 1831 and was to remain in his post throughout the heyday of the Romantic ballet until his retirement in 1850. The infusion of new blood from the boulevard theatres was not confined to Coralli, for two other dancers from those popular surroundings had joined the Opéra in 1830: Jules Perrot and Joseph Mazilier, the first a man of unprepossessing appearance who danced with astonishing skill and agility, and the second an exceptionally talented mime.

Véron's boldest step was unquestionably the elevation of Marie Taglioni to the rank of star ballerina over the heads of dancers like Noblet and Montessu, who had previously been her equals in the hierarchy. Taglioni was given a six-year contract at the unprecedented salary of 30,000 francs a year, and at the same time her father, who was her mentor and teacher, was invited to produce ballets for her. This breach of hallowed tradition was a stroke of genius that no director under the old system, tied to the apron strings of the Royal Household, could have attempted. Other changes soon followed, some long overdue, others vital for the theatre's financial prosperity. The age-old division of the dancers into three genres – the *noble*, the *demi-caractère* and the *comique* – was discarded, unregretted and with its disappearance barely noticed, and roles that had previously been the exclusive property of certain artists were now shared.

At the same time, continuity was maintained in the School of Dance, and although Gardel and Milon were no longer there, Auguste Vestris, now a wizened old man, still taught a select number of pupils. Because of the excellence of its dance training, the influence of the Opéra reached out far beyond the frontiers of France: dancers came from all over Europe to study in Paris, and everywhere French dancers were in great demand. London, where the vogue for ballet reached extraordinary proportions in the 1840s, regarded ballet as a fundamentally French art in much the same way as it looked to Italy as the source of opera. A more modest, but more enduring, example of this influence is today to be found in Copenhagen, where August Bournonville established the French style, which he had absorbed in Paris under Vestris. He reproduced a dance class such as he himself had experienced in his ballet *Konservatoriet* (Copenhagen, 1849), and this scene has survived intact in the repertory of the Royal Danish Ballet.

Another of Véron's innovations was to allow the more important *abonnés* to pass backstage into the Foyer de la Danse and mingle with the dancers as they prepared for the performance. For old and young men alike this acted as an irresistible attraction, and the Opéra prospered greatly as a result. For a long time, the Foyer de la Danse was to be an important centre for male society. Many friendships and sometimes closer associations were formed there with the dancers, but the strictest decorum was enforced and the demands of the profession allowed a dancer on duty little time for dalliance. Nevertheless, in the popular mythology of the day the Opéra dancer became an object of sentimental yearning and physical desire, taking her place as a sort of sister to the pleasure-loving *grisette*. And through the writings of journalists such as Nestor Roqueplan and

Albéric Second, the public became aware for the first time of the humbler members of the company, and particularly the skinny child who emerged out of obscurity and often poverty to enter the glittering make-believe world of the Opéra ballet – the *petit rat*.

Having shaken the Opéra into the modern world, Véron would be able to retire four years later with a considerable fortune. This happy result was not due to administrative measures alone. Of much greater significance was that the gates had been opened to the forces of Romanticism, and the Opéra began to make a greater contribution to the musical and artistic life of the capital. Already in preparation when Véron took over was a new opera by Meyerbeer, *Robert le Diable* (1831), which was to inaugurate his management with a resounding flourish. Its ballet was given a new character by a young man whom Véron had placed in charge of the scenic department, the same Henri Duponchel who had thrown the bouquet to Taglioni at her debut. In place of the conventional divertissement originally planned, Duponchel conceived a moonlit scene in a ruined cloister, which was brilliantly realised by Ciceri. The Ballet of the Nuns was an integral part of the opera, developing naturally at the point where spectres of lapsed nuns rise from their graves to entice the hero. The choreography of Filippo Taglioni was perfectly in accord with the Romantic mood of the setting. In the words of an American visitor, the future Mrs Longfellow, it was all 'magnificent and terrific and diabolical and enchanting', the dancers appearing as 'very charming witches with their jaunty Parisian figures and most refined pirouettes'. As the Abbess Héléna, Marie Taglioni was given a role with certain erotic overtones, and it was perhaps for that reason that she found it uncongenial and, despite Meyerbeer's protest, withdrew from the opera after a few performances.

The impact of this manifestation of Romanticism was shattering. That the Opéra was set on a new course was soon demonstrated by the ballet that was conceived when *Robert* was in preparation. The scenario of *La Sylphide* (1832) was written by the tenor Adolphe Nourrit, who created the role of Robert and mimed opposite Taglioni in the Ballet of the Nuns. Nourrit had imagined a theme that was to become a pattern for countless ballets in later years: the love between a mortal and a spirit that can find no fulfilment in the world of reality. Such a situation was essentially Romantic, for it mirrored the Romantic artist's obsession with the infinite and the unattainable. In *La Sylphide* Taglioni immortalised the role of the aerial spirit who appears to a young Scot, tempting him to abandon his betrothed and pursue the wraith into the forest, where he discovers to his cost the hopelessness of his quest. Divided into two contrasting acts, the first a rustic scene of the interrupted betrothal celebrations and the second a *'ballet blanc'* set in a mysterious forest where the sylphides dwell, the ballet revealed the two opposing facets of Romanticism – the exotic, with its obsession with local colour, and the supernatural. With Schneitzhoeffer's music, sets by

Ciceri and costumes by Eugène Lami, it was not only the perfect setting for Taglioni's artistry, but also a dance work of unprecedented sublimity. For the first time, ballet had taken flight in the higher reaches of poetic fancy.

Filippo Taglioni was never to equal the achievement of *La Sylphide*, but he continued to produce ballets for his daughter that displayed her artistry with an insight of which only a parent could have been capable. In *La Révolte au serail* (1833), an enormously popular ballet, he presented her as the leader of a feminine revolt. Although the plot was unremarkable save for a curiously prophetic call at the end for women's rights, it contained a wealth of dancing, including a wonderful *pas de deux* for Marie Taglioni and Perrot. These two dancers were superbly matched, but Taglioni, who was conditioned to supremacy, resented sharing the applause with a male partner. For his part, Perrot began to feel he was inadequately rewarded for his services; but the Opéra took a different view of his value, and when his contract expired early in 1835, he was unable to negotiate satisfactory terms and left Paris.

Having established Taglioni in a position of pre-eminence, Véron conceived a plan to stimulate the receipts by pitting her against a younger rival. His attention had been drawn to an Austrian ballerina, Fanny Elssler, who was beginning to gain a promising reputation, and he made a special journey to London to see and engage her. Shortly after her arrival in Paris, she began to study intensively under Vestris, while Véron prepared a publicity campaign in which he cynically exploited an unfounded rumour that she had been the last love of the Duc de Reichstadt, the ill-fated son of Napoleon who had died in Vienna two years before. Any embarrassment that this may have caused her was amply offset by the curiosity it aroused, and her debut in Coralli's *La Tempête* (1834) showed how sure had been Véron's intuition. Not only was she remarkably beautiful, but she danced in a manner that contrasted strongly with Taglioni's style: she was a creature of the earth rather than the air, performing in a style that connoisseurs called *'tacqueté'* to distinguish it from Taglioni's *'ballonné'* manner. Her point work was strong and intricate, and she projected a voluptuous, sensual quality that appealed particularly to the male section of the audience.

Her first creations at the Opéra were in mediocre ballets, and not until 1836 was she given a role that measured up to her talents. Florinda in Coralli's *Le Diable boiteux* (1836) is a passionate Spanish dancer who is involved in a series of fast-moving adventures in a balletic treatment of Le Sage's novel. Towards the end of the ballet Florinda assumes male disguise to challenge the hero to a duel, but the highlight of the role was the Cachucha, a character dance based on the Spanish classical dance vocabulary and skilfully stylised for the stage. It became the sensation of the hour, and made history as the first dance to be encored at the Opéra. Elssler was to perform it, as an isolated number, throughout her career; it was to become identified with her, just as the role of the Sylphide was associated with Taglioni, a parallel that was taken up by the sculptor Jean-Auguste Barre when he made his celebrated statuettes of the two rival ballerinas.

A few months later it was to be Taglioni's turn. Her father's new ballet, *La Fille du Danube* (1836), was somewhat disappointing; but it presented her in another striking role perfectly suited to her style, and at the same time introduced a young ballet composer of exceptional promise, Adolphe Adam. Shortly after this, Taglioni's contract expired and was not renewed by Duponchel, who had succeeded Véron as director. This decision prompted a macabre protest from one of her admirers. He dispatched invitations to Duponchel's funeral, and the director arrived one morning to be astonished to find a funeral cortège drawn up in the courtyard of the Opéra and his friends arriving to pay their last respects.

Taglioni's departure in 1837 left Fanny Elssler in sole possession. After appearing in a ballet by her sister Therese, *La Volière* (1838), notable only for being the first ballet to be produced at the Opéra by a woman, she fell under the influence of the Marquis de La Valette, who unwisely encouraged her to appear in two of Taglioni's most celebrated roles. Fanny Elssler's interpretation of the Sylphide captivated Théophile Gautier, who was just embarking on his career as a theatre critic and was inspired to make the famous analogy of her and Taglioni as being respectively a pagan and a Christian dancer. However, such a presumption infuriated Taglioni's admirers; and when Elssler appeared in *La Fille du Danube*, a riot broke out in the theatre that had to be quelled by the police.

The lesson to be learned was to be true to one's genre, and shortly afterwards Mazilier's *La Gipsy* (1839) provided Elssler with a role that brought out her qualities as a dancer-actress as never before. This was Mazilier's first ballet, and its strong dramatic narrative revealed what was to be the distinguishing feature of most of the works he was to produce at the Opéra over the next twenty years. The scenario was in fact so effective that a few years later it would be adapted for an opera, the highly popular *Bohemian Girl* by Balfe. As the heroine Sarah, a girl of noble birth who has been stolen as a child by gypsies and is restored to her family only to be tragically killed by her distraught gypsy lover, Elssler appeared in a new light: she was acclaimed as a second Bigottini, and even classed with the Shakespearean actress Harriet Smithson. Among the dances was a pendant to her famous *Cachucha* – the *Cracovienne*, which she danced in true military-style costume with clinking spurs on her boots.

Coralli's *La Tarentule* (1840), which followed a year later, was a work of a lighter texture, a witty comedy that she performed with the light touch of a true comedienne, proving that she could arouse laughter as easily as she could draw tears. Its highlight was yet another stirring *pas de caractère* – the *Tarantella*.

In spite of these triumphs, Fanny Elssler was becoming increasingly disillusioned with Paris, for she had been deeply wounded by the hostility shown to her by a section of the public and certain critics. In this mood she grasped at an opportunity to escape, and signed a contract to visit America. Crossing the Atlantic was a hazardous undertaking in those days, but once in the United States she found a wealth of enthusiasm that surpassed her wildest imaginings, and financial rewards to match. Persuaded to overstay the leave of absence that the Opéra had granted her, she remained in America for more than two years, bringing her art to places that had never seen a dancer of her quality before. The Opéra brought proceedings against her for breach of contract, and she was never to dance in Paris again.

The Opéra was thus bereft of its star ballerinas with no obvious replacement to hand. Two promising foreigners had flashed fleetingly across its stage – the Danish ballerina Lucile Grahn, and a coltish young American, Augusta Maywood – but neither stayed, and for a time the ballet was headed by a French dancer, Pauline Leroux. Leroux appeared in Mazilier's *Le Diable amoureux* (1840) with considerable success, but no one really expected her to succeed Taglioni and Elssler, and one observer compared the Opéra to a widow bereaved.

Happily, the period of mourning did not last, for a new star appeared in the person of Carlotta Grisi, a remarkable young dancer whom Jules Perrot had discovered in Italy and brought to Paris in the hope of obtaining engagements at the Opéra for them both. To his chagrin, Perrot's personal ambition was to be disappointed, for the post of leading male dancer had only recently been filled by Lucien Petipa, and the former's flair for choreography was still untried. The loss of French ballet was to be London's gain, for in 1842 Perrot would be engaged as ballet-master at Her Majesty's Theatre, where he produced a series of masterpieces that established him as the greatest choreographer of his time: *Ondine, Esmeralda, Caterina,* the *Pas de Quatre* and others.

Among the men who lost their hearts to Carlotta when she made her debut at the Opera in 1841 was the poet and theatre critic, Théophile Gautier, who became her adoring cavalier and a lifelong friend. The ballet was already a source of passionate interest for him, and in his reviews he not only set new standards of dance criticism but described the performances he saw with such a vivid insight that the modern reader can almost share the thrill of his own experience. Now he was to be drawn by Carlotta into the more active role of scenarist. His involvement began when he read a description by the German Romantic writer, Heinrich Heine, of the wilis of German legend, malign spirits of girls who have died on their wedding eve and waylay young men in the forest to take a posthumous revenge by dancing them to death. From this idea, augmented by a poem by Victor Hugo about a girl who dies after a night of frenzied dancing at a ball, was born the scenario of *Giselle* (1841), which Gautier wrote in collaboration with the dramatist Saint-Georges.

It was submitted, perhaps intentionally, at the very moment when a new ballet was required to launch Carlotta. She had just turned down one proposal, and this new scenario, with an action requiring only two sets, had the merit of being simple to produce. It was accepted immediately, and Adolphe Adam threw himself into the task of writing the music, working closely but privately with Perrot and Carlotta. Perrot seems to have accepted that there could be no question of his producing the ballet himself. This task fell, by right, to the *premier maître de ballet*, Coralli; but perhaps because it was considered only as a stopgap to give time for a more substantial ballet, Coralli was content to allow Perrot to arrange the scenes and dances for Carlotta. It was generally known that Perrot 'had a finger in the pie', but he received neither acknowledgement nor fee for his contribution, nor, as far as is known, did he expect any. It was only much later, on Lifar's prompting, that the Opéra officially recognised him as one of the ballet's creators. Outside France, however, Perrot was to continue to work on this ballet: he revived it first in London and then in St Petersburg, where he produced his definitive version which, with retouchings by Marius Petipa, forms the basis of the ballet as it has been handed down to us today.

Giselle established Carlotta as the true successor to Taglioni and Elssler, and in her Gautier discovered his muse. He was seldom more inspired than when extolling her beauty and artistry. Her feet, he rhapsodised, would have 'driven an Andalusian to despair', not just because of their delicate beauty, but on account of their strength, which enabled her to perform feats of *pointe* work of coruscating intricacy. Almost too much for his impressionable nature was the limpid 'nocturnal' blue of her eyes that reminded him of violets in the twilight. He noted also a 'childlike artlessness, a happy and infectious gaiety, and sometimes a little pouting melancholy', and it was this delicate touch of melancholy that haunted her Giselle. Her interpretation was conceived more in terms of dance than was then the custom, and in that contrasted strongly with the more dramatic performance of the other great Giselle of her time, Fanny Elssler, who, alas, never danced the role in Paris.

Giselle had much in common with *La Sylphide*, being based on the same formula, with its action taking place on the two levels of the real and the supernatural. Dramatically, however, it was a profounder work, and today it is universally considered the greatest achievement of the Romantic ballet. Strangely enough, its significance was not recognised in Paris until long afterwards: after being dropped from the Opéra repertory in 1868, it was not considered worthy of revival until 1924.

As the 1840s rolled on, Carlotta's supremacy at the Opéra was consolidated by a varied series of creations. Gautier supplied her with another scenario, for Coralli's *La Péri* (1843), an oriental fantasy, again based on a mortal – spirit relationship, and containing as its highlight an incredible leap by Carlotta into Lucien Petipa's arms from a platform two metres high. It was a feat of great daring, which she was not able to accomplish every time. When she misjudged it once in London, the audience responded to her courage and begged her not to attempt it again, but the Opéra public was harder to please and on one occasion made her perform it three times before being satisfied. It was also reported that a certain sensation-seeking Englishman never missed a performance of the work at the Opéra because he was convinced that one day she would kill herself.

On a more earthly level, but even more successful, was Mazilier's *Le Diable à quatre* (1845), a sparkling comedy ballet of exchanged identities to music by Adam. As the simple basket-maker's wife who is transformed by magic into a countess for one day, Carlotta showed a new side to her talent. She made the audience laugh by the wit of her acting, but although her part included a dancing-lesson scene in which she had to appear gauche, she also had opportunities to display her spectacular technique. 'Her satin ballet slipper seems to end in a blade of steel,' wrote one critic. 'She stays poised on her *pointe*, immobile as a marble statue.' In *Paquita* (1846), a melodramatic ballet set in Spain during the First Empire, Mazilier exploited her astonishing technical skill to such an extent that she was heard to complain in the wings of the pain that so much point work caused her. Her ordeal can be imagined when one reflects on the light, unblocked slippers, strengthened only by darning and wadding, on which Romantic dancers rose on their toes to give the illusion of weightlessness and flight.

For her last creation at the Opéra, *La Filleule des fées* (1849), Carlotta had the satisfaction of working once again with the man to whom she owed her first successes, Jules Perrot. Now a choreographer of European repute, Perrot was able to spare a few months between engagements in London and St Petersburg to produce his only ballet for the Opéra. After the artistic freedom he had enjoyed in London, he may have been disappointed to find himself hamstrung by the conventional fairy tale imagined by the scenarist, Saint-Georges, but he nevertheless created some enchanting choreography for Carlotta and revealed his exceptional ability in handling a large *corps de ballet*.

With Carlotta Grisi's departure from the Opéra at the end of 1849, the golden age of the Romantic ballet came to an end. In a space of only twenty years, three '*déesses de la danse*' – Taglioni, Elssler and Carlotta Grisi – had caught the imagination of the public and given ballet a popularity it had never enjoyed before; but in doing so they had also helped to sow the seeds of future decadence. They had inaugurated the cult of the ballerina, which was to retain its hold until the twentieth century; but it was at the expense of the male dancer, who found himself consigned, not so much by a lack of talent as by the taste of the increasingly bourgeois public, to a sorry state of subservience. Gone were the days when a Dupré or a Vestris was the main pillar of the Opéra. Lucien Petipa, admired though he was, was neither applauded nor rewarded in the same proportion as the dancers he partnered, and for nearly a hundred years his successors in Paris were to fare even worse. This eclipse of the male dancer emasculated the art of ballet, as would be revealed all too clearly by the decline that set in when the first flush of Romanticism faded.

VI

Romanticism in Decline

Carlotta Grisi was the first in a long and virtually unbroken line of Italian ballerinas who were to dominate the ballet of the Opéra for nearly a century. She was not wholly a product of the Italian school herself, having perfected her style under Jules Perrot, but her strong technique, and particularly her point work, portended the fertilisation of French ballet with the brilliant virtuosity being developed in Milan. In the second half of the nineteenth century, the Scuola di Ballo of La Scala supplied ballerinas for most of the opera houses of Europe, but with rare exceptions their technical mastery was achieved at the expense of lyricism and feeling. Technique was in danger of becoming an end in itself. Ballet began to lose touch with the trends that vitalised other arts and to degenerate into a mere entertainment built up around the person of the star ballerina.

In Paris this decline was at first hardly noticeable. For twenty years after Carlotta Grisi's retirement until the close of the Second Empire, the Opéra remained the main centre of European ballet. Its repertory was replenished with new ballets with no observable loss of importance relative to the operatic productions; the style taught in the School of Dance was still distinctively French; and, most significantly, the presence of Mazilier, Saint-Léon and Marie Taglioni was an ever-present reminder of the link with the golden age of the 1830s and 1840s.

Arthur Saint-Léon, who dominated French ballet first from 1847 to 1852, and later from 1863 until his death in 1870, was a man of exceptional dynamism and versatility. As a dancer, he possessed a spectacular technique that placed him among the foremost male virtuosos of his time; but he was also a brilliant violinist, a choreographer with a facile turn of invention, no mean teacher, and a man who thought deeply about his art. He had become both partner and husband of Fanny Cerrito, the Neapolitan ballerina who was London's special favourite, and when they were both engaged at the Opéra in 1847 they were regarded, professionally, as an inseparable team.

Cerrito was then thirty and had lost something of the fresh physical appeal that had overwhelmed London, but she still possessed an exciting attack and a voluptuous charm. She and Saint-Léon had been travelling around Europe with a repertory of tried successes for some years, and most of Saint-Léon's early ballets for the Opéra were revivals, which he was able to mount with considerable speed and efficiency. They made their Paris debut in *La Fille de marbre* (1847), an adaptation of *Alma* (London, 1842), one of Cerrito's greatest successes. This was followed by *La Vivandière* (London 1844, Opéra 1848), a slighter work notable mainly for its sparkling character dance, the *Redowa*, and *Le Violin du Diable* (Venice 1848, Opéra 1849), in which the versatile choreographer appeared as a violinist as well as a dancer. These three ballets also had music by Cesare Pugni, probably the most prolific ballet composer of all time, whom Saint-Léon had come across in London, producing great quantities of ballet music to order for Her Majesty's Theatre. Pugni also wrote the score of *Stella* (1850), a ballet with a colourful Neapolitan setting, culminating in a brilliant tarantella. Saint-Léon's choreographic pretensions were at this time relatively modest. These early ballets were all primarily vehicles for Cerrito, but some of the distinctive features of his later work were already apparent, particularly his interest in national dances.

More than any of his colleagues, Saint-Léon was concerned about the ephemeral nature of a choreographer's creative work, the survival of which depended entirely on human memory. To remedy this he invented an ingenious method of dance notation, called *Sténochorégraphie*, and wrote a manual which, with an eye to his future, he dedicated to Tsar Nicholas I of Russia. Although he hardly ever put the system to practical use, he preserved for posterity, as an appendix to his book, the whole of the *pas de six* from *La Vivandière*, including his own and Cerrito's variations.

His partnership with Cerrito came to an end when their marriage broke up in 1851. He produced one more ballet for her, *Pâquerette* (1851), to a scenario by Gautier, and left the Opéra in 1852. Cerrito remained at the Opéra until 1855, her last creation being in *Gemma* (1854), a ballet she choreographed herself, again with Gautier as scenarist. After her retirement she settled in Paris, living in such untroubled tranquillity that her death more than fifty years later passed completely unnoticed. It was the summer of 1909, and the public was so preoccupied with the forthcoming opening of Diaghilev's first season of Russian ballet that it gave no thought to the passing of one of the great Romantic ballerinas. *Sic transit gloria mundi!*

At the Opéra, Cerrito's place was to be filled by Carolina Rosati and Amalia Ferraris, for whom Mazilier produced his last ballets. Although both ballerinas were pupils of Carlo Blasis, the great teacher who had revitalised the Italian school, they could hardly have been more different in temperament and style. Rosati was volatile by nature, stirring memories of Elssler by the intensity of her acting and the 'earthly' quality of her dancing, while Ferraris possessed a tranquil personality and a technique that was distinguished by a feather-light elevation.

With his predilection for dramatic narrative, Mazilier found an ideal interpreter in Rosati, for whom he produced two powerful ballets, *La Fonti* (1855) and *Le Corsaire* (1856). *La Fonti* reaches its climax with an unforgettable mad scene in which the betrayed heroine appears, her mind deranged, in the midst of a carnival crowd who jeer at her as she dances a crazy tarantella before faltering and falling to the ground dead. It was this role that drew from Blasis the tribute that she was the perfect example of a ballerina who was equally dancer and mime. *Le Corsaire* was based on Byron's poem, its score being the last work that Adolphe Adam composed before his death a few months after the first performance. For local colour and dramatic interest it was only to be compared with Fanny Elssler's successes, *Le Diable boiteux* and *La Gipsy*, of a generation before. Rosati had a great triumph as the heroine Medora, and the final scene was a *tour de force* of the machinist's art – an incredibly realistic shipwreck, which Gustave Doré depicted in a vivid engraving for one of the illustrated papers.

Ferraris made her Paris debut in 1856, and the following year Mazilier boldly presented her and Rosati together in the same ballet, *Marco Spada* (1857). Based on a comic opera by Auber, it was a strongly dramatic work containing contrasting ballerina roles tailored for the two principals: the bandit's daughter for Rosati and the Marquise for Ferraris. It was the first time that two such prestigious stars had appeared in the same ballet at the Opéra; neither Camargo and Sallé, nor Taglioni and Elssler, had confronted one another in this way. More remarkable still was the effect of the last act, when the whole stage rose to reveal a double-storeyed scene – a battle between bandits and soldiers taking place on the upper level, and beneath, Marco Spada expiring in his underground cavern.

Ferraris's most interesting work at the Opéra was in Lucien Petipa's first ballet, *Sacountala* (1858). Théophile Gautier had based the scenario on a drama by the Hindu poet Kalidasa, and the ballet had an unusually distinguished score by Ernest Reyer, whose operas *Sigurd* and *Salammbô* were to enter the Opéra repertory later in the century. As befitted Ferraris's talent, the leading role was designed primarily to bring out her technical virtuosity, with dazzling turns, aerial leaps, *tours de force* on *pointe*, and in the *pas de deux* of the first act a breath-catching lift in which Petipa held her aloft at the full stretch of his arm.

After the departure from the Opéra of Rosati in 1859 and Ferraris in 1863, a French ballerina might have broken the sequence of Italian stars if Fate had not cruelly ordained otherwise. In October 1858 the debut was announced of an unknown sixteen-year-old dancer called Emma Livry in a revival of *La Sylphide*. Considering that this would be her first stage appearance, it was a singularly bold undertaking, for there were many who could remember Taglioni in her most famous role. In addition to her inexperience, the young dancer had other handicaps: she was skinny in an age that admired curvaceous women, and she was plain. She was judged therefore solely on her performance as a dancer and an interpreter, and the extent of her triumph was a complete vindication of those who had faith in her, bringing immediate renown both to herself and to her devoted teacher, Mme Dominique. Taglioni, then living in retirement by the shores of Lake Como, was very curious to see the new Sylphide and came post-haste to Paris. She was overwhelmed. 'It is true that I never saw myself dance,' she was heard to say, 'but I must have danced like her.' She needed little persuasion to remain in Paris to watch over the development of the new star, and took over the *classe de perfectionnement* at the School of Dance.

More than that, she decided to turn choreographer, and produced *Le Papillon* (1860) especially for the gifted young Livry. With its sparkling score by Offenbach, this ballet gave Livry a creation that was to be associated with her no less indelibly than the Sylphide had been with Taglioni. Had her career not been cut short, the ballet would doubtless have survived much longer in the repertory, for it was dropped principally because no one had the heart to see another dancer in the title role. At the time of its creation it aroused exceptional interest: Napoleon III saw it twice, both of London's opera houses begged Livry to bring it to England, and Barre added a statuette of Livry in her butterfly costume to the figures of Taglioni and Elssler he had made nearly a quarter of a century before. The world was at Emma Livry's feet.

Plans were soon made for another ballet by Taglioni, and while this was being prepared Livry agreed, with some reluctance, to play the mime role of Fenella in Auber's opera, *La Muette de Portici*. It was a fateful decision, for it was during a rehearsal of this work that her career was cut short in a horrifying accident that long cast its gloom over French ballet. As she stood up to enter the stage, her skirt touched a naked gas flame. She ran screaming on to the stage with flames blazing high above her head. By the time a fireman caught her, she was frightfully burned. She endured eight months of agony before death finally claimed her on a summer night in 1863. Her body was interred in the Montmartre Cemetery, and as the cortège made its way sadly through the streets, Gautier, with his poet's eye, observed two white butterflies hovering ceaselessly above the coffin.

At this time, the Opéra was faced with a considerable problem because it had no resident choreographer who could shoulder the responsibility of replenishing the repertory. Lucien Petipa had succeeded Mazilier as *premier maître de ballet* in 1860, but apart from divertissements in opera, his ballets were rare. Alphonse Royer, the director of the Opéra at this time, attributed the decline of ballet that followed Mazilier's retirement to the lack of a ballerina capable of supporting a major role in a *ballet d'action*: there were now, as he put it, only 'danseuses de pas'. But Petipa's inadequacy as a creative artist was clearly recognised, for in the early 1860s the Opéra turned frequently to other choreographers to produce important works: Marie Taglioni, Pasquale Borri and Giuseppe Rota. Lucien Petipa's younger brother Marius, who was developing a prodigious talent in St Petersburg, also came to Paris, producing with his brother's help a minor work, *Le Marché des innocents* (1861).

Eventually the Opéra's dilemma was resolved, without dispossessing Lucien Petipa, by the reappearance of Saint-Léon. Since leaving the Opéra some ten years before, Saint-Léon had succeeded Perrot in the prestigious post of ballet-master to the Russian Imperial Theatres, but the theatrical season in Russia was so short that he was free for half the year. Consequently, for eight successive years, from 1863 to 1870, he was able to spend the summers working for the Opéra. In this way he achieved the unique distinction of dominating both French and Russian ballet simultaneously.

Under its new Tsar, Alexander II, Russia was then encouraging much closer ties with the rest of Europe, and it became easier for Russian dancers to visit Paris. Maria Petipa, the first wife of Marius Petipa, was granted permission to appear at the Opéra in 1861 and 1862, and the following year an invitation was sent to Marfa Muravieva. Nervous at the thought of being so far from home, Muravieva expressed the desire to work with a choreographer she knew, such as Saint-Léon. The new director, Émile Perrin, invited Saint-Léon to produce a new ballet for her, and was so impressed by his personality that he soon came to rely on his advice in preference to Lucien Petipa's on matters relating to the ballet.

During Muravieva's visits to Paris in 1863 and 1864 she danced in a revival of *Giselle* and two ballets by Saint-Léon, *Diavolina* (1863) and *Néméa* (1864), both being variants of works he had produced earlier in Russia. *Néméa,* the more substantial of the two, had a score by his close friend, Ludwig Minkus, and brought into prominence Eugénie Fiocre, who created a sensation as a beauty in the role of Cupid. Muravieva was expected in Paris for a third season in 1865, but suddenly decided to retire from the stage – in obedience, it appeared, to the wish of her future mother-in-law.

The Opéra was now in desperate need of a ballerina to fill the gap left by Rosati, Ferraris and Livry. A distinguished Italian dancer, Amina Boschetti, appeared briefly in 1864, but her figure was too opulent to please, and her compatriot, Guglielmina Salvioni, who danced in Paris from 1864 to 1867, proved little more than a highly proficient virtuoso. The problem seemed solved when Saint-Léon recommended Adèle Grantzow, a young German dancer who, although under contract in Russia, was, like him, free to appear in Paris in the summer. With the dearth of ballerinas of the class required, such an arrangement was acceptable to the Opéra, particularly since Grantzow was a pupil of Mme Dominique and possessed a style that was refreshingly French.

Her debut at the Opéra in *Giselle* in 1866 revealed her as a dancer of great charm and promise, and Paris looked forward to her first creation, in the new ballet, *La Source* (1866), which Saint-Léon was preparing. But this was not to be: for various reasons the production was delayed, and she had to be replaced by Salvioni. The most important ballet to have been presented in Paris for some years, *La Source* introduced a combination that seemed an exciting augury for the future. Saint-Léon had discovered two collaborators with whom he could work in the closest sympathy: Léo Delibes, a young composer with a brilliant melodic gift that was ideally suited to the dance, and as his scenarist, Charles

Nuitter, a wealthy theatre-lover who had undertaken the task of organising, gratis, the Opéra's archives. Nuitter's scenario was not exceptional, but Delibes's music for two of the four scenes was infinitely superior to that of Minkus, who was responsible for the remainder of the score. Although deprived of the opportunity of creating the part of Naïla, Grantzow took it over in 1867 with such success that one critic said it was like seeing the ballet for the first time.

Saint-Léon, Delibes and Nuitter soon set to work on a new creation which, in spite of all the trouble and delays in its production, was to become the most frequently performed ballet in the whole history of the Opéra – *Coppélia* (1870). Grantzow, the original choice for the principal role, was again unlucky. After rehearsing it throughout the summer of 1868, she fell so seriously ill that Saint-Léon had to start all over again with another ballerina the following year. So desperate had been the search for a replacement that Delibes had even been sent to Italy to scour the ballet schools there for talent; but while he was away the choice had fallen on a fifteen-year-old girl who was being carefully groomed by Mme Dominique in the School of Dance. This young dancer, Giuseppina Bozzacchi, had never appeared in public, and Saint-Léon had to reshape very radically the role of Swanilda, which he had originally conceived for an experienced ballerina.

Nuitter's scenario for *Coppélia* could hardly be faulted. The story of two young lovers who play a rather cruel joke on an eccentric old doll-maker was almost perfectly suited for the medium of ballet. Delibes's music expressed all the turns of the plot and the quirks of the characters in a way that no ballet score had done previously, while Saint-Léon, who usually worked too hastily, had this time been forced by circumstances to prepare his choreography with exceptional thoroughness. The result was a polished masterpiece that has retained its popularity for more than a century. Outside Paris, *Coppélia* has been reproduced by many other choreographers, but Saint-Léon's version, which long remained the basis of the Opéra's production, remains unmatched for its delicacy and charm.

At its first performance *Coppélia* was an immediate success for authors and performers alike. The public took the gentle Bozzacchi to their hearts, and Eugénie Fiocre appeared opposite her *en travesti* as a charming Frantz – continuing a convention that had been growing over the past few years, partly as a result of the disfavour shown to male dancers, and partly no doubt because of Fiocre's piquant charm in roles such as this, in which she could show off her shapely figure without the concealing effect of a ballet skirt.

But tragic events were at hand. That summer, war broke out with Prussia. After a few weeks of military disasters, the Second Empire fell and Paris was besieged. Bozzacchi's dreams of glory faded, the Opéra was closed, and Saint-Léon died of a sudden heart attack at the age of forty-nine. A few months later, when the rigours of winter were added to the hardships of the besieged population, Bozzacchi died of smallpox on her seventeenth birthday. Today her grave is

1. Jean-Baptiste Lully. 2. Pierre Beauchamp.

3. Louis Pécour.

4. Marie-Thérèse Subligny.

5. Françoise Prévost.

6. Marie-Anne Cupis de Camargo.

7. Marie Sallé.

8. Anne Heinel.

9. Louise Madeleine Lany.

10. Jean-Georges Noverre.

11. Maximilien Gardel.

12. Pierre Gardel.

13. Marie Gardel.

14. Emilie Bigottini.

15. Geneviève Gosselin.

16. Marie and Paul Taglioni in *La Sylphide*.

17. Fanny Elssler dancing the *cachucha*.

18. Carlotta Grisi as Giselle.

19. *Giselle*, Act I.

20. Arthur Saint-Léon and Fanny Cerrito in *Le Violon du Diable*.

21. Carolina Rosati in *Le Corsaire*.

22. Emma Livry and Louis Mérante in *La Sylphide*.  23. Marfa Muravieva in Act II of *Giselle*.

24. Adèle Grantzow.

25. Giuseppina Bozzacchi as Swanilda in *Coppélia*.

26. Eugénie Fiocre as Frantz in *Coppélia*.

27. Scenes from the first production of *Sylvia*.

28. Rita Sangalli in *Yedda*.

29. Rosita Mauri.

30. Carlotta Zambelli.

unmarked, for she was buried in the *fosse commune*, but she has her memorial, far more lasting than any tomb, in the immortal character of Swanilda.

The war of 1870–71 and the Commune that followed interrupted the activities of the Opéra for nearly a year. In the development of French ballet this break marked very sharply the close of a period. The deaths of Mazilier and Saint-Léon and the retirement of Taglioni had deprived the Opéra of three vital links with the past. The prestige of the ballet was greatly diminished. Louis Mérante, who had been appointed *premier maître de ballet* in 1869 when the post was little more than that of assistant to Saint-Léon, still had to prove his choreographic talent, and the company was sadly deficient in star material: never was the loss of Livry and Bozzacchi more sorely felt.

The new director, Olivier Halanzier, was very conscious of the decline of the ballet and devoted much thought to restoring its prestige, even if not all his ideas bore fruit. As a replacement for Saint-Léon he considered Jules Perrot, who was at that time giving classes at the Opéra; but Perrot, it seems, had no desire to resume his creative activity. Among the proposals for new ballets were two imaginative projects, which unfortunately never materialised. The last work that Gautier wrote before he died in 1872 was a scenario on the theme of *The Pied Piper of Hamelin* which Jules Massenet was to set to music, but Mérante rejected it – surely, as a wit suggested, on the ground that the *abonnés* would not stand for rats being represented in a ballet. There was also talk of engaging Hippolyte Monplaisir, a French choreographer who had produced many successful ballets in Italy, but nothing came of that. In his search for a ballerina, Halanzier was to be more fortunate: although his first choice, Erminia Pertoldi, was ill-conceived, he then secured the services of Rita Sangalli, who was to dominate the Opéra ballet for many years. Changes were also required in the School of Dance, where Mme Dominique took over the *classe de perfectionnement*, relinquishing the children's class to Zina Mérante.

In 1871, ballet performances at the Opéra were resumed with a diminished repertory and with French dancers such as Léontine Beaugrand, Annette Mérante, Eugénie Fiocre and Laure Fonta taking the leading roles. Nearly two years were to pass before a new ballet was produced. This was Mérante's *Gretna Green* (1873), an insubstantial piece to music by Ernest Guiraud, which is worthy of note only because it was the last ballet to be created at the theatre in the Rue Le Peletier before it was burnt to the ground in October that same year. The fire was a further setback for the ballet, for the scenery and costumes for nearly all the current repertory, including *Coppélia, La Source* and *Gretna Green*, were destroyed. For the theatre itself, whose walls had echoed with applause on so many great occasions of opera and ballet, it was a spectacular and not unfitting end. It was as if it had taken a hand itself in determining its fate, to avoid the ignominy of demolition that inevitably awaited it when Charles Garnier's palatial new opera house a few blocks away was completed.

VII

The Decadence

The fire in the Rue Le Peletier had the timely effect of hastening the completion of the new opera house, which by then had already taken twelve years to build. Throughout 1874, when the finishing touches were being applied, the displaced singers and dancers gave their performances in the cramped surroundings of the Salle Ventadour, which they had to share with the Italian opera company. Mercifully, this spell of acute inconvenience was short, for the gala opening of the new theatre was announced for 5 January 1875.

A few weeks before the inauguration, Halanzier took Rita Sangalli to see the new stage. Recalling how, in Boston, she had once misjudged the depth of the stage and fallen into the orchestra pit, he turned to her and said jokingly: 'Well, is it large enough this time?'

She did not reply, but instead walked to the back of the stage and from there darted forward with three great leaps that took her to the very edge of the prompter's box.

For a building conceived in the flamboyant style of the Second Empire, it was sad that its inauguration should be deprived of imperial pageantry. But if an Emperor and his Cent Gardes were absent, it was nonetheless a glittering occasion, with the King of Spain and the Lord Mayor of London among the distinguished guests.

Sangalli's presence in the final item in the programme, a scene from *La Source*, underlined the continuing Italian influence in French ballet. When Halanzier engaged her in 1872, she already had behind her an experience that was extraordinary in a dancer still in her early twenties. A product of La Scala, Milan, she had left her native city to win laurels further afield, first in Turin and London, and then in the United States, where she spent three adventurous years and crossed the newly opened-up continent from east to west. In Paris she had filled a much-felt want, bringing a glamour and excitement that the French dancers, for all the orthodox purity of their style, were unable to supply. Typically Italian in appearance, she was as strong and supple as an acrobat, performing daring *tours de force* with energetic panache.

The Italian school did not have all its own way, for Léontine Beaugrand had established herself as a French star of a magnitude not known since the time of Noblet fifty years before. She was a 'daughter of the house' in the truest sense of the term, having been trained from childhood in the School of Dance, gained her early experience in the *corps de ballet* and gradually worked her way to the top. Her progress was at times almost despairingly slow. Being French was in itself a disadvantage. As Gautier observed when writing about her, 'there are several dancers who have great talent and are just as worthy as the exotic personalities who are imported at great expense, but they have been seen since they were very young, and people hardly notice a plant that has all the time been growing before their very eyes'.

Her opportunity came after the war of 1870–71, when in the absence of foreign stars she found herself heading the company. She took over the role of Swanilda with the most conspicuous success, and created that of Pretty in *Gretna Green*, but although she acquired a host of admirers who refused to be seduced by Italian virtuosity and saw her as the personification of the French school, she was somehow never able to impose herself fully on the public. She had an irreproachable technique, and was so consistent that it was said that her execution never varied from one performance to another, but she lacked charm and warmth.

It was clear to all but her most fervent followers that the Opéra ballet could flourish only with the support of an Italian star, and it was Sangalli who was cast in the new ballet for which Delibes was writing his second complete ballet score, *Sylvia* (1876). The composer had been initiated into the world of ballet by two collaborators with whom he had enjoyed an unusual sharing of minds. The driving force of this combination, Saint-Léon, was now dead, and the other, Nuitter, was given no part in the creation of the new ballet. Delibes must have missed them greatly, for the scenario he was given lacked dramatic interest and contained no scope for the sort of characterisation that had inspired him in *Coppélia*. Further, the choreographer, Louis Mérante, although highly competent, lacked the flair and experience of Saint-Léon. Fortunately these difficulties did not inhibit Delibes from producing a masterpiece of a score, which was not only wonderfully rich in melody but also written in a symphonic manner that was novel for its time. It was to be universally acknowledged as an important landmark in the development of ballet music, and a young Russian composer, Piotr Ilyich Tchaikovsky, who was beginning to write for the ballet himself, was so overwhelmed by it that he despaired of producing anything to match it. 'It put me to shame,' he confessed to a friend. 'If I had known that music, I would never have written *Swan Lake*.'

But for its music, *Sylvia* would have soon been forgotten. For its first three performances it was presented on its own, without an accompanying opera, an experiment that was not to the public's taste. Generously served by the choreographer, Sangalli enjoyed a personal triumph, but the ballet itself was only moderately successful.

The direction had placated Beaugrand with the promise of a new ballet, but all she was offered was a wretched one-act piece, *Le Fandango* (1877). She made what she could of it, only to find that its failure was attributed, not to Mérante's shortcomings as a choreographer, but to herself for being no longer a box-office attraction. Not surprisingly, she and Mérante had little liking for one another. When she heard that he had said she was growing too old to dance, she commented sourly: 'He says I am no longer young because I made him look old-fashioned'. In 1880 she was driven to retire; and as a final indignity, her offer to become a teacher was spurned. There was general astonishment that the direction had bowed to 'petty backstage intrigues' and yielded 'to the demands of an all-powerful rival'. Beaugrand received offers to dance elsewhere, but she had no desire to continue her career in unfamiliar surroundings. 'I have never danced anything but the French school,' she explained, 'and I have danced it only at the Opéra.'

Her departure came as a shock, but the French school did not of course disappear with her. It was, nevertheless, coming increasingly under Italian influence, not only through the presence of Sangalli, but also from the Italian ballet company of the Eden Théâtre, a brash entertainment house which opened in 1883 within a stone's throw of the Opéra. The renowned Italian choreographer, Luigi Manzotti, came there to produce *Excelsior* and *Sieba*, and Paris was overwhelmed by the novelty of it all: by the vertiginous spinning of Elena Cornalba and the passionate miming of Virginia Zucchi, by the almost military precision of the *corps de ballet*, and by the titillatingly short skirts of the ballerinas. The ballet of the Eden was the sensation of the hour, and some critics were so carried away that they made unfavourable and unfair comparisons with the Opéra. In time a more balanced outlook prevailed, and it was realised that French ballet as practised at the Opéra possessed qualities of finesse and expression that were more valuable than the eye-catching effects of the Italians.

Although the French dancers absorbed a certain amount of Italian virtuosity, they retained their distinctive qualities. While it was found necessary to have an Italian prima ballerina at the head of the Opéra ballet, the company was trained exclusively by French teachers and there were still openings for French talent. Beaugrand's place was soon filled by Julia Subra, who took over the role of Swanilda in *Coppélia* in 1882. Some purists would have wished her to be more in Beaugrand's mould and were shocked to find that she had been somewhat infected by the Italian school. But her quality was fundamentally French, and for many years she was to rank alongside Sangalli, Mauri and Zambelli.

Even Sangalli had been upset by the exaggerated praise bestowed on the productions at the Eden, exclaiming in a moment of exasperation: 'But I do the same thing'. She need have had no fears about the Eden, which lasted only a short time as a centre of ballet, but within the Opéra itself a very real threat to her position had materialised in the person of Rosita Mauri. Mauri was a Spaniard who had been partially trained in the French school, her father having brought her to Paris, at great personal sacrifice, to study under Mme Dominique. She had then gone to Milan, where Gounod had seen her dancing at La Scala and immediately wanted her for the new opera he was writing, *Polyeucte*. Mérante gave his blessing, Halanzier went to Milan to engage her, and she made her debut in 1878.

Sangalli's supremacy was in jeopardy from the very beginning of Mauri's engagement, and within a few months she found herself compelled to share her latest creation and invite a direct comparison. This was the title role in Mérante's *Yedda* (1879), a ballet with a Japanese setting that lasted only a short time in the repertory but was exceptional for its time in having a tragic ending. Sangalli, who was the more expressive mime, acted Yedda's death scene with convincing pathos, but Mauri unquestionably proved her superiority as a dancer. While she was in no way deficient in virtuosity, she danced with a harmonious, flowing style that was in marked contrast with Sangalli's displays of energy and strength. The question of who was the finer artist was never really in doubt, and this rankled with Sangalli. For some time the two ballerinas were hardly on speaking terms, but eventually a public reconciliation was skilfully arranged. In a performance of *La Muette de Portici* to celebrate the centenary of Auber's birth, a new *pas* was inserted in which they danced together as two jealous women who begin by hurling abuse at one another and then, forgetting their differences, fall into each other's arms. It was a touching moment for the public, and for Mauri a satisfying acknowledgement of her supremacy, which she had firmly established in *La Korrigane* (1880).

This ballet, with its charming Breton theme imagined by the poet François Coppée, was one of Mérante's most successful productions. Charles Widor's music attracted unusually serious attention and, twelve years before Tchaikovsky discovered the liquid tones of the celeste for *Casse-Noisette*, introduced a similar instrument by the same inventor, Mustel, known as the typophone. The ballet's peasant-girl heroine was perfectly portrayed by Mauri, who at one moment put on wooden clogs to dance a spirited *sabotière*. Her dancing was full of joy, and Coppée searched his imagination for parallels. 'She whinnies and darts like a young foal,' he wrote, 'she soars and glides like a bird on the wing. Indeed, in her dark and somewhat wild beauty is to be found something both of the Arab steed and of the swallow.'

The improving standard of ballet music was one of the redeeming features of French ballet at this period, but there were limits beyond which it was dangerous to stray. Vaucorbeil, Halanzier's successor as director, commissioned Edouard Lalo to compose the score for the ballet *Namouna* (1882) as a consolation for not producing his opera, *Le Roi d'Ys*. 'It seems that I can only enter the Opéra through a ballerina's door,' sighed the composer as he conscientiously set to work. The task proved so exhausting that he fell seriously ill, and in a selfless gesture of friendship Charles Gounod completed the orchestration. This was not the end of Lalo's troubles. It was believed that Sangalli disliked his music, but in fact her illness turned out not to be feigned, as had been suspected, and when the Opéra threatened to give the role to Mauri, she announced that she would dance it even if it killed her. Lucien Petipa had emerged from retirement to produce this ballet, which was musically so much in advance of its time that it was not to be fully appreciated until nearly a quarter of a century later. The role of Namouna was Sangalli's last creation, for shortly afterwards, in 1884, she retired.

Mauri, now the unchallenged star of the Opéra ballet, was provided by Mérante with two more triumphs: the divertissement in Massenet's opera *Le Cid* (1885) and the role of Gourouli in *Les Deux Pigeons* (1886). Gourouli was one of Mauri's happiest creations: she appeared in the first act virtually unrecognisable in a blonde wig, but in the second scene in the gypsy camp she let her long black hair flow over her shoulders. *Les Deux Pigeons* was remarkable on two other counts: it introduced André Messager to ballet, and it proved to be Mérante's swansong as a choreographer. Messager's music was in the direct tradition set by Delibes, being equally inventive in the delicate passages and in the rousing gypsy dances. Mérante responded to this score, arranging the ensembles with a care that revealed a lesson learned from the Eden Théâtre. But within a year this hard-working, dignified man was dead, at the age of only fifty-nine, deeply mourned by his dancers.

As *premier maître de ballet* for seventeen years, he had given the ballet of the Opéra a period of remarkable stability. He had ruled his charges with a kindly authority, leaving the harsher duties of maintaining discipline to his *régisseur de la danse*, Édouard Pluque, a stern martinet who held that post from 1870 to 1895. Mérante, however, must bear much of the responsibility for the loss of the old repertory. He had little sense of tradition, it seemed, for he allowed the ballets of Mazilier and Saint-Léon to sink into oblivion while producing little of any distinction to take their place.

Mérante's choreographic heritage has long since vanished, yet we can visualise the life of the dancers as it was in his day with miraculous clarity through the eyes of one of the greatest painters ever to have become absorbed by the dance. To connoisseurs of painting, the name of Edgar Degas is virtually synonymous with the ballet. For more than twenty years, first in the Opéra of the Rue Le Peletier and then at the Palais Garnier, this solitary artist haunted the classrooms and the wings, observing everything about him with a determined concentration, endlessly and patiently sketching. He revealed an insight into the mysteries of ballet that has never been surpassed, and which his friend Manet could relate only to Chardin's treatment of still life. In his drawings and paintings, the dancers, the teachers (Perrot and Mérante among them), the violinist-accompanist, even the mothers, all come to life in a veritable microcosm in which the fatigue of the anonymous ballet girl sinking onto a bench after an exhausting class is portrayed with no less immediacy and care than the proud elation of the ballerina taking her bow before the public.

The male dancer was conspicuously absent in Degas's pictures, an oversight that was not unintended, reflecting as it did the public's indifference to men in ballet. This attitude was to reach a peak of absurdity in 1891 when a certain deputy, taking part in a debate on the Opéra budget, proposed that since 'those strange creatures called male dancers' were needed only to support the ballerinas, they should be replaced by bus drivers at a cost of three or four francs an evening! In the face of such prejudice the travesty role appeared as a natural solution, but Mérante, to his credit, resorted to it relatively sparingly. He had himself played leading roles in his ballets almost to the end of his life, and only twice, in *Gretna Green* and *Les Deux Pigeons*, did he conceive his hero in feminine guise. In the School of Dance the consequences were more serious: few boys were taking up ballet as a career, those that did being embarrassingly outnumbered by the girls, and the teachers were now almost exclusively female. Without a man to learn from and emulate, it was not surprising that the standard of male dancing fell disastrously. During the last thirty years of the century the Opéra possessed only one male dancer of any real calibre, Michel Vasquez.

Even the Foyer de la Danse was losing its attraction. The palatial room that Garnier had designed in the new Opéra lacked the intimacy of the Foyer de la Danse at the Rue Le Peletier, and the policy of admitting anyone who had subscribed for all three performances in the week took away the cachet of exclusivity. Fewer dancers bothered to assemble there now, and the stars often preferred to receive in their spacious dressing rooms.

Such was the state of the ballet in 1887, when Mérante died. There was no obvious successor to be found in the company, and the Opéra turned to a Belgian ballet-master, Joseph Hansen, who had worked in Brussels, London and Moscow. His experience seemed promising: he knew the Saint-Léon version of *Coppélia,* and in Moscow he had staged a new production of *Swan Lake*, a ballet still unknown to Western Europe. During his twenty years at the Opéra, from 1887 to 1907, he proved to be a competent but not particularly successful choreographer. As Antonin Proust put it, 'he lacked neither the will, nor the desire to please, but he was not helped by circumstances'.

Nor was the cause of ballet helped by the presence, in the director's chair, of Pedro Gailhard, a former baritone who guided the fortunes of the Opéra from 1884, with one interval of just over a year, until 1907. The upkeep of the Opéra at the Palais Garnier had become ruinously costly, and in fixing his financial priorities Gailhard deliberately starved the ballet, concentrating almost exclusively on the opera. Even there he was forced to play for safety by producing revivals of works that had succeeded elsewhere. He was much helped by the vogue for Wagner, and it was during his regime that amends were made for the dishonourable fiasco of the first Paris production of *Tannhäuser* in 1860, when members of the Jockey Club created a scene because the obligatory ballet had been inserted in the first act, at an hour when they were accustomed to be still at dinner. In 1895 *Tannhäuser* was much more respectfully received. It was notable for its Venusberg scene, which had been arranged by Virginia Zucchi, who herself appeared in the first few performances as one of the Graces.

The ballet company was disgracefully underprivileged. While the stars of the opera successfully demanded higher salaries, and the musicians of the orchestra enjoyed the right of sending a substitute if they wished to play in concerts elsewhere, the dancers had to make do on a budget that had stayed static for years. It was perhaps no fault of Hansen's that the ballet repertory continued to dwindle. In 1894 it suffered a shattering blow when the scenery store in Rue Richer was destroyed by fire. The sets and costumes for all but two ballets were lost, and of the fifteen works chosen to be restored, fourteen were operas. Hansen's output was small. In the fourteen years before the century's end, he produced only four major ballets, and of these only one, *La Maladetta* (1893), could be rated a success. With a score by Paul Vidal, and a scenario that Hansen had worked out in collaboration with Gailhard, it was a variant on the *Sylphide* formula, leading to a denouement when the Fairy of the Snows, having no further use for the hero, turns him into stone. The cast was headed by the finest dancers of the company: Mauri as the Fairy, Subra as the Fiancée and the brilliant Vasquez as the Gypsy Chief.

Rosita Mauri was now approaching the end of her career, and it was once again to Milan that the Opéra turned for a successor. At the end of 1894, on the occasion of the 1000th performance of *Faust*, the name of Carlotta Zambelli appeared for the first time on an Opéra playbill. This slender girl of nineteen, whom Gailhard had chosen from the graduates of the school of La Scala, quickly proved to be an exceptional acquisition. For the first few years of her engagement, however, she had to be content with dancing very much in Mauri's shadow, but her clean and brilliant technique made a strong impression, particularly in her multiple *fouettés* – the hallmark of the Milan-trained ballerina – with which she astonished the Parisians at the same time as Legnani was introducing them to St Petersburg. In 1898 Mauri retired, and Zambelli was naturally accepted as her successor. Mauri's service to the Opéra was by no means at an end, for the post of *professeur de la classe de perfectionnement* was revived for her, and she continued to teach until 1920.

Zambelli first took over Mauri's roles in the meagre repertory that had survived. Suddenly Paris was aware that it possessed a star who combined great technical skill with a personality of immense charm. As the years passed, she established herself as a leading figure of the French theatre in a way that no other dancer had done since the Romantic period. Modest in her private life and completely dedicated to the dance, she earned respect not only for herself but also for her much neglected art. A visit to St Petersburg in 1901 greatly enhanced her prestige. The Russians offered a longer engagement on advantageous terms, but out of loyalty to the Opéra she declined, a gesture that was all the more remarkable in the light of the stagnant condition of French ballet. She had to wait eight years from her debut before creating a role in a new ballet. This was in Hansen's *Bacchus* (1902), an over-opulent spectacle with an obscure action and unremarkable choreography. Another three years passed before her next creation, *La Ronde des saisons* (1905), another ballet by Hansen, to a carefully written score by Henri Busser, and memorable only for Zambelli's performance, in which her sparkling technique was matched by the delicate wit of her interpretation. *Le Lac des Aulnes* (1907), which followed, was an ill-starred work. Hansen fell ill and died while preparing it, and the ballet, which was a failure, was completed by Vanara.

At this stage in her career, Zambelli had little to show for her thirteen years in Paris. The combined effect of an impoverished repertory and the eclipse of the male dancer had brought French ballet to an abysmal level of decadence. Greater vitality was to be found even in London, where ballet had taken root in the plebeian surroundings of the music hall. Other cities, which had once looked to Paris for leadership in the field of dance, were now becoming guardians of ballet's tradition. In Copenhagen's Royal Theatre the male dancer still played an honourable part in a repertory that was rich with the ballets of Bournonville, while in St Petersburg the standing of the Imperial Ballet was more prestigious than ever, with a repertory built up by Marius Petipa and a brilliant new generation of dancers coming to the fore. To all this activity the ballet of the Opéra seemed completely impervious. In its lacklustre isolation it was like a sleeping beauty, clad in the faded robes of yesteryear, waiting for the kiss of her prince to waken her into life again.

VIII

A Time of Transition

The year 1908 was one of change and promise. The parsimonious Gailhard was dislodged at last from the position of Director, and on New Year's Day handed over to the composer André Messager and his partner, Broussan. A few weeks later, when the Opéra opened under this new management, the interior gleamed with a fresh coat of paint that seemed to presage a return to past splendours. Eager new faces appeared in the administration, and a bold new policy was announced. Under the previous regime, ballet had been so neglected that it could hardly fail to benefit from the change. The post of ballet-master was offered to Léo Staats, an articulate and gifted dancer who had been trained at the Opéra, and the company was further strengthened by the engagement of Aïda Boni, a ballerina from Milan. The future offered exciting prospects, but these lay mainly in the field of opera. A much-publicised feature was the proposed 'Slav season' of operas to be performed by Russian singers, as was the declared intention to add one or two Russian operas to the permanent repertory.

For some years now, Paris had been discovering the treasures and delights of Russian art, largely through the efforts of Serge Diaghilev. This remarkable man had presented a memorable exhibition of Russian historical portraits in 1906, and the following year had returned to organise a series of concerts of Russian music at the Opéra. These concerts made a deep impression. Paris thrilled to the resonant bass voice of Fyodor Chaliapin in excerpts from operas by Rimsky-Korsakov and Mussorgsky. A guest visit by a strong contingent from the Imperial Opera of St Petersburg in 1908 – the first-ever visit to the Opéra of a complete company from a foreign opera house – was a logical consequence, and Chaliapin revealed a new facet of his genius by his hypnotic acting in *Boris Godunov*.

As yet, there was no question of bringing Russian ballet to Paris in the same way, but its excellence was not unknown. As long before as 1894, the wealthy few who wintered in Monte Carlo had seen Matilda Kshessinskaya and Olga Preobrajenskaya in their youthful prime, and in 1907 Vera Trefilova had come to Paris with Nicolai Legat to dance at the Opéra-Comique. When Broussan had gone to St Petersburg at the end of that same year to make arrangements for the visit of the Russian singers, he had also extended an invitation to Kshessinskaya to give a series of guest performances during the summer of 1908.

Appearing in *Coppélia* and *La Korrigane*, Kshessinskaya was not seen to best advantage, and she was doubly disappointed to find the ballet relegated to a sort of after-piece to the opera instead of being accorded a whole evening on its own, as was the custom in St Petersburg. The lot of the ballet at the Opéra had hardly yet had time to improve, but there were already hopeful signs of increased activity, even if along traditional lines. A new production of *Faust*, with the ballet rearranged by Staats, had inaugurated the new regime; Zambelli had appeared as Swanilda in *Coppélia* for the first time; and Staats's revival of *Namouna* not only gave her another major role but brought a belated recognition of Lalo's score. It was also music – that of Saint-Saëns – that motivated the choice of the next ballet to be produced, *Javotte* (1909). This had originally been produced at Lyons in 1896 with choreography by Mariquita, who had later revived it at the Opéra-Comique. The Opéra now chose it as a companion piece to Saint-Saëns's *Samson et Dalila*. With new choreography by Staats, it was to enjoy a new lease of life at the Opéra, and the authority with which Staats partnered Zambelli seemed to announce that the tradition of travesty roles would now become a relic from the past.

While ballet was very slowly gathering momentum at the Opéra, Diaghilev had returned to Russia after his operatic triumph in 1908 with an ambitious plan for the following year forming in his mind – to present a season of Russian opera and ballet, but with the distinction that the ballets would not be selected from the classical repertory but be specially created with music, choreography and decorative design each contributing towards a cumulative theatrical effect. However, the Opéra was not yet ready to accept ballet as an art of such consequence, and for that and other reasons the honour of receiving the Ballets Russes for their first season fell to the Théâtre du Châtelet.

The shattering impact of Diaghilev's Paris season of 1909 has passed into theatrical legend. For the art of dancing, it marked the moment of regeneration. With almost unbelievable suddenness, ballet was recognised as a major aesthetic force, spreading its influence into many areas of life, from the other theatre arts to fashion in dress and interior decoration. Never before had the dance, or any other form of spectacle, been accompanied by décor and costumes so evocative and distinguished, nor in human memory had Paris seen choreography of such inspiration as that of Michel Fokine. These performances were a feast of visual and plastic beauty that no one who saw them could ever forget. To a public that had always been receptive to ballerinas' charms, Pavlova and Karsavina were greeted with anticipated enthusiasm; but the overwhelming revelation lay in the strength and, above all, the beauty of the male dancer – strength in the rippling muscles of Adolph Bolm, and beauty personified by the miraculous Vaslav Nijinsky, who was lauded, with no false flattery, as 'the new Vestris'.

In the presence of this sensational event, the Paris critics could be under no illusions about the decadence of their own ballet. One went so far as to deny any hope of a similar resurgence at the Opéra, giving as his reason the background of social unrest which, he declared, was unfavourable to such a reform. Only on one point were they prepared to champion their national company. One and all, they remained unswerving in their loyalty to Zambelli.

In fact, the Opéra needed time to assimilate the new aesthetic that Diaghilev had introduced into the art of ballet. With a season of the Diaghilev ballet becoming an annual event, the Opéra could not remain unaffected by the influence of the Russians, and gradually – almost imperceptibly at first – changes began to appear. In the few years of peace that were left before the outbreak of war, ballet at the Opéra enjoyed an increasing activity. Standards rose, the male dancer became more prominent with the emergence of young Albert Aveline, and a Russian *maître de ballet*, Ivan Clustine, was even engaged; but the concept of ballet as a collaboration between artist, musician and choreographer, each working on equal terms with the others, was still foreign.

There can be no more convincing proof that the significance of Diaghilev's message lay in this new concept than the comparative lack of interest shown in the visit of Kshessinskaya and Preobrajenskaya to the Opéra in 1909. Their guest performances in the regular repertory took place simultaneously with Diaghilev's season at the Châtelet, but are remembered only for the fact that Kshessinskaya's partner, Nicolai Legat, became the first man to dance the part of Frantz in *Coppélia* at the Opéra, drawing a shocked protest from Messager by interpolating a galop by Drigo for his variation.

There was no revolutionary spirit within the Opéra. Staats was soon replaced by Mme Stichel, who produced only one ballet – *La Fête chez Thérèse* (1910) – before leaving in her turn. This was a charming evocation of the Romantic period, with a plot that revolved around the anxieties of a pretty milliner whose sweetheart's head is turned by the flattering attentions of a duchess. In the part of Mimi Pinson, Zambelli added another wittily conceived characterisation to her laurels, while Aïda Boni supported her as the beautiful duchess. The music was by Reynaldo Hahn, who was shortly to write the score of *Le Dieu bleu* for Diaghilev.

In a single season Diaghilev had achieved the feat of making ballet, at least in the exotic form in which he presented it, acceptable to the musical and artistic establishment of Paris; for in 1910 no obstacles were placed in his way when he proposed a season at the Opéra entirely devoted to ballet. Thus it was that Stravinsky's music for *The Firebird* was first heard at the Opéra, and that *Giselle* was shown there after an interval of more than forty years, with Karsavina and Nijinsky. To the audiences of 1910, however, whose ears were attuned to Wagner, Adam's melodies sounded thin and old-fashioned. The time was not yet ripe for *Giselle* to be recognised, as it is today, as the masterpiece of the Romantic ballet.

A year later the Opéra took another step forward by engaging a Russian *maître de ballet*. It was, however, a hesitant step, for the choice carefully avoided any direct contact with Diaghilev. Ivan Clustine was a product of the Bolshoi, Moscow, where he had danced for many years and been ballet-master from 1898 to 1903. He had then emigrated to the West, being engaged for several seasons as ballet-master in Monte Carlo. His arrival at the Opéra brought about a noticeable improvement in discipline, and he introduced several timely innovations. Travesty roles were anathema to him, and he endeavoured with some success to improve the lot of the male dancer at the Opéra. He also had ideas of his own on the subject of costume; in his first work for the Opéra, *La Roussalka* (1911) – a ballet inspired by a poem by Pushkin and having a general similarity with *Giselle* in its theme – he discarded the abbreviated tutu and dressed his dancers in simple close-fitting dresses for the peasant girls in the first act, and in Romantic skirts reaching below the knees for the *roussalka* spirits in the second. Although he had not worked with Diaghilev, he was intelligent enough to recognise the developments that were taking place in the art of choreography. In the lavishly produced *Les Bacchantes* (1912) he was patently influenced by Nijinsky, for he wove into Zambelli's role poses in profile, inspired by bas-reliefs, which were reminiscent of *L'Après-midi d'un faune*. His most successful work during his three years at the Opéra from 1911 to 1914 was *Suite de danses* (1913), the Opéra's reply to Fokine's *Les Sylphides*, and performed to a selection of pieces by Chopin orchestrated by Messager and Vidal. Derivative though it was, it was an admirable showpiece for the talents of the whole company, and survived in the repertory for many years.

There was, during these pre-war years, another significant indication of the increasing importance of the ballet. Although it was still regarded as of secondary importance to the opera, the dancers had gained a new confidence and would never again submit to the indignities that Gailhard had inflicted on them. In 1912, Messager and Broussan had to contend with a crisis without precedent in the annals of the Opéra – a strike of the *corps de ballet*. The dancers' union was inexperienced and the strike was broken by the firm action of the management, but the justice of the dancers' complaint was recognised and the new contracts that were drawn up after the company had been dismissed stipulated an acceptable increase in their salaries.

The fateful summer of 1914 produced a final glow of splendour with a season of the Diaghilev Ballet at the Opéra, made memorable by the debut of Leonide Massine in Fokine's *La Légende de Joseph* to music by Richard Strauss. But sadly the early promise of the Messager–Broussan partnership had not been fulfilled; the two men had irreconcilably fallen out with one another, and were driven to resign some months before their term was due to expire.

No one could have been better qualified than their successor, Jacques Rouché, who was to rule the Opéra with paternal benevolence and unparalleled knowledge and taste for thirty years and guide it safely through two World Wars. Unlike most of his predecessors, he was already an influential figure in the theatre when he was appointed. Highly cultured, experienced in business, and accepted in government circles as well as in high society, he had also made a profound study of the experimental work of Stanislavsky, Appia, Craig and others in freeing stage productions from the stifling grip of naturalism. He had travelled widely to gain personal experience of the dramatic and scenic innovations that were taking place abroad, and in 1910 had written an important book, *L'Art théâtral moderne*, in which he called for a radical rethinking of the principles of stage design, maintaining that it should reflect the vision of art as expressed by the painters of the time.

Between 1910 and 1913 Rouché had put his ideas into practice at the Théâtre des Arts, launching a new school of designers by his encouragement of such artists as Maxime Dethomas, Drésa and René Piot. His programmes were astonishingly eclectic for so modest a stage. He presented dramatic works that ranged from Molière and de Musset to Copeau and Bernard Shaw, reconstructions of lyric works by Monteverdi, Lully, Lalande and Rameau, and a series of original ballets by Léo Staats, Jeanne Chasles and Jane Hugard. His interest in the dance had also led him to organise a series of dance concerts at the Châtelet for Natalia Trouhanova, for whom Clustine produced four ballets that were later to enter the repertory of the Opéra: *Adélaïde, La Tragédie de Salomé, Istar* and *La Péri*.

The outbreak of the First World War shortly before Rouché was to take up his new duties brought the activities of the Opéra to an abrupt halt. More than a year passed before he was authorised to reopen the theatre for matinées, and it was not until 1916 that evening performances could be resumed. With so many of the male artists and stage staff at the front, a return to normal activity was out of the question. Programmes had to be made up to suit the exceptional circumstances, and Rouché soon showed the originality and flexibility that were to distinguish his management to the end. Appreciating the importance of the Opéra's long tradition, he presented a number of divertissements that recreated past periods in the history of the lyric theatre. *Mademoiselle de Nantes* (1915) was the most successful of these works, being a reconstruction of a fête at Versailles under Louis XIV. Léo Staats, who arranged the dances, was able to work for the Opéra only when his military duties allowed, and Rouché also had to make use of the services of François Ambrosiny, a ballet-master from Brussels, who produced a new version of *Adélaide* (1917) to the *Valses nobles et sentimentales* of Ravel, for Aïda Boni and Aveline.

Staats found time to stage *Les Abeilles* (1917), a ballet to Stravinsky's *Scherzo fantastique*, in which Zambelli appeared as the Queen Bee against an ingeniously geometrical setting by Dethomas; but he was unable to obtain leave to participate in Rouché's only major production of the wartime years – the revival of Rameau's opera-ballet, *Castor et Pollux*. The rediscovery of Rameau, who had remained totally neglected throughout the nineteenth century, was due mainly to Rouché. At the Théâtre des Arts in 1911 he had presented the celebrated *entrée* of *La Danse* from *Les Fêtes d'Hébé*, and a critic had then written: 'since the art of ballet is once again in fashion, thanks to the Ballets Russes, why should not the Opéra ... revive, for example, *Les Indes galantes*?' Seven years later Rouché made his reply when, on the very day in March 1918 that the German armies launched their last great offensive, Rameau's masterpiece, *Castor et Pollux*, was revived at the Opéra for the first time since the eighteenth century. In the absence of Staats, the choreography had been entrusted to Nicola Guerra, an Italian ballet-master who had gained his reputation largely in Vienna and Budapest. Aïda Boni, Anna Johnsson and Aveline were the leading dancers, dressed in sumptuous costumes, which, set off by Drésa's décor, provided a welcome splash of colour in war-worn Paris. The revival was acclaimed as a musical event of the first importance; but owing to circumstances wholly unconnected with art, more than seven months were to separate the first two performances. The bombardment of the city by German long-range artillery brought new dangers, and the authorities were fearful lest the wide panniers might hinder the dancers if the theatre had to be hastily evacuated.

With the signing of the armistice in November, life in Paris began to return to normal. Evenings at the Opéra resumed an elegance that had long been suppressed throughout the terrible years of war. Confirmed in his position as Director in January 1919, Rouché accepted a challenge that would have daunted a more conventional administrator, and throughout the decade known as 'the crazy years' played a vital part in restoring the cultural supremacy of Paris. His aim was twofold: to renovate the operatic repertory, and to enhance the status of ballet.

For the latter objective the climate was particularly favourable, for the vogue for the dance was reaching new heights. Never before had so many different manifestations of the dance been offered to the Paris public: the annual seasons of the Diaghilev Ballet, the Ballets Suédois of Jean Börlin, Boris Romanoff's Ballets Romantiques, Ida Rubinstein, Anna Pavlova, La Argentina; and on a more popular level, the adagio dancers and the girls of the music halls, and the new dances such as the Charleston that became the rage in ballrooms. In front of the curtain at the theatre a new breed of journalist was emerging: the knowledgeable dance critic who was not content with the vapid reporting that all too often had filled the columns in earlier times, but who could discourse perceptively and constructively on the aesthetics of the dance and was to educate the public to a deeper awareness of what that art had to offer. Foremost among these writers was André Levinson, who had left Russia at the time of the Revolution and was to leave a precious record of the dance events of the 1920s and early 1930s.

In the midst of all this activity, the Opéra stood firmly as a conventional stronghold of ballet. At its centre, unrivalled and supreme, was Carlotta Zambelli, recognised as the very personification of the classical dance, and probably the model for Athikté, *'la danseuse extrême'* of Paul Valéry's classic essay, *L'Âme et la danse*, which appeared in 1921.

The Opéra was by no means impervious to change, however, and the new ideas and influences of the time were gradually absorbed, partly by the rise of new generations of dancers and audiences to whom they were a natural expression of their time, and partly by the deliberate policies followed by Rouché. Realising the effectiveness of direct contact with outside forces, he continued to invite the Diaghilev Ballet, which presented four of their Paris seasons in the 1920s at the Opéra. Ida Rubenstein was another frequent guest, sometimes appearing in works destined for the repertory – Guerra's new version of *La Tragédie de Salomé* (1919) to the music of Florent Schmitt, Staats's revival of *Istar* (1924) to music by Vincent d'Indy, and in 1922 Debussy's *Le Martyre de Saint Sébastien* – and later with her own company, as its star and impresario, presenting a repertory created for her by the leading choreographers, musicians and designers of the time.

Rouché's interest in new trends in the dance went further than inviting Diaghilev and Rubinstein. In the course of his investigations into innovations in the theatre, he had come across the work of Emil Jaques-Dalcroze, who had devised a method of education based on the understanding of rhythm. Dancing was an important element in the method, but not originally an end in itself. Rouché was so impressed that shortly after the war he introduced a class of eurhythmics at the Opéra's School of Dance. The experiment grew somewhat out of hand, for the teachers he engaged began to develop the work into a new style of dance and to form a group of specialised eurhythmic dancers within the company. Some of these dancers, such as Yvonne Daunt and Alice Bourgat, had had a sound classical training, but the regular dancers soon began to resent them as interlopers. There were several attempts to introduce eurhythmics onto the stage as an independent dance form – *La Petite Suite* (1922), arranged by Rachel Pasmanik and Jessminn Howarth to the music of Debussy, and Placido de Montoliu's *Fresques* (1923) to music by Philippe Gaubert – but the experiment was quietly dropped after a few years, although some of the eurhythmic dancers were retained in the company for a short time afterwards.

The strength of the classical training in the School of Dance was not, however, diluted. Since Mauri's retirement as a teacher in 1920, Zambelli had taken over the perfection class, teaching strictly according to the principles she had herself learnt in Milan. Consequently, French ballet continued to absorb the influence of the Italian school, and to move further away from the old French style as had once been taught by Auguste Vestris – a style that still existed almost unchanged in Copenhagen, where it had been introduced by Vestris's pupil August Bournonville nearly a century before.

Meanwhile, in stage design the new approach that Rouché had initiated at the Théâtre des Arts was being applied at the Opéra. The day of naturalistic scenery and costumes was over, and décor was now generally recognised as an important and integral part of a production. Rouché saw that ballet benefited no less than opera from this new development, and most of the creations of the 1920s were designed by one or other of the artists who had first spread their wings at the Théâtre des Arts – Dethomas, Drésa and Piot. Diaghilev's two great collaborators, Benois and Bakst, also worked occasionally for the Opéra, and by the end of the decade other distinguished French painters such as Raoul Dufy and Marie Laurencin were commissioned by Rouché to design ballets.

Rouché also looked back to his days at the Théâtre des Arts in selecting his *maître de ballet*. Léo Staats had won his confidence then, and had given further proof of his ability during the war. On his return to civilian life he was rewarded by being officially appointed as *maître de ballet* of the Opéra, where, from 1919 until he was tempted to go to America in 1926, he produced a number of ballets that established him as the outstanding French choreographer of the first third of the century. His choreography, however, tended to be uneven in inspiration, and he lacked that final touch of authority needed to bring about a real transformation in the company's attitude towards their art.

Staats's first important task was to revive *Sylvia* for Zambelli. It was virtually a new work, for the ballet had not been performed since 1894 and Mérante's original choreography was largely forgotten. Levinson, who had been brought up on the richer fare of the pre-Revolution Maryinsky, found the production rather colourless, but Staats succeeded in providing Zambelli with a role that suited her physique and style to perfection. The critic Maurice Brillant called her 'the ideal Sylvia… No one who saw her,' he continued, 'will ever forget her radiant entrance at the head of the huntress-nymphs, nor the ethereal poetry of her *valse lente* … nor her celebrated pizzicato, danced with sparkling *pointes*, like an exquisite piece of embroidery.' Aveline shared in her triumph, partnering her in a memorable *adage* in which they seemed to move as if impelled by a single force.

Within the next few years, Zambelli appeared in three new ballets by Staats. In *Taglioni chez Musette* (1920) she was cast appropriately as Taglioni in a charming evocation of the Romantic period, with music culled from works of that time. *Cydalise et le Chèvre-pied* (1923) was a more ambitious production, and deserved more success than it achieved. The scenario told of a young faun falling in love with a dancer at the court of Versailles but being drawn back by the voices of the forest to his existence as an elemental spirit. The conjunction of civilisation in its most artificially refined form with forces of primitive mythology offered opportunities for wit, which were seized both by the composer, Gabriel Pierné, and by the choreographer, Staats. One of the highlights was a danced scene in which Zambelli, as the dancer Cydalise, reads her love letters in a mocking mood. It was a perfect cameo of comedy. As Levinson wrote:

> The ballerina has wit down to the very tips of her toes, as you realise when you think of those bursts of laughter, echoed by the orchestra, that are

mimed by her arms and marked by her agile *pointes*. This is then followed by a delicately sensual dialogue in which the artful girl swoons in the arms of her guileless lover, a dialogue which in texture recalls *Le Spectre de la rose*.

But such moments of inspiration were all too rare, for Staats's choreography was disappointingly thin in invention. More modest in scale, *La Nuit ensorcelée* (1923) had greater success. It was the brainchild of an experienced master, Léon Bakst, who not only conceived the theme but designed the production. Unhappily, it was to be his last completed work for the theatre, for he died just a year later. To a score woven from the works of Chopin, children in a Second Empire nursery dream of their dolls coming to life. It was ingeniously simple, but wonderfully evocative, with Zambelli in a role that brought out her inimitable vivacity, and Staats himself playing the part of her Paganini doll.

As early as 1921, Rouché judged the time to be ripe for a direct injection of Russian influence, and that summer he boldly presented a Russian evening, which included Fokine's *Daphnis et Chloé* (Diaghilev Ballet 1912, Opéra 1921), with the choreographer and his wife Vera Fokina in the leading roles, and Clustine's *La Péri* (Châtelet 1912, Opéra 1921), performed by Anna Pavlova and Hubert Stowitts. The choice of *Daphnis et Chloé* was particularly appropriate, because it was the first Diaghilev ballet to have been produced with music composed by a Frenchman, Maurice Ravel's score being already recognised as a classic. Fokine, who had not worked for the Opéra before, discovered that the French dancers lacked the dedication of his compatriots, but he did not allow himself to be troubled by that. One day, when the dancers were chatting among themselves more than usual, he stopped the rehearsal and quietly said to them: 'I am going out to smoke a cigarette, Mesdemoiselles, and when you have finished your conversation, I shall return'. As a result of his perseverance, *Daphnis et Chloé*, with Bakst's scenery and costumes, was an impressive production, and after the Fokines left Paris it remained in the repertory, with the leading roles taken over by Zambelli and Aveline. *La Péri* was a slighter work – an extended *pas de deux* with a Persian flavour, to a lush score by Paul Dukas. Dukas had written it originally for his mistress, Natalia Trouhanova, who had none of the classical purity of Pavlova, and Clustine revised his choreography considerably for the revival at the Opéra. It, too, was to hold a place in the repertory for many years, but the significance of this Russian evening lay not in the mere addition of two works to the repertory but in demonstrating that the Diaghilev Ballet and the ballet of the Opéra were manifestations of the same art.

Shortly afterwards, faced with the problem of finding a new star ballerina, Rouché had recourse to the Russians again. Zambelli's dancing career was approaching its end, and there was no obvious successor in the company. Aïda Boni had retired in 1922, and the other *premières danseuses étoiles* – Jeanne

Schwarz, Anna Johnsson and Yvonne Daunt – lacked the necessary authority and renown. It was clearly the moment for the sort of bold, imaginative choice that it was in Rouché's character to make. Ignoring the time-honoured precedent of applying to Milan, he looked this time to Russia and found Olga Spessivtseva.

Spessivtseva was a product of the Imperial Russian ballet who had risen to stardom in Petrograd in the early years of the Soviet regime, dancing her first Giselle in 1919. Diaghilev had long wanted her for his company, and in 1921 succeeded in drawing her to London to be one of the pleiad of ballerinas who shared the role of Aurora in his historic revival of *The Sleeping Princess*. She had then returned to Russia, but was soon being importuned again by Diaghilev. It was at this moment that Rouché was favoured by a stroke of good fortune. Spessivtseva's advisor in Paris was Bakst, who had fallen out with Diaghilev, and it was he who persuaded her to accept Rouché's offer of an engagement at the Opéra, with the added inducement of appearing in the revival of *Giselle* planned for the end of 1924.

Rouché had originally thought of inviting Preobrajenskaya to stage this ballet, but in the end he entrusted the task to Nicolai Sergueyev, the former *régisseur* of the Maryinsky who had fled from Russia with the choreographic records of the repertory in the Stepanov notation. The shy, dedicated young ballerina was happy to be working with a compatriot. When the French dancers first saw her at rehearsal, they were amazed at her fragile physique, but they soon fell under the spell of her artistry. Watching her rehearse the mad scene in the Rotonde of the Opéra, they were awed into silence as if suddenly finding themselves in the presence of a great mystery. With Aveline as her partner, Spessivtseva created a sensation when she made her Paris debut as Giselle. Levinson hailed her as a genius, no less.

During her first engagement at the Opéra, until 1926, Spessivtseva also created the principal role in Staats's *Soir de fête* (1925), a divertissement arranged to a selection from Delibes's music for *La Source*, took over Zambelli's role in a revival of *Les Abeilles*, and succeeded Pavlova in *La Péri*. But she became dissatisfied with the secondary place that ballet still occupied at the Opéra, and in 1926 left to rejoin the Diaghilev Ballet. She did not completely abandon the Opéra, however, for she returned a year later, and in 1928 danced in a revival of *La Tragédie de Salomé*.

Meanwhile, Staats had not been ignoring the stars of lesser magnitude. For Camille Bos and her gifted young partner, Serge Peretti, he produced *Siang-Sin* (1924), with music by Georges Hue, a successful piece of orientalism as seen through Western eyes, the choreography being lightly inspired by the dances of Cambodia. The following year, to mark the fiftieth anniversary of the opening of the Palais Garnier, he collaborated in a very different work – a revival of Lully's *Le Triomphe de l'Amour*, in which Jeanne Schwarz danced to the music that had been played when Mlle de Lafontaine had appeared as the Opéra's first ballerina nearly two and a half centuries before.

Rouché was seemingly under no illusions about Staats's shortcomings as a choreographer, for well before his departure for America he was actively seeking a replacement. Becoming even bolder in his leaning towards the Russians, he invited Bronislava Nijinska to produce a ballet. The sister of Nijinsky, she had already given proof of her original talent for choreography in several ballets for Diaghilev, including *Les Noces* and two works that mirrored the social world of her time, *Les Biches* and *Le Train bleu*. Her first ballet for the Opéra was *Les Rencontres* (1925), to music by Ibert, and featuring Spessivtseva and Peretti. She followed this by arranging the dances in Gluck's *Alceste*, and in 1927 produced *Impressions de music-hall*, a daring work for the solemn surroundings of the Palais Garnier. Never before had the Opéra stooped to parody, but times were changing and Rouché perhaps felt compelled to follow the example set by the Ballets Russes in some of its more avant-garde works. As a burlesque of the popular theatre, it was a little restrained, but it had its moments. Aveline appeared in a variation caricaturing the clown Fratellini; another number evoked the Dolly sisters; and the illustrious Zambelli – appearing in the last creation of her career – made her entrance from an enormous hatbox to dance a cakewalk.

The vacancy left by the departure of Staats was filled in 1927 by the return of Nicola Guerra, who was to be remembered by those dancers who were *petits rats* at the time as a rather frightening figure with a pointed beard and a black cloak. In his year at the Opéra he made little impression as a choreographer, but he proved an excellent teacher and did much to form the style of a future *étoile*, Solange Schwarz. After his departure a series of short-lived creations followed. The Swedish dancer Carina Ari produced a charming piece, *Rayon de lune* (1928), to music by Gabriel Fauré, which was remembered with pleasure long after it was dropped from the repertory. Camille Bos, who had recently been appointed an *étoile*, appeared with Ari in this work, and played the principal role in Staats's *L'Écran des jeunes filles* (1929), a slight work to a score by Roland-Manuel. Equally evanescent was *L'Éventail de Jeanne* (1929), a pleasing divertissement for children to pieces of music by ten contemporary composers, staged by two former eurhythmic dancers, Yvonne Franck and Alice Bourgat, and noteworthy for the appearance of a nine-year-old pupil of Preobrajenskaya who dazzled the audience with a precocious display of virtuosity – Tamara Toumanova.

As the 1920s drew to a close, the Opéra ballet seemed to be in danger of losing the momentum that Rouché had so successfully stimulated only a few years before. Zambelli was dancing only rarely now – she retired finally as a dancer in 1930 – and the repertory was languishing for want of substantial new works. Levinson, who had been brought up on the rich repertory of St Petersburg with its canon of classics from the past, saw it differently. To him, it was shameful that 'the work of Coralli, Petipa, Saint-Léon and Mérante, a precious patrimony, the cream of French choreography and, it follows, of the French spirit, should remain unknown'.

Such was the state in which the Opéra ballet found itself in August 1929, when the news reached Paris that Diaghilev had died in Venice. Deprived suddenly of its founder and director, the company of the Ballets Russes disintegrated at once. No one could have foreseen the effect that this turn of events was to have on the fortunes of the Opéra ballet, but Rouché was gifted with the instinct that is the hallmark of the great theatre director. Realising that many dancers who had served Diaghilev would be seeking employment, he seized his opportunity and sent an urgent message to the youngest and most flamboyant of Diaghilev's discoveries, Serge Lifar. The consequences that flowed from this single act were to change the whole course of French ballet.

IX

The Lifar Years

Serge Lifar, the last of the prestigious male dancers to be moulded by Diaghilev, had found his calling almost by accident. The son of a civil servant, he was a student in Kiev when the Revolution shattered his comfortable existence. An injury to his hand then destroyed his dream of becoming a professional pianist, and in 1921 chance led him into the school of Bronislava Nijinska, sister of the great Nijinsky. He had entered out of bored curiosity, but once inside he found his life transformed. Nijinska herself was then in the West working for Diaghilev, and one day a telegram arrived from her calling for the five most promising pupils to be dispatched to Diaghilev's company in Paris. One of them failed to turn up, and Lifar took his place.

Perceiving the potential of the rawly trained boy, Diaghilev sent him to Italy to improve his technique under Cecchetti, and watched personally over his artistic education, as he had done earlier with Nijinsky and Massine. On rejoining the company, Lifar found himself entrusted with roles of increasing importance, becoming, in a short time, the principal male dancer. He was given roles in new ballets to create, and danced also in what there was of the classical repertory, partnering Nemchinova, Karsavina and Spessivtseva. By 1929 his supremacy was unchallenged. Not only had he stirred the public by his vibrant personality and innate beauty of line, but he had also produced his first ballet, *Renard*.

Diaghilev's death ended a chapter in Lifar's life. Now a new one was to open with his meeting with Jacques Rouché at the Opéra. The two men, so different in almost every way except in their commitment to the dance, understood one another from the outset. Rouché explained that he was planning a new version of *Les Créatures de Prométhée* (1929), using Beethoven's only ballet score. In his memoirs Lifar relates that he was asked to produce the ballet as well as to dance in it, but that, being apprehensive because of his lack of experience, he declined the first part of the offer, and suggested that Balanchine be engaged as the choreographer. Balanchine arrived to undertake the task, but fell seriously ill almost at once. According to Balanchine's biographer, it was on his advice that Rouché then gave Lifar the opportunity to finish the work. The two versions are not necessarily incompatible, and which of the two recommended the other is unimportant – except perhaps to themselves.

It soon became apparent that Lifar's conception of the ballet differed fundamentally from that of the scenarists, who angrily demanded his dismissal. Rouché refused to intervene. Lifar had shifted the emphasis of the action from the creatures to his own role of Prometheus. He freely admitted that as an egotist he composed the choreography for himself, and the impression it made on the public was due more to the dancer than to the choreographer. However, the choreography, uneven though it was, revealed a talent of unusual originality though little experience, and Levinson somewhat apprehensively described Lifar as 'the living symbol of revolt and challenge, a sublime "factionist", hero and martyr of free will struggling against established order'.

On the strength of the first performance, Rouché decided that Lifar was the man to complete the revitalisation of the Opéra ballet that he had long desired. Engaged as dancer and ballet-master, Lifar brought a touch of the Diaghilev magic to the Opéra, where he was to exercise a sway over French ballet that for its duration and authority has only one parallel in its history – that of Pierre Gardel more than a hundred years earlier.

Not surprisingly, the company viewed the arrival of the young Russian with considerable reserve. To Léo Staats, who had rejoined the staff as a ballet-master and had seen Fokine, Nijinska and Guerra come and go, Lifar appeared as yet another threat, and the two men were to clash fundamentally over their very different conceptions of ballet. The principal teachers, Zambelli, Aveline and Gustave Ricaux (who was the formative influence of many of the leading French dancers of this period, from Peretti to Renault and Babilée), were also apprehensive, but here, counselled no doubt by Rouché, Lifar proceeded with caution. At first he did not interfere, but once he had consolidated his position he began encouraging some of the younger dancers to supplement their training privately with lessons from one or another of the great Russian teachers working in Paris – Kshessinskaya, Preobrajenskaya, Trefilova, Egorova, Volinine – and in 1932 he himself took charge of the *classe d'adage*. In this way the Italian element in the French school was to be tempered by the more lyrical Russian school, which had itself developed out of the old French school.

Lifar had also to contend with the influence of the *abonnés*. Their support was particularly important to Rouché, because his personal fortune was at risk in the enterprise owing to the insufficiency of the subsidy. Ever since they could remember, they had enjoyed the right of entry into the Foyer de la Danse, a tradition that Lifar found wholly incompatible with the dignity of the dance as he saw it. Rouché agreed with him, but his own earlier attempts to cut down the privileges granted to the *abonnés* had foundered. With Rouché's encouragement, Lifar began by instituting pre-performance rehearsals in the Foyer de la Danse that required the presence of the male dancers, who had hitherto been excluded from that 'holy of holies'. As expected, there were vigorous protests from the old guard, but the argument that the innovation was necessary to maintain a high standard of performance was unanswerable. This and other reforms began to give the company a new pride in their calling.

By providing it with Lifar instead of Balanchine, fate may have been kind to the Opéra. Although Balanchine was unquestionably the greater choreographer, it is doubtful if he would have accepted the conditions that existed there for very long, or been willing to divert some of his creative energy to the task of reinvigorating a company that lacked any strong sense of artistic mission. Lifar, on the other hand, conceived for the Opéra a passionate attachment which never relaxed. He also caught the imagination of Paris. Something of a solitary bohemian in his way of life, he possessed a flamboyant allure that won him fervent supporters in society, in artistic and intellectual circles, and among the general public. Furthermore, he enjoyed his reputation as an iconoclast and a 'barbarian'. He threw himself wholeheartedly into the struggle to impose changes and reforms. Having a natural gift for expressing himself in words and print, he relished controversy, not only for its publicity value, but also because it brought the dance into the polemics of public debate.

Lifar's early ballets were, understandably, tentative, even immature. In *Prélude dominical* (1931), *L'Orchestre en liberté* (1931) and the more ambitious *Bacchus et Ariane* (1931), with its fine score by Albert Roussel and décor by Chirico, he was clearly still seeking a means of blending his individual conception of movement with the classical dance.

As a choreographer, Lifar does not fit into the traditional mould because, unlike Massine and Balanchine, he had not been conditioned since childhood in a particular school. This lack of background had to be replaced by personal experience and experimentation gained as his career progressed, and consequently his development was to be affected, more strongly than with most other choreographers, by such influences as chance happened to throw in his path. The economic depression of the early 1930s, for example, had a very significant effect, for the cuts that Rouché had to make in his budget, coupled with the grumblings of the *abonnés*, forced Lifar to turn his attention to reviving classics from the past. Although he had never known the great theatres in Russia where the classical tradition had been nourished, he had savoured it during his years with Diaghilev, and in Paris there were many *émigré* Russian dancers on whose advice he could, and did, rely. The production of Fokine's *Le Spectre de la rose* (Diaghilev Ballet 1911, Opéra 1931) required little expense, and proved a turning point by winning the support of such connoisseurs as Levinson, who had been severely critical of Lifar's early ballets but was now delighted to see him discovering the rich treasury of the past. Next came a revival of *Giselle*, and then *Divertissement* (1932), a 'digest' of dances from Petipa's *Sleeping Beauty*.

Spessivtseva's Giselle has perhaps never been surpassed for its penetrating combination of lyrical beauty and tragic intensity, but until this point she had always carried the ballet virtually on her own shoulders. Her former partners, Aveline and Ricaux, had remained self-effacingly in the background; but now Lifar, building on the advice of the former Moscow dancer, Pierre Vladimirov, reshaped the role of Albrecht so that it became almost as prominent as that of Giselle. It was a breach of convention, but it made dramatic sense. Levinson was so impressed that he acclaimed the partnership of Spessivtseva and Lifar as matching, and at moments surpassing, that of Karsavina and Nijinsky.

Sadly, this new partnership, like its predecessor, was to be short-lived. Spessivtseva, who was on the verge of a mental breakdown, had never been truly happy at the Opéra, and Lifar's consciously self-centred policy of exalting the male dancer – at times, seemingly at the expense of the ballerina – was a development she could neither comprehend nor accept. In her confused state of mind, this dilemma assumed ungovernable proportions, and the breaking point was reached when she attempted to throw herself from a window during rehearsal. After that incident she never set foot in the Opéra again.

These revivals were of great importance in Lifar's development. *Giselle* had shown him the value of tradition, which in the later period of the Diaghilev Ballet had been somewhat submerged in the frantic search for novelty, while *Divertissement* obliged him to give prominence to some of the excellent young dancers in the company: Camille Bos, Suzanne Lorcia (who had been nominated *étoile* in 1930), Lucienne Lamballe and – most promising of all – the young Solange Schwarz. Lifar's commitment to the classical tradition was to be wholehearted and sincere, although he always viewed it from a completely personal standpoint, as he showed in several of the books that now began to flow from his pen. *Giselle* itself inspired him to write an important study of the ballet – the first to be published outside Russia – as well as a biography of Carlotta Grisi; *Divertissement* brought him into contact with Petipa and the golden age of the Imperial ballet, whose history was to be told in another of his books.

It was impossible to deny the stimulating spirit that was beginning to permeate the Opéra. By 1933 this venerable institution had been transformed into 'a centre of choreographic activity such as it seldom was and such as no other exists today, unless it be the excellent but ambulating Ballets Russes de Monte Carlo'. As a dancer, Lifar had reached his peak. Levinson, now completely won over, described him unreservedly as 'the greatest dancer of our time'. The combination of his vital personality and his impressive physical prowess had an electrifying effect on the public, and was a powerful inspiration to the company, from principals to *corps de ballet*.

Lifar's objective as a choreographer was to discover a personal conception of the classical dance while remaining within its tradition, and this was the basis of what he called his neo-classical style. In his early years at the Opéra he had been groping; but now, in the space of a few months, the influence of the Italian *commedia dell'arte* gave him two resounding successes: *La Vie de Polichinelle* (1934) and *Salade* (1935). In these well-constructed *ballets d'action* he controlled his fixation on his own role, while giving excellent opportunities to other dancers and achieving a better balance than ever before. With décor by Pedro Pruna and music by Nicolai Nabokov, *La Vie de Polichinelle* was a series of joyous scenes set in eighteenth-century Venice. It contained one particularly striking moment when dancing broke out simultaneously on several different levels of a public square, with a variety of movement that recalled the choreography of Fokine. Lifar played the part of Polichinelle with an appealing mixture of roguery and tenderness, and among the others who stood out were Serge Peretti, precise and elegant, as a dancing-master, and Marie-Louise Didion, who displayed her brilliant virtuosity as a young acrobat. By contrast, *Salade*, colourfully designed by André Derain and robustly set to music by Darius Milhaud, presented the Neapolitan Pulcinella, whom Lifar played as a comic, empty-headed figure whose pranks often rebound on himself.

The success of these two ballets led to an important, and very belated, development – the introduction of regular evening performances devoted entirely to ballet. Rouché had attempted to do this when Fokine had been briefly engaged in 1921, but had been thwarted by the opposition of the *abonnés*. The memory of this defeat was still vivid when Lifar raised the idea again, and Rouché insisted on asking the *abonnés* for their views. Only a handful out of two hundred were in favour, and once again the proposal seemed doomed to failure. But then Lifar's successes restored Rouché's courage, and he authorised a single performance as an experiment. To his surprise and delight, the opponents of the plan were confounded. The public flocked to the Opéra, and the experiment became a permanent feature. Wednesdays were established as ballet nights, and later, from 1940, a complete month of the year was reserved for ballet alone.

Although very much dominated by Lifar, the mid-1930s saw the last ballets of Léo Staats, which seemed colourless by comparison. At the same time, Albert Aveline began to reveal a refined, if somewhat conventional, talent for choreography with *La Grisi* (1935), a charming work produced to a selection from the dance music of Olivier Métra, in which Camille Bos portrayed the ballerina with the elegant Peretti as her lover.

Lifar's philosophical mind was now turning to more fundamental problems. The failure of his ballet *Sur le Borysthène* (1932), for which Serge Prokofiev had written a score that the choreographer had found unsuitable, had led him to ponder on the relationship between music and dance. From this emerged his pamphlet, *Le Manifeste du chorégraphe,* in which he propounded the theory that rhythm, rather than music, is the essence of the dance, and that the dance should derive its rhythms from within itself rather than from external resources.

This was succeeded by an attempt to apply these ideas in practice. The first seeds of *Icare* (1935) had been sown during a visit to Greece. Igor Markevitch was originally commissioned to write the music, but Lifar became convinced that no pre-composed music could adequately accompany the sort of dance he was envisaging to match the sublimity of the ancient myth. Deciding to arrange his choreography in complete isolation, he noted down the rhythms and then asked Arthur Honegger if he would orchestrate them for percussion instruments. Because Honegger was working on an important commission for Ida Rubinstein, who disapproved of his undertaking another task at the same time, the orchestration had to be credited to the conductor J.-E. Szyfer, who had assisted Honegger in his work.

Far from being a *'scandale'*, as had been feared, *Icare* proved to be a decided success. Some connoisseurs, who had welcomed the more lyrical style that Lifar had shown in *La Vie de Polichinelle*, were disappointed to see him revert to the distorted movements they had found objectionable in his early works; but the ballet contained an inner force when performed by Lifar himself that enabled it to survive for many years.

Since the departure of Spessivtseva, the Opéra had been managing without a foreign ballerina for the first time for more than sixty years, and the guest appearance of the Soviet ballerina Marina Semyonova in the winter of 1935–36 came merely as a brief interlude in the theatre's activities. Semyonova's Giselle was too realistic and unsubtle for French taste, but her prodigious technique and her grand manner aroused great enthusiasm in *Divertissement* and in fragments from *Le Lac des cygnes* (1936), which Lifar arranged specially for her final performance.

Of the three ballets that Lifar staged that year, *Promenades dans Rome* (1936) was the most noteworthy. Full of humour and *joie de vivre*, its scintillating choreography was well matched by the sparkling Italian melodies that Marcel Samuel-Rousseau had woven into the score.

Amid all this activity, the classics were not neglected. *Coppélia* had been restored to the repertory with Camille Bos, but it was not until Solange Schwarz returned from the Opéra-Comique in 1937 that the Opéra was to find its ideal Swanilda. *Giselle* had presented an understandable problem after the departure of Spessivtseva, but in 1936 three young dancers – Marie-Louise Didion, Lycette Darsonval and Paulette Dynalix – were given the opportunity to contend for the privilege of succeeding her.

Lycette Darsonval was the victor in this interesting contest, and was rewarded with a major creation – the title role in Lifar's *Oriane et le prince d'amour* (1938) – and elevation to the rank of *étoile*. With music by Florent Schmitt and décor by Pruna, this ballet marked a significant step in Lifar's development as a choreographer, on account of the importance given both to the role of the ballerina and to the *corps de ballet*. Lifar was to admit that it had required time for him not only to understand the symphonic possibilities of the *corps de ballet*, but also to gain confidence in its qualities, and in this work he made handsome amends. The experience of seeing Fokine and Massine at work when he was engaged by Col. de Basil's Ballets Russes de Monte Carlo in 1936 may have been a significant influence.

Between Lifar the dancer and Lifar the choreographer there was a continual conflict, and this was very apparent in the works that followed. It seemed he was reverting to his earlier egotistical manner, for each ballet revolved around the part he played. Two of them, *David triomphant* (1937) and *Le Cantique des cantiques* (1938), were based on biblical themes and were performed to his own arrangements of rhythms in the manner of *Icare*, while *Alexandre le Grand* (1937) had a conventional score by Philippe Gaubert. He did not, however, entirely neglect his fellow dancers in these ballets. Lorcia, Schwarz and Carina Ari were each rewarded with interesting roles, and in *David* a remarkable young dancer first attracted notice – Yvette Chauviré.

These controversial works were offset by three new ballets by Aveline that entered the repertory in the last years of peace: *Elvire* (1937), a romantic work to music by Scarlatti; a charming Christmas ballet, *Les Santons* (1938), to music by Henri Tomasi; and *Le Festin de l'araignée* (1939), in which Lorcia gave an impressive rendering as the spider to the score that Albert Roussel had written for Rouché in 1913, shortly before the first world conflict.

The grim, tragic years of the Second World War saw a brilliant flowering of ballet at the Opéra. Like the embattled Londoners on the other side of the Channel, the people of Paris turned to ballet as a momentary release from the miseries of the German occupation. Every Wednesday evening the Opéra was filled to capacity with people eager to drink in beauties that only the dance, it seemed, could offer. In the depths of winter the unheated theatre was just as full as in the summer months, and the public appeared cheerfully oblivious to the thick woollen leg-warmers that the ballerinas sometimes had to wear over their tights.

Most of the dance talent of France was concentrated at the Opéra in those years. Lifar was still in his prime as a dancer, but the boyish allure of his earlier years was being tempered by a dramatic presence that had come with maturity. Peretti, who became an *étoile* in 1941, had emerged as a classical dancer of a nobility such as had not been seen in Paris for more than a century, and Suzanne Lorcia, the senior *danseuse étoile*, was to be joined, and overshadowed, by three remarkable younger ballerinas. Lycette Darsonval's aristocratic blonde beauty and commanding style were effectively displayed in Lifar's new production of *Sylvia* in 1941; and coming into prominence at the same time were Solange Schwarz, with her exceptional technical gifts, and Yvette Chauviré, who was to become one of the great international ballet stars after the war.

Solange Schwarz owed her nomination as *étoile* to her performance as the Degas dancer in Lifar's *Entre deux rondes* (1940) only a few weeks before the Battle of France and the Armistice. The ballet itself was slight, but the part bristled with technical difficulties, which she overcame with consummate ease and an effervescent charm.

As if to emphasise that art stands above man's mundane differences, the ballet of the Opéra left Paris for a tour of Spain at the very moment when the German armies were pouring into northern France. A few weeks later the company returned, heavy-hearted, to witness the final phase of their country's disaster and the entry of the Germans into Paris. They found that Rouché and the administration had left for Cahors with the French Government, and Lifar was formally confirmed as *maître de ballet* by the French authorities in Paris with the object of maintaining activity and preventing German interference with the running of the Opéra. It was not long before Rouché returned to his desk, and under his wise direction the Opéra reopened and remained a bulwark of French culture throughout the four years of the Occupation.

A year was to pass before a new ballet was presented. In the opinion of many, *Le Chevalier et la Damoiselle* (1941) was Lifar's finest work. Founded on a legend of medieval Burgundy about a princess who must assume the form of a hind each night until she meets a man who can teach her to suffer, it was a brilliant *ballet d'action*, creating a mood of romance and chivalry that struck a responsive chord in those times of national anguish. Philippe Gaubert's sumptuous score – his last composition, for he died only a few days after the triumphant première – and the luminous colours of A.-M. Cassandre's sets were equally inspired. The honours of the performance were shared by Schwarz, as the damoiselle, and Lifar as the knight errant who wins her heart and emerges the victor in a brilliant tournament scene. Alongside them Peretti had a personal success as the blue knight.

Chauviré's opportunity came a few months later with Lifar's new version of *Istar* (1941). It was virtually an extended solo, in which she was joined by a partner only in the final minutes. As a result of her triumph, she was elevated to the supreme rank of *étoile*.

All three of these young *étoiles* were given important roles in Lifar's next major creation, *Joan de Zarissa* (1942), which took its place as a sort of companion piece to *Le Chevalier et la Damoiselle*. A version of the Don Juan story, it was acted out to a theatrical score by Werner Egk, with impressive sets and costumes by Yves Brayer. Lifar produced it as a gripping dance drama, giving a powerful performance himself as Joan, whose arrival creates havoc in the castle of the Duc de Fer. Darsonval played the Duchess, Schwarz portrayed an exotic prisoner from the East, and Chauviré was the innocent girl for whom the Don abandons the Duchess.

A month later, during the darkest period of the Occupation, Lifar produced a ballet that had a very special meaning for Parisians at that time. *Les Animaux modèles* (1942), to music by Poulenc, was based on the fables of La Fontaine, and contained inspired roles for Lifar, Peretti, Lorcia, Schwarz, Chauviré, Dynalix and others. Wholly French in its spirit, it was a source of much-needed encouragement, a reminder that French culture was, after all, imperishable.

The talents of the three young *étoiles* were again exploited to brilliant effect in Lifar's *Suite en blanc* (1943), produced to an arrangement of some of the music from Lalo's *Namouna*. According to Lifar's own definition, it was 'a suite of dances in the manner of 1943, a real parade of stars'. It was to become the most frequently performed of all his ballets, and it remains to this day an impressive display of the accomplishments of the company.

As the fortunes of war turned in favour of the Allies, Lifar continued to create. *Guignol et Pandore* (1944), with music by André Jolivet, was the last ballet to be created during the Occupation. At the time of the Allied breakthrough in Normandy in July 1944, Lifar had virtually completed another major work, *Les Mirages*, which had just been shown in general rehearsal when the Opéra was closed on account of the military situation.

The Liberation of Paris was greeted with delirious joy, but other less savoury passions rose to the surface. With little regard for justice or truth, a purge committee decreed the expulsion from the Opéra of several dancers who were thought to have had unacceptable links with the Germans. One of these was Solange Schwarz, who sadly never rejoined the company and returned only once to the stage of her early triumphs – for her farewell performance in *Coppélia* in 1957. Lifar was given a travesty of a trial, and in spite of overwhelming support from the dancers – Chauviré gave her evidence in ballet costume – the purge committee ruled that he be excluded for life from the Opéra and other state theatres. Some months later this verdict was reviewed by another committee, which reduced the period of exclusion to one year.

It was the end of an era, marked also by the retirement of Rouché. Courageously, but without much success, Peretti undertook the task of replacing Lifar as choreographer of *L'Appel de la montagne* (1945), for which Honegger had written the music. The Opéra ballet languished without a leader and with a savagely depleted repertory, for Lifar's own works could no longer be given. It was in this dark moment that Aveline arranged the *Grand Défilé du corps de ballet* to Berlioz's *Marche Troyenne*, which has been used ever since on gala occasions to parade the company on the full expanse of the stage, extended into the brilliantly lit Foyer de la Danse in the far distance.[1]

Meanwhile the search for a *maître de ballet* continued. Victor Gsovsky, Robert Quinault and Marcel Bergé came and went without making any appreciable mark. Morale dropped and several indispensable dancers left, among them being Peretti, Chauviré (who preferred to join Lifar in Monte Carlo) and a number of younger talents including Roland Petit, Jean Babilée and Renée Jeanmaire, who were to play a notable part in French ballet in the coming years, but outside the Opéra.

Georges Hirsch, who directed the Opéra from 1946 to 1951 and again from 1956 to 1959, hesitated to import a *maître de ballet* from outside France, but necessity forced him to offer a short engagement to George Balanchine, who arrived in Paris with his wife, Maria Tallchief, and Tamara Toumanova in 1947.

---

[1] An earlier *défilé* had been arranged by Staats to the march from *Tannhäuser* in 1926, but was given on only two occasions.

Within a few months, Balanchine enriched the repertory with four new productions, three of which were revivals of existing ballets: *Sérénade* (American Ballet 1935, Opéra 1947), *Apollon Musagète* (Diaghilev Ballet 1928, Opéra 1947), *Le Baiser de la fée* (American Ballet 1937, Opéra 1947) and *Le Palais de cristal* (1947). *Sérénade*, to Tchaikovsky's *Serenade for Strings*, brought into prominence Christiane Vaussard, a pupil of Zambelli, who was nominated *étoile* that same year. In *Apollon Musagète*, with music by Stravinsky, Michel Renault, who at the age of eighteen in 1946 had become the youngest *étoile* ever to be nominated, proved himself a worthy successor to Peretti, dancing with Tallchief, Dynalix and Jacqueline Moreau as the muses. *Le Baiser de la fée*, also to a Stravinsky score, featured Toumanova as the fiancée, Tallchief as the fairy, and Alexander Kalioujny – a dancer with the physique and allure of an athlete, who in 1947 had been engaged as *étoile* from outside the Opéra, an unusual departure – as the young man. The world première of *Le Palais de cristal* presented the full company, headed by Darsonval and Kalioujny, Toumanova and Roger Ritz, Micheline Bardin and Renault, and Madeleine Lafon and Max Bozzoni respectively in the four movements of Bizet's exhilaratingly youthful symphony, which had only recently been discovered. In recognition of the increasing strength of the company, a number of new *étoiles* were nominated at this time: Ritz and Bozzoni in 1947, and Bardin in 1948.

Balanchine had restored some of the confidence that the company had lost, but inevitably the Opéra could no longer retain the virtual monopoly of ballet that it had enjoyed during the war. The flame it had then carried alone now passed into other hands as well – first, the Nouveau Ballet de Monte-Carlo, which Lifar had joined, and then Roland Petit's Ballets des Champs-Élysées, which in 1946 gave London its first exhilarating contact with French culture since the war. Keenly aware that the Opéra ballet was losing its supremacy, and fearing a relapse into stagnation after Balanchine's return to America, the dancers who had remained desperately petitioned Hirsch to recall Lifar.

Lifar returned to the Opéra in September 1947 as *maître de ballet*, but not as a dancer, for the political forces that had ejected him from the Opéra in 1944 still had to be reckoned with. At the same time, Chauviré returned. Lifar's first concern was to present *Les Mirages* (1947), on which he had been working at the time of the Liberation. Conceived in collaboration with the designer Cassandre to a score by Henri Sauguet, it was a study of a man struggling with his conscience in a land of dreams. With Renault and Chauviré in the principal roles, it was one of Lifar's most profound and poetic works.

During his last ten years at the Opéra, Lifar's creativity showed no signs of flagging, and the repertory expanded rapidly with ballets both new and revived. By no means were all successful, but hardly a year passed without the addition of one substantial work. When he was permitted to dance again, in 1949, Lifar staged a number of productions containing important roles for himself. He

31. Lycette Darsonval as Salome, with Paulette Dynalix as Herodias and M. Blanc as Herod in Albert Aveline's *La Tragédie de Salomé*.

32. Alexandre Kalioujny and Tamara Toumanova in *Le Baiser de la fée*, one of the four ballets staged by George Balanchine in 1947.

33. The world premiere of Balanchine's *Palais de crystal* took place at the Opéra in 1947 with spectacular scenery and costumes, as seen here. Today, it is given without scenery and in simple costumes as *Symphony in C*.

34. Lifar's *Les Mirages* had reached the dress-rehearsal stage when the allied armies broke through the German line in Normandy in 1944. Its first performance did not take place until three years later, with Michel Renault and Yvette Chauviré, here seen as the Young Man and his shadow, with Paulette Dynalix as the Moon.

35. Nina Vyroubova and Serge Lifar as Arzigogola and Scapin in *Les Fourberies*, the latter's interpretation of Molière's comedy.

36. Yvette Chauviré revealed a gift for comedy in John Cranko's light-hearted ballet, *La Belle Hélène,* to Offenbach's sparkling music. On the right is Michel Renault.

37. Cyril Atanasoff in *La Damnation de Faust*.

38. Claude Bessy with Gene Kelly during the rehearsals of the latter's *Pas de dieux*.

39. Wilfride Piollet in Maurice Béjart's version of *Les Noces*.

40. Jacqueline Rayet and Jean-Pierre Franchetti in Maurice Béjart's *Webern Opus V.*

41. Rudolf Nureyev and Carolyn Carlson in Glen Tetley's *Tristan*.

42. Jacqueline Rayet, Christiane Vlassi, Georges Piletta, Nanon Thibon and Claire Motte in a moment from Roland Petit's *Turangalila* to Messiaen's symphony of that name.

43. Zizi Jeanmaire and Michaël Denard in Roland Petit's *La Symphonie fantastique*, danced to Berlioz's symphony of that name.

44. Michaël Denard in Maurice Béjart's *L'Oiseau de feu*.

45. Jean Guizerix and Dominique Khalfouni in Yuri Grigorovich's *Ivan le terrible.*

46. Ghislaine Thesmar and Pierre Lacotte in the latter's reconstruction of *Coppélia*.

47. Maurice Béjart rehearsing *La IXe Symphonie*, with Élisabeth Maurin.

48. Roland Petit during a rehearsal of *Clavigo*.

49. *Raymonda*, choreography by Rudolf Nureyev, after Marius Petipa. Aurélie Dupont, Jean-Guillaume Bart.

appeared as Don Quixote in *Le Chevalier errant* (1950), to music by Ibert, in which Dulcinea appeared in a series of different forms, portrayed by four separate ballerinas: Darsonval, Vaussard, Bardin and Españita Cortez. *Phèdre* (1950) was perhaps Lifar's most outstanding ballet of this period. The theme of Euripides's tragedy had obsessed him for years, and just before the war he had prepared a ballet, which was to remain unperformed, with Hippolytus as the central character. The immediate inspiration of *Phèdre* came from Jean Cocteau, who not only wrote the scenario – originally intended by Lifar for Greta Garbo – but also designed the scenery and costumes. With its powerful score by Georges Auric, it was an impressive tragedy in plastic movement. Lifar played the role of Hippolytus, but the ballet centred around Toumanova's mimetic *tour de force* as Phèdre. *Blanche-Neige* (1951), a brave but unsuccessful attempt to create a popular fairy-tale ballet, had the newly nominated *étoile* Liane Daydé in the title role, Lifar as the Huntsman, and, as the Queen, Nina Vyroubova, a Russian dancer who had made her name in the Ballets des Champs-Élysées and who entered the Opéra as an *étoile* in 1949. *Fourberies* (1952), to music based on themes by Rossini, was a hilarious interpretation of the Molière comedy with Lifar as Scapin, and with Vyroubova making the most of the fantastic character of Arzigogola.

Vyroubova was an interpretative ballerina with a very wide range, equally at ease in comedy and in romantic roles such as Giselle, the Shadow in *Les Mirages*, which she rendered no less lyrically than Chauviré but in a manner all her own, and the high tragedy of Phèdre. Lifar also chose her for the role of the Firebird, with Youly Algaroff as the prince, in his new version of *L'Oiseau du feu*, which he staged in 1954 to Stravinsky's celebrated score to mark the twenty-fifth anniversary of Diaghilev's death.

The last role that Lifar created for himself was Friar Laurence in a condensed two-act version of *Roméo et Juliette* (1955), to music by Prokofiev. A year later he made his final appearance at the Opéra as a dancer, as Albrecht in *Giselle*, the role he had marked more than any other with his personal imprint.

His last productions for the Opéra included two ballets that were fundamentally romantic in theme and treatment: *Nautéos* (Nouveau Ballet de Monte-Carlo 1947, Opéra 1954), with music by Jeanne Leleu, and *Les Noces fantastiques* (1955), with music by Marcel Delannoy. The heroes of these works were both shipwrecked mariners who fall under the spell of a spirit of the deep and return, each in a different form, to their village community. While *Nautéos* ended with the water-spirit resuming her solitude and leaving the mortal lovers to their happiness, the Océanide in *Les Noces fantastiques* was unrelenting, and the hero returned only as a ghost to haunt his native village. In the former ballet, Chauviré reappeared in the role she had created in Monte Carlo just after the war, with Michel Renault as Nautéos. In *Les Noces fantastiques* Peter Van Dyk, a young German dancer who had been engaged as *étoile* in 1955, and Vyroubova gave highly charged performances as the drowned captain and his fiancée, and Claude

Bessy, who was to join the ranks of *étoiles* in 1956, was the Océanide. Lifar's last important creation for the Opéra was *Chemin de lumière* (1957), to a score by Auric, a ballet in the manner of *Les Mirages* – a parallel emphasised by the designer Cassandre – in which the hero, played by Van Dyk, overcomes a series of trials in a dreamlike setting before finding the path of light with his chosen companion.

Lifar left the ballet of the Opéra incalculably stronger in dancers of quality than he found it, and in two sets of variations he had proudly displayed his *étoiles* – the women (Darsonval, Vaussard, Bardin, Daydé, Vyroubova and Madeleine Lafon, nominated in 1952) in *Variations* (1953) to music by Schubert, and the men (Renault, Kalioujny, Bozzoni, Algaroff, who had been engaged as an *étoile* that year, and a young dancer of exceptional strength, Jean-Paul Andréani, who also became an *étoile* in 1953) in *Grand Pas* (1953) to music by Brahms.

Lifar's unremitting activity did not absorb the energies of the Opéra ballet to the exclusion of all else. Aveline, with the devoted support of Zambelli, continued to watch over the repertory, and was always ready to produce a competent ballet or divertissement when called upon. Two of his ballets stand out in sharp contrast from one another: a new version of *La Tragédie de Salomé* (1944) and *La Grande Jatte* (1950), a charming scene of the 1900s to a score by Fred Barlow.

In 1952 the Opéra ballet had been strengthened by the arrival of Harald Lander, who had been the ballet-master of the Royal Danish Ballet for many years and had raised it to a level of excellence that it had not enjoyed since the time of Bournonville. He, Lifar and Aveline were all involved in the monumental revival of Rameau's *Les Indes galantes* in 1952, but it was Lander's contribution that was the most effective – the *entrée* of *Les Fleurs*, an elegant evocation of eighteenth-century style made doubly memorable by the injection of rose-scented perfume into the auditorium at the moment that Micheline Bardin, as the Rose, made a dramatic entrance, rising from the depths, centre-stage, on a trap. In Copenhagen, Lander had been reared on a repertory rich in classical works from the past, and it was appropriate that his first work for the Opéra should be a successful revival of the oldest ballet extant – Galeotti's *Les Caprices de Cupidon* (Copenhagen 1786, Opéra 1952). Unfortunately he was never given the opportunity to stage any of the Bournonville ballets he knew so well, nor was he able to capture the creative spark in any of the new ballets he produced at the Opéra. *Hop-Frog* (1953), to music by Raymond Loucheur, was hopefully designed to give Jean Babilée, the brilliant star of the Ballets des Champs-Elysées and the Ballets de Paris, a creation worthy of his talents; but it was not a success, and his stay at the Opéra was as disappointingly short-lived as the ballet. The only ballet of Lander's that remained in the Opéra's repertory was a revival of *Études* (Copenhagen 1948, Opéra 1952), a brilliant showpiece of classical technique from classroom exercises to dazzling virtuosity, performed to Riisager's arrangement of Czerny pieces.

Two distinguished choreographers from outside made brief appearances as guests in the 1950s. John Cranko, a product of the Sadler's Wells Ballet in London who was later to gain international renown at Stuttgart, produced a hilarious parody of Offenbach's *La Belle Hélène* (1955), with Chauviré as Helen and Renault as Paris; and Leonide Massine reproduced his *Symphonie fantastique* (Ballet Russe du Col. de Basil 1936, Opéra 1957) to the Berlioz score, with the original designs by Christian Bérard, in which the leading roles were taken by Christiane Vaussard and Youly Algaroff.

In the post-war period Lifar never regained the dominance that had been his before and during the war, and his resignation as ballet-master of the Opéra in 1958 resulted from his increasing dissatisfaction at not being consulted, as he considered was his due, on policy matters affecting the repertory and the company. It pained him grievously to leave the theatre to which he had given so much of himself, but the legacy he left was both significant and lasting. In the absence of a firmly adopted policy of notating and recording ballets, most works must inevitably disappear in time if a repertory is to be continually replenished, and the greater part of Lifar's choreographic life-work was to be dropped after his departure. It was a fate similar to that which had overtaken Noverre and Gardel, and a number of works worthy of preservation as representative of his period were lost. However, the direction in which he had guided French ballet during the previous three decades was an unquestionable fact of history, and the inspiration he had given to the company formed a solid base upon which its future development would be built. In a wider sense, particularly through the Institut Chorégraphique, he had raised the dance to a level where it commanded consideration and respect as an expression of French culture. Egotistical and controversial though he was, his identification both with his art and with the theatre he served was absolute. The sum of his achievements lies embedded in the strength of the company and the enhanced status of the dance in the Opéra's activities.

X

A New Strategy Emerges

Problems and changes inevitably followed in the wake of Lifar's departure. Not since the time of Gardel had a ballet-master wielded such authority in Paris. But Lifar had left no assistant or disciple to step into his shoes, and many years were to pass before the Opéra ballet would come under another personality of his stature.

Lifar's immediate successor was George Skibine, a Russian like himself, but one brought up from infancy in Paris. He had studied under Preobrajenskaya, and in the 1950s he and his wife, the American ballerina Marjorie Tallchief, had become internationally celebrated as principal dancers of the peripatetic Grand Ballet du Marquis de Cuevas. Discovering a bent for choreography, Skibine had also produced several successful ballets. In 1957 both dancers were engaged by the Opéra, she as a replacement for Vyroubova, and he to be appointed ballet-master one year later.

His tenure of this post was to be notable less for his creative contributions than for the introduction of ballets by outside choreographers. Most of Skibine's own productions were in fact revivals: *Idylle* and *Annabel Lee* (both 1958) had been created for the Cuevas repertory; *Concerto* (1958), to music by Jolivet, had earlier been staged in Strasbourg; and *Pastorale* (1961) was a minor offering devised for Mrs Jacqueline Kennedy's visit to Versailles.

During his term at the Opéra he presented only two true creations, one of which, *Conte cruel* (1959), was little more than a *pas de deux*. The other, however, was a substantial work by any standard – a new version of Ravel's *Daphnis et Chloé* (1959), with luminous designs by Chagall, in which the choreographer and Claude Bessy created the title roles.

After so many years dominated by the works of Lifar, there was a strong case for bringing ballets by outside choreographers into the repertory, but the move was also a response to a growing internationalisation in a world that was becoming seemingly smaller as it moved into the jet age. Skibine himself had been nurtured in a touring company, gaining experience in many cities in the Old World and the New. His cosmopolitan outlook would inevitably have an influence on his contribution to the Opéra, and his years there were to be marked by a number of revivals of works created elsewhere.

Thus, in 1959, Balanchine revived his interpretation of Gounod's symphony, *Symphonie*, for Josette Amiel (recently nominated *étoile*) and Jean-Paul Andréani; Anton Dolin staged his evocation of the *Pas de quatre* for the emotional farewell performance of Lycette Darsonval; and Tatiana Gsovsky produced an expanded version of her *Dame aux camélias*, to a score by Sauguet, in which Yvette Chauviré, partnered by Skibine, repeated the triumph she had gained in Berlin two years before.

The additions of the following year, 1960, were even more impressive. Only one was a creation in the true sense, Gene Kelly's *Pas de dieux*, the first jazz ballet to be seen on the stage of the Palais Garnier. Set to Gershwin's piano concerto and designed by André François, it was joy to behold – and also, in the performances of the long-limbed Bessy and Attilio Labis, to dance. In recognition of his success, Labis was nominated *étoile* within a month of its première. In severe contrast was Harald Lander's restaging of his Eskimo ballet, *Qarttsiluni*, a work of primeval power, but inevitably less accessible to the sophisticated Paris public.

A much greater triumph awaited Vladimir Bourmeister's full-length production of *Le Lac des cygnes*, which had caused a sensation four years previously when brought to Paris by the Ballet of the Stanislavsky Theatre, Moscow. It was to remain in the repertory of the Opéra for many years, appealing not only to the dancers, to whom it offered a challenge to stretch their interpretative talent, but also to the public, whose presumed antipathy towards the full-length ballet seemed at last laid to rest.

There were no additions to the repertory in 1961, which saw the nomination of two new *étoiles*, Claire Motte and Jacqueline Rayet, and the engagement of the Danish dancer, Flemming Flindt, who was to remain as an *étoile* with the company for three years before leaving to assume the post of ballet-master in Copenhagen.

Skibine's resignation at the end of 1961 was followed by a period of uncertainty and crisis. There were rumours that Bourmeister might be tempted out of Moscow to take over, but in the end a successor was chosen from within the company.

Under Michel Descombey, who was to remain in charge until 1969, the policy of inviting guest choreographers continued. In 1962 Lifar came out of retirement to revive *Les Mirages*, *Salade* and *Icare*, and the following year four Balanchine revivals were presented: *Bourrée fantasque*, *Scotch Symphony*, *Concerto Barocco* and *Four Temperaments*.

Of greater significance, however, was the appearance of two French guest choreographers of international repute, each of whom would have had an ample claim to be considered for the supreme post of ballet-master, had he cared to press it. The first of these was Maurice Béjart, acclaimed by some as the most influential French choreographer of the modern generation. In 1964 he staged at the Opéra a sensational production of Berlioz's *La Damnation de Faust*, devised as 'a choreographic fresco', with the singers, apart from those representing the principal characters, discreetly positioned as a static chorus. In the aftermath of this work, its three principal dancers were all to be nominated *étoiles*:

Christiane Vlassi (Marguerite) and Cyril Atanassoff in 1964, and Jean-Pierre Bonnefous in 1965. In 1965 Béjart staged a new version of *Renard* for a Stravinsky programme, which was completed by revivals of his *Les Noces* and *Le Sacre du printemps*. In 1966 he returned to revive another of his works, *Webern Opus V*.

Slightly more senior, and with the aura of a distinguished career outside the Opéra, was Roland Petit, who contributed two major ballets: *Notre-Dame de Paris* (1965), a dark, impressionist piece in which he gave an unforgettable performance as Quasimodo alongside Claire Motte's authoritative Esmeralda, and an even greater masterpiece, *Turangalila* (1968), designed by Max Ernst, in which the Oriental quality of Olivier Messiaen's grand hymn to love and joy was ingeniously captured in the inventive choreography. On a more intimate level, Petit also created *Paradis perdu* (1967) for Margot Fonteyn and Rudolf Nureyev, who were guest artists, and *Extase* (1968) for Nureyev, with Noëlla Pontois, Wilfride Piollet and Martine Parmain.

Descombey himself also had ambitions as a choreographer, producing a number of ballets, only one of which – *Symphonie Concertante* (1962), to music by Frank Martin – achieved a real measure of success. Another of his ballets, *But* (1963), was an amusing attempt to convey the skills of basketball in terms of dance. Much of his later work, however – including a misguided and happily transitory reworking of *Coppélia* – revealed a modernistic trend which at that time seemed out of place at the Opéra and, towards the end of his term, was arousing protests from a section of the public. However, the technical standards of the company in no way suffered under his direction, and indeed the dancers benefited from the experience of supporting a succession of distinguished guest artists: Fonteyn and Nureyev, Maya Plisetskaya and Nicolai Fadeyechev, and Erik Bruhn. It was also in Descombey's time that Noëlla Pontois achieved her nomination as *étoile*.

Descombey's successor was John Taras, an American ballet-master of wide experience who had developed under the wing of Balanchine. From him a firm guidance, allied to a respect for tradition, was to be expected, but unfortunately his term at the Opéra was prematurely cut short by a dispute that finally had to be settled in the courts. Taras's term was too short to leave a permanent mark, but the tempo of activity was maintained. Two new *étoiles*, Wilfride Piollet and Georges Piletta, were nominated in 1969, and early in 1970 the company paid a highly successful visit to Russia.

Taras's departure took place against a background of impending crisis. The need for a radical re-appraisal of the structure of the Opéra ballet was becoming urgent, and negotiations had been opened with Roland Petit who, it was hoped, would be persuaded to direct the company. But after being appointed in 1969 on condition that his term would commence the following year, he never took up his duties, withdrawing when his ideas proved too drastic and draconian for the dancers. Maurice Béjart was also approached, but he too declined, preferring to remain with his own company, for which he could create with total freedom.

The Opéra provisionally appointed Claude Bessy as *maître de ballet*. The Palais Garnier then had to be closed for structural works, and the ballet company enjoyed a successful season under Maurice Béjart at the Palais des Sports, where Béjart revived his *Boléro* and *Damnation de Faust*, and produced a new version of *L'Oiseau de feu* (1970), in which the Firebird became a young revolutionary leader who emerges from among a group of partisans. That role was designed for Michaël Denard, who, with Jean-Pierre Franchetti, was shortly afterwards nominated as *étoile*.

Autonomy had now become an issue, and in April 1971 Raymond Franchetti was appointed as Delegate-General for the Dance to the Administrator, with the task of settling the conditions under which this could be achieved. Franchetti, father of the new *étoile*, was a retired dancer whose dance academy in the Cité Véron attracted many celebrated names in the world of dance at one time or another, and his rare gift as a teacher had led to an engagement as guest teacher at the Royal Ballet School in London. Now that he was invested with full powers over choice of programmes, casting and promotions at the Opéra, he announced his intention to introduce a number of reforms. Instead of weekly performances, alternate months would be devoted to ballet; there would be more sharing of roles; annual examinations would be reintroduced, but on a voluntary basis as a means of discovering talent; there would be exchanges with artistes from foreign countries; the repertory would be videotaped; and an experimental group would be formed to encourage young choreographers.

At this time, because of a change of status at the Opéra-Comique, its ballet company was amalgamated with that of the Opéra, and its ballet-master, Michel Rayne, rejoined the staff at the Palais Garnier.

The Opéra reopened in the autumn of 1971. Early in 1972 Alicia Alonso, the celebrated Cuban ballerina, staged *Giselle* in a traditional staging that replaced Carzou's designs. A few months later another classic was added to the repertory, Pierre Lacotte's evocation of Taglioni's *La Sylphide*, which had previously been screened on television. To the score that Schneitzhoeffer had composed for Taglioni, Noëlla Pontois and Cyril Atanassoff had the privilege of bringing the ballet back to life, being succeeded by Ghislaine Thesmar and Michaël Denard, who had featured in the television film. Thesmar's triumph was to earn her an engagement as *étoile*.

The appointment of Rolf Liebermann as director of the Opéra was to mark a historic turning point, bringing to an end a long period of instability and restoring the Palais Garnier to its rightful place among the opera houses of the world. At the same time, its ballet company was becoming increasingly recognised in the international arena, not only for the technical and artistic excellence of its personnel, but also for the catholic spread of its repertoire.

This was to be increasingly reflected in its programmes, and the choice of Balanchine to choreograph the ballet in Gluck's *Orphée et Eurydice* for the inaugural performance of the Liebermann administration was a portent of a promising eclectic policy to come.

A marked shift of policy soon became apparent. Whereas, until Lifar's retirement, ballet at the Opéra had been primarily regarded as an expression of French culture with a slight nod of recognition towards the influence of the Ballets Russes, it was now to be offered as an art without frontiers. Works by acknowledged masters the world over would take their place alongside those of native choreographers. The change of the artistic chief's title from ballet-master to director of dance was no empty gesture, but signified the extent to which the world had shrunk with the increased availability and speed of transport. Paris was becoming an international hub to which visitors flocked in ever-increasing numbers. In such circumstances, artistic chauvinism was fast becoming a dead letter.

With Liebermann now installed, this was now to be reflected in the Opéra's ballet programmes. After a somewhat disappointing start with Flemming Flindt's *Jeux* (1973) and Norbert Schmucki's *L'Apprenti sorcier* (1973), the fortunes of the ballet rose with a programme in honour of Stravinsky. This included five gems from the repertory of the New York City Ballet: three by Balanchine – *Orphée, Agon* and *Capriccio* (the 'Rubies' section from the full-length *Jewels*) – and Jerome Robbins's *Scherzo fantastique* and *Circus Polka*. To these was shortly added another Robbins revival, the poetic *Afternoon of a Faun*, while Leonide Massine was asked to restage Nijinsky's masterpiece to the same score.

In stark contrast was a new ballet by another American choreographer, Glen Tetley. His *Tristan*, given to music by Henze, was full of tormented complexities, and performed by a strong cast, including Nureyev as guest artist, Denard, Guizerix, Piollet and Carolyn Carlson.

That the Opéra was not forgetful of its tradition was displayed by Lacotte's loving restoration of the traditional version of *Coppélia*, with scenery and costumes based upon the designs of the 1870s. The only concession he made to modern taste was to abandon the travesty role. Daringly, he even restored the third act, which he had to re-choreograph afresh in period style, since it had been dropped in 1872 and had long been forgotten.

A start was also made in building a repertory of classics from another main stream of balletic tradition, that of the golden age of Imperial Russian ballet when Tchaikovsky was devoting his genius to the dance. In 1974 Alicia Alonso was invited to stage *La Belle au bois dormant*, in which Pontois added to her laurels alongside Atanassoff as her Prince, and Patrice Bart, who had been nominated an *étoile* two years before, displayed his clean technique in the Blue Bird *pas de deux*. Also in that year, Rudolf Nureyev returned to mount and dance in the 'shades' act of *La Bayadère*, another jewel from the St Petersburg ballet, with eminently danceable music from a lesser composer, Minkus.

Notwithstanding these revivals from the past, the Opéra did not neglect the present. In 1975 Roland Petit was invited to present the company in a programme of his own works, including an old favourite, *Le Loup*, created for the Ballets de Paris twenty-two years before. With Dutilleux's score given a new orchestration and Carzou's forest setting lovingly restored, it provided Pontois and Franchetti with a triumph in the roles created by Violette Verdy and Petit himself. Petit then proposed his own version of Berlioz's *Symphonie fantastique*, designed by Josef Svoboda. Brilliantly theatrical in conception, it caught the mood of the music in depicting the Romantic artist's frenzied search for inspiration. Denard gave an outstanding performance as the artist, but the main interest of the première was focused on Zizi Jeanmaire, who, although still suffering from an injury, was able to appear for just this one night as a guest artist.

Every summer from 1973 to 1977, the Opéra organised the Festival of the Louvre, during which the ballet gave open-air performances in the Cour Carrée. *La Belle au bois dormant* and *Le Lac des cygnes* were presented in the earlier seasons, and in 1977 a more recent work was given, *Ivan le Terrible*, with music by Prokofiev and choreography by Yuri Grigorovich, director of the Bolshoi. This work was noted for its powerfully dramatic roles, which earned two dancers their nomination as *étoile*: Dominique Khalfouni and Charles Jude, who, after being a magnificent Prince Kourbsky, in the same year gave a powerful performance of a tormented Ivan.

On his retirement in 1978, Franchetti was succeeded as director of dance by Violette Verdy, a French-trained ballerina whose varied international career had been spent with such companies as the Ballets des Champs-Élysées, American Ballet Theater and New York City Ballet.

During her three years as director of dance, she introduced a number of changes, including the appointment of a music director for the ballet. Her term, short though it was, was marked by several interesting creations, as well as by works new to Paris but previously seen elsewhere. The first of the creations was *Mahlers Lieder* (1977) to music by Mahler and choreography by the Argentinean choreographer Oscar Araiz. This abstract piece aimed, not entirely successfully, to weld classical dance with elements of modern style based on Limon technique. The following year, the English choreographer Kenneth MacMillan staged a new work for the Opéra, *Métaboles,* to music by Dutilleux, which proved one of his less happy creations – a disappointment partly assuaged by the acclaim awarded to a revival of his Mahler masterpiece, *Song of the Earth*.

A close relationship with Moscow's Bolshoi Ballet, established during a guest season at the Opéra in 1977, led to its ballet-master, Yuri Grigorovich, being invited to stage his *Romeo and Juliet* for the Opéra. This was presented in February 1978 with Michaël Denard and Dominique Khalfouni as the star-crossed lovers, and Georges Piletta and Jean Guizerix as Mercutio and Tybalt. Grigorovich had been given complete freedom to choose cast, designer and conductor; but unfortunately the result was far from happy. The choreography was found lacking in distinction and imagination, too much of the rich detail of the story had been omitted, and the settings and costumes were condemned as drab and wholly lacking in Italian flavour.

In 1978 two new *étoiles* were nominated, Claude de Vulpian and Florence Clerc, for their roles in the great classical ballets, respectively *La Belle au bois dormant* and *Giselle*.

Much more substantial was the last ballet creation of the Liebermann administration, Roland Petit's full-length *Le Fantôme de l'Opéra* (1980). Liebermann himself had initiated this work by commissioning Marcel Landowski to compose a score on the subject of Gaston Leroux's celebrated novel. Originally conceived as an opera-ballet, it finally emerged as a ballet. Petit first envisaged Nureyev as his phantom, but owing to a misunderstanding over the latter's availability, the role was created by the Danish dancer, Peter Schaufuss. The singer-heroine of the novel was predictably transformed into a ballerina and created by Dominique Khalfouni. Petit greatly admired her, and later that year, feeling herself stagnating at the Opéra, she left to join the Ballet de Marseille, of which Petit was director. The hero who rescues the heroine was played with engaging panache by the rising young dancer Patrick Dupond.

Le Fantôme de l'Opéra was to have been featured in a tour of the United States that summer, but a condition imposed by the American impresario that the company should be led by Nureyev met with such sustained opposition from the dancers that the visit had to be abandoned.

Liebermann's retirement in 1980 coincided with the departure of Carolyn Carlson, whom he had engaged at the beginning of his term, with the title of *étoile*, to direct the GRTOP (Groupe de Recherche Théâtrale de l'Opéra de Paris). The establishment of a contemporary dance group within a bastion of classical ballet had been a revolutionary innovation, and under a less inspirational artist than Carlson the experiment might have foundered. She had first come to Paris with Alwin Nikolais's modern dance company, but her style was intensely personal. For six years, programmes danced by members of the GRTOP were interspersed among the main repertory, arousing increasing interest and admiration. Her own ballets were not narrative pieces in the strict sense, but evoked a strange harmonious dream-world bound within a gentler conception of time. There was a great clarity in her compositions, and they provided an enriching experience for the young classical dancers who appeared in them.

Jacques Garnier, dancer and choreographer, succeeded Carlson in 1981 with a slightly different title – director of the Groupe de Recherche Chorégraphique de l'Opéra de Paris (GRCOP). He thus returned to the Palais Garnier; he had left it in 1972, with Brigitte Lefèvre, to found the Théâtre du Silence, a contemporary dance company that played a pioneering role in the context of the Ministry of Culture's policy of choreographic decentralisation.

Liebermann's retirement was accompanied by other changes, notably the appointment of a new director of dance, Rosella Hightower. One of the most celebrated American dancers of the 1940s and 1950s, Hightower had spent much of her career with such great international touring companies as the Ballets Russes de Monte Carlo and the Grand Ballet du Marquis de Cuevas. While her roots were firmly planted in traditional soil, her extensive travels had given her a broad view of the dance activity of her time; on her retirement as a dancer, she settled in Cannes to found an international ballet school and had the additional experience of directing the ballet in Marseilles and Nancy.

Her three-year term at the Opéra was to be notable for the production of more full-length ballets. The first, however, another version of *La Belle au bois dormant*, based on the spectacular production presented by the Cuevas company shortly before the Marquis's death, was staged, not at the Opéra, which was then undergoing extensive repairs, but at the Palais des Sports.

That same year, Elisabeth Platel and Jean-Yves Lormeau joined the ranks of the *étoiles* after their performances respectively as Princess Aurora and the Prince. Patrick Dupond was also nominated *étoile* in that year.

For the reopening of the Palais Garnier, Hightower planned two important productions, John Neumeier's *Le Songe d'un nuit d'été* and Rudolf Nureyev's version of *Don Quichotte*. However, owing to Neumeier's illness, this order had to be reversed, and *Don Quichotte* became the centrepiece of the ballet season of 1981. Nureyev had become a cult figure in the world of ballet ever since his spectacular defection from the Kirov Ballet at Orly airport twenty years before. For several years his career had centred on the Royal Ballet in London, where he and Margot Fonteyn formed one of the historic dance partnerships of all time. Now, at forty-three, he had passed his prime as a dancer, and was turning increasingly to production and choreography. For his first offering at the Palais Garnier he was to stage Petipa's *Don Quichotte*, which he had first produced in Vienna in 1966 and revived several times since. What Paris saw was thus a polished version that respected the traditional production as handed down in Russia, but to which Nureyev had added the gloss of his personal vision of Cervantes's Spain. By tightening the action, Nureyev had given it an exuberant vitality, and his personal inspiration galvanised the dancers to new heights of brilliant virtuosity. Noëlla Pontois and Claude de Vulpian gave contrasting interpretations as Kitri, with Cyril Atanassoff and Patrick Dupond sharing the role of Basile.

The summer of 1981 also saw a somewhat eccentric version of *La Fille mal gardée* by Hans Spoerli that was to give Dupond another rounded character-study in the role of Alain.

Neumeier's *Le Songe d'un nuit d'été*, when eventually presented in May 1982, proved well worth waiting for. Originally produced for the ballet of the Staatsoper of Hamburg, over which Neumeier presided, it was a profoundly penetrating translation of Shakespeare's comedy into dance. With its psychological insight into the relationship of the characters, it was very modern in conception. In a stroke of brilliance, the choreographer had distinguished the three levels of characters by accompanying their action with widely contrasting music: the mortals by Mendelssohn, the fairies by Ligeti, and the mechanicals by popular tunes played on a hurdy-gurdy. The dancers were well served by choreography firmly based on classical technique while providing scope for characterisation. In this revival, Noëlla Pontois and Jean-Yves Lormeau created the dual roles of Hippolyta-Titania and Theseus-Oberon, but the strongest impression was made by Dupond's witty portrayal of Puck.

That summer, during the performances given by the company at the Festival of Nervi, Monique Loudières was nominated *étoile* after a memorable performance as Kitri in *Don Quichotte*.

Hightower's term as director of dance closed in 1983 on another high note, a revival of John Cranko's widely acclaimed *Romeo and Juliet* – the fourth interpretation of Prokofiev's Shakespearean score to be presented at the Opéra. Cranko, who had died tragically some years before, was still remembered in Paris for his hilarious *La Belle Hélène*; and quite recently the Stuttgart Ballet, which he had virtually created, had introduced his later masterpieces to Paris. To many, his *Romeo and Juliet* was of all versions the most faithful to Shakespeare. It was full of finely observed character studies that were now to give junior members of the Opéra ballet new opportunities to hone their dramatic skills. However, the ballet depended largely on those who played the title roles, which were to be generously shared, the honour of creating them in Paris falling to Pontois and Denard as the lovers and Dupond as an engaging Mercutio.

Taking stock at this juncture, when the question of who was to succeed Hightower had to be faced, it was clear that the policy of interspersing new ballets with selected masterpieces from outside was paying excellent dividends. The Opéra had always been a centre of ballet, but now its prestige beyond the borders of France was noticeably on the rise. For the future, the choice of a director of dance to continue the progress made in the past decade would be crucial.

XI

Nureyev and After

In naming Hightower's successor, the Opéra stunned the dance world with its choice of Rudolf Nureyev, certainly the most prestigious figure to have emerged in the world of ballet since Nijinsky, and by reputation an *enfant terrible* fully conscious of his worth and well able to exploit it. Rolf Liebermann, at the beginning of his term, had already thought of approaching him, but the time was not ripe for the dancer to consider such a change. When negotiations opened more than a decade later, their path was not smooth, and the Opéra was forced to yield to Nureyev's demand that, for tax reasons, he would give his services for no more than 180 days in each year. That an organisation so conventionally bound by tradition would be so bold as to take on Nureyev, and even more that he would bind himself to it, was a source of general amazement. Many must have thought that the arrangement could not last, but last it did until the end of 1989.

There was much curiosity as to the policy Nureyev would adopt. However, fears that he might contemplate rapid and radical changes were put to rest when he announced his plans. He made it clear that he was prepared to be patient. He denied any intention of overturning the existing order, although there were a few reforms that he hoped to introduce, such as having a freer hand in choosing teachers and the possibility of not taking strict account of the hierarchy. As to the repertory, he willingly embraced the existing policy of introducing full-length ballets, without prejudice to the encouragement of new choreography. There was nothing controversial in all this, and Nureyev took up his duties amid a general spirit of good will. The only serious concern, which later events would show to be well founded, was whether his desire to continue his international career might clash with his obligations to Paris.

His first offering, at the end of 1983, was a full-evening version of *Raymonda*, a Russian classic that the octogenarian Petipa had created in St Petersburg in 1898, and which Nureyev remembered from his early days at the Kirov. This was also the first classic he had revived after his escape to the West. Although hampered by a colourless plot, it owed its survival to Glazunov's lush score and a surfeit of brilliant dances, both classical and national. In Paris, the brilliance of the dancing carried the day. The honour of creating the leading roles fell to Elisabeth Platel and Charles Jude, with Jean Guizerix playing the villain and, in the mime role of the spectral Countess Sybille, Yvette Chauviré, returning to the scene of so many of her former triumphs.

Nureyev also had ambitions as a creator in his own right. In the spring of

1984 he presented *La Tempête*, which had earlier suffered an indifferent reception when created for the Royal Ballet in London. It came as no surprise that this long Shakespearian epic proved even less comprehensible to the Parisian public, which found it pretentious and obscure, notwithstanding Nureyev's compelling performance as Prospero.

Infinitely more accessible was Pierre Lacotte's *Marco Spada*, a reinterpretation of Mazilier's long-forgotten ballet of 1857. The original choreography had been lost, and Lacotte produced it afresh in the Second Empire style. It had a mixed reception from the critics, but the public seemed content with its melodramatic plot and its generous proportion of dancing.

Classics from the more recent past were not, however, ignored, and a programme devoted to ballets with scores by Stravinsky brought together revivals of works by three major choreographers – Balanchine's *Violin Concerto*, Paul Taylor's *The Rehearsal*, and MacMillan's *Danses concertantes* – which were accompanied by one new work, Nils Christe's *Symphonie en trois mouvements*. Later in the year, Lifar's *Icare* and Béjart's *Sacre du printemps* were revived, accompanied by Lucinda Child's charming bagatelle to music by Shostakovitch, *Premier Orage*.

Nureyev seemed filled with an irrepressible urge to produce versions of full-length classics, even at the cost of jettisoning an existing production, and for the reopening of the season in the autumn of 1984 he staged yet another version of Prokofiev's *Romeo and Juliet*, which replaced Cranko's more modest but much admired interpretation. Nureyev's was a very grandiose production, which was found somewhat wanting in its depiction of the characters, despite an impressive performance by Nureyev himself as Mercutio. A few weeks later, Bourmeister's acclaimed *Le Lac des cygnes* was superseded by a new production from Nureyev that was considered by many to be inferior. On the other hand, it afforded splendid opportunities to some of the younger dancers to be tested in the dual role of Odette/Odile. Most notable of these was a brilliant aspirant with a technique that owed much to her early training as a gymnast and was to make her a role model for the next generation of dancers – Sylvie Guillem. On the evening before Christmas, in a historic departure from tradition, she was nominated *étoile* on stage in the presence of the public.

Among the new ballets that followed in 1985, Christe's *Before Nightfall*, to music by Martinu, was favourably received, as was *Quelques Pas graves de Baptiste*, a graceful essay in the baroque style by Francine Lancelot, a specialist who was both scholar and dancer – the Baptiste of the title being, of course, Lully. In it Nureyev appeared alongside Jean Guizerix and his wife, Wilfride Piollet, both of whom had become fascinated by the study of early dance.

Nureyev's own ballet, *Washington Square*, an ambitious work based on Henry James's novel and constructed to music by Charles Ives, was a brave failure, its narrative swamped by much parading of drum majorettes, a Salvation Army band, jazz singers and cowboys. Much more impressive was the extended *pas de deux*, *Mouvement-Rhythme-Étude*, which Maurice Béjart constructed to a score by Pierre Henry for the astonishingly pliant Guillem and another rising young dancer, Éric Vu An. That winter two new *étoiles* were nominated: Isabelle Guérin and Laurent Hilaire.

At the end of 1985, to the satisfaction of many, the Bourmeister *Lac des cygnes* was restored, and Nureyev philosophically consoled himself for what was to be only a temporary eclipse of his own version by staging *Casse-Noisette* – a reworking of a production that had been first produced in London and later revived elsewhere in Europe and South America. The choreography owed little to the traditional version that had come down from Russia, and the familiar *pas de deux* was missed; but the dances in the second half of the ballet gave splendid opportunities to some of the younger dancers.

The first new programme of 1986 was devoted to works by Maurice Béjart. In addition to reviving his *Sonate à trois*, a ballet version of Jean-Paul Sartre's *Huis clos* to music by Bartok, he created a fascinating piece entitled *Arepo*, performed to a patchwork of operatic melodies. The title ('opera' spelt backwards) disclosed that he was drawing on childhood memories of a performance of *Faust*, which inspired a sequence of comic and sinister scenes that stretched his dancers to the limit. A few weeks later he presented another startlingly original work. Created for Patrick Dupond in New York, *Salomé* presented this very masculine dancer with the extraordinary challenge – accepted with triumphant effect – of impersonating the *danseuse fatale* of Biblical history who demanded the head of John the Baptist.

That summer Manuel Legris had the honour of being nominated *étoile* on the stage of the Metropolitan Opera House in New York during a tour of the United States, the Opéra ballet's first visit to that city since 1948. This was the sequel to an unfortunate misunderstanding earlier in the year when Béjart, believing he had authority, announced the nomination of Legris and Éric Vu An. Cruelly for the two dancers, this was swiftly followed by a denial. Legris was wise enough to swallow his pride and remain, but the more volatile Vu An left to embark on a freelance career.

Before the new season opened in the autumn of 1986, it was announced that Patrice Bart had been appointed *maître de ballet*, a subsidiary post that would become of increasing importance in the long absences of Nureyev, ever careful not to extend his annual stays in Paris.

A full-length creation with popular appeal at the end of the year was now becoming a tradition, and the dawning of 1986 saw Nureyev's outrageous but highly original version of Prokofiev's *Cendrillon*, transposed into the tinsel world of Hollywood. In spite of amusing gags and cameo-studies of famous film stars, his inspiration appeared to flag after the first act. The production was saved by Guillem's Cinderella. Charles Jude was her Prince

Charming, and Isabelle Guérin and Monique Loudières excelled themselves in the comic roles of the stepsisters.

Two interesting works were added before the end of 1986, a revival of Robbins's *In memory of...* for Guillem, and David Parsons's amusing sketch, *The Two Brothers*, in which Nureyev and Jude appeared as two adolescent boys at play.

The new year, 1987, opened with another novelty, *Sans Armes, citoyens!*, a pretentious work by Rudi Van Dantzig that had little success. Much more successful was Joseph Lazzini's version of *La Fille mal gardée*, which had long been applauded in the provinces, but had not until now been seen in the Palais Garnier. Nureyev had been very keen for Frederick Ashton to stage his much-acclaimed version in Paris, but the ageing English choreographer was not to be persuaded. In Lazzini's charming and well-crafted recreation of this historic ballet, Florence Clerc and Jean-Yves Lormeau seemed ideally matched as the lovers. It was coupled with a sombre modern work by Maguy Marin to Couperin's *Leçons de ténèbres*, an evocation of the sufferings of Jerusalem under Saracen rule that brought to the fore two young dancers of unusual promise, Marie-Claude Pietragalla and Kader Belarbi.

Nureyev's absorbing interest in modern dance was revealed in the invitation to William Forsythe to create *In the middle, somewhat elevated*, a work of great power in which he exploited Guillem's extraordinary pliancy. A few weeks later there followed another revival in a modern genre from an earlier period – José Limon's *La Pavane du maure* to music of Purcell, featuring Jean Guizerix and Claude de Vulpian as Othello and Desdemona, Charles Jude as Iago, and Françoise Legrée as Emilia – and, less successfully, Van Dantzig's *Quatre derniers Lieder*.

The ballet of the Opéra was now consolidating its transatlantic reputation. Its successful tours in 1986 and 1987 were followed by a more elaborate one in 1988 when, for the first time, it was accompanied by its School of Dance. As well as giving two complete performances at the Juilliard School of Music in New York, the pupils of the School presented a full-day demonstration of its syllabus before an appreciative audience of American teachers.

With this American visit and another tour of the Far East taking up much of the company's time and energy, Paris was somewhat neglected in 1988, during which no new work was added to the repertory. It might even have seemed that there was a slackening of momentum, and there was certainly cause for concern when the Opéra lost two of its brightest stars: Patrick Dupond, who left to direct the Ballet de Nantes, and in 1989 Sylvie Guillem, who embarked on a freelance international career, signing a contract as guest artist with the Royal Ballet in London.

However, there was talent aplenty waiting for opportunities, and in December 1988 Elisabeth Maurin joined the select group of *étoiles*, having the unprecedented privilege of being nominated in the television studio where she was being filmed as Clara in *Casse-Noisette*.

In July 1989 the Opéra-Bastille opened with a great flourish, only to be closed for further works once the celebration of the bicentenary of the Revolution was over. It would not formally reopen for another eight months. Meanwhile, in Nureyev's absence, uncertainty as to what the future held was not surprisingly affecting the dancers' morale. This, however, hardly showed in their performances, and in spite of everything 1989 had opened with an interesting programme of ballets never seen before at the Palais Garnier: Tatiana Leskova's revival of Massine's ballet to Tchaikovsky's fifth symphony, *Les Présages*, and two works by the American choreographer Twyla Tharp – a revival of *As Time Goes By* to music by Haydn, and a creation, *Rules of the Game*, to music by Bach and Colombier. This was followed by a revival of *La Belle au bois dormant*, the run of which was interrupted when the dancers went on strike in protest against a proposed law imposing a compulsory examination on anyone wishing to become a teacher.

That summer, Nureyev's contract, which had already been once extended, came up for renewal. For one reason and another his relationship with the Opéra had become strained. Although it was not generally known, he was suffering from AIDS, which was beginning to have a debilitating effect on his stamina. The rift proved too wide to be bridged; the negotiations foundered, and Patrice Bart and Eugène Poliakov, who had virtually been running the company for some time, were placed in temporary charge.

Care had been taken not to close the door too firmly, and a joint press statement announced Nureyev's departure as a 'mutual decision'. Further, to ensure that his productions would remain in the repertory, he was to be given the honorary title of '*premier chorégraphe*'. A main factor of the breach had been Nureyev's desire to embark on a lengthy tour of North America in the musical *The King and I*, which now meant that the planned production of his full-length *Bayadère* for the Opéra would have to be deferred *sine die*.

Appropriately, in view of Nureyev's absorbing interest in modern dance and his friendship with Paul Taylor, the last programme he planned was devoted to works by three of America's leading choreographers: *Speaking in Tongues* by Taylor himself, Merce Cunningham's *Points in Space*, and – the sole creation – Mark Morris's *Ein Herz*.

Another programme offered in the spring of 1990 was a tribute to the work of Roland Petit, containing revivals of two classic works he had created for the Ballets de Paris more than forty years earlier: *Carmen*, with Fanny Gaïda and Kader Belarbi, and *Le Jeune Homme et la mort*, in which Éric Vu An and Belarbi shared the role so indelibly associated with Jean Babilée. To these two masterpieces Petit added a joyful new work, *Debussy pour sept danseurs*.

The cloud of uncertainty that had settled over the dancers was finally dispelled by the announcement that the Palais Garnier was to become exclusively a ballet house. To open the new season in the autumn of 1989, the Czech choreographer Jiří Kylián staged two works. One was a tried success, *Tantz-Schul*, inspired by Lambranzi's early-eighteenth-century manual of dances in the *commedia dell'arte* style; the other was a ballet composed specially for Paris, *Sinfonietta*, to music by Janáček. Both were received with enthusiasm, as were the two programmes that followed, one of Diaghilev revivals, and the other devoted to ballets by Balanchine and Robbins.

In the summer of 1990 it was announced that Patrick Dupond would be Nureyev's successor as director of dance. In his two years at Nancy, Dupond had given proof of his leadership qualities, and his popularity both within the Opéra and without augured well and gave the company's morale a much-needed boost. There was no shortage of new blood to replace the older dancers at the end of their careers. Patrice Bart and Jean-Pierre Franchetti retired in 1989 and Jean Guizerix in 1990, their departures being accompanied by two nominations to the grade of *étoile*: Kader Belarbi, honoured after an impeccable performance as the Blue Bird in *La Belle au bois dormant*, and Marie-Claude Pietragalla.

A Lifar retrospective was followed by an important production from the repertory of the Royal Ballet, Kenneth MacMillan's *Manon* (retitled *L'Histoire de Manon* at the request of the composer's heirs), a three-act ballet to music by Massenet, based on the Abbé Prévost's classic novel. MacMillan's skill in depicting character was appreciated by public and company alike, giving opportunities to younger dancers as well as extending the dramatic range of the principals. Cast changes enabled the public to judge between various interpreters of the leading roles. Monique Loudières, Fanny Gaïda and Claude de Vulpian presented contrasting portrayals as Manon, and public interest was further whetted by Sylvie Guillem's return, as guest artist, to add her interpretation of the part.

Few new works were added in 1991, but to compensate for this there was a surfeit of interesting revivals. A Diaghilev programme presented a revival of Nijinska's *Les Biches* and a scholarly reconstruction by Millicent Hodson and Kenneth Archer of Nijinsky's *Le Sacre du printemps*, meticulously based on surviving evidence. It had not escaped notice that the summer would mark the 150th anniversary of *Giselle*, and a new production was prepared to honour that auspicious occasion. The sombre costumes and modernistic sets, inspired by Breton models, cast something of a gloom over the occasion – Yvette Chauviré's initial reaction was one of shock – but did not detract from the successful restaging by Bart and Poliakov, in which no less than nine ballerinas shared the role of Giselle.

In July the versatility of the company was put to the test in a programme devoted to works from American choreographers, including Twyla Tharp's justly celebrated *Push Comes to Shove*, in which Dupond played the part created for Baryshnikov. There followed a programme of ballets by Jerome Robbins, including revivals of *Dances at a Gathering*, to music by Chopin, and *Glass Pieces*.

Early in 1992 three more masterworks from the past were presented: two from the Diaghilev era, Massine's *Le Tricorne* and Nijinska's *Le Train bleu*, and one of Roland Petit's early works, *Le Rendez-vous*. Then followed a programme composed of ballets by young French choreographers, Daniel Larrieu's *Attentat poétique* and Odile Duboc's *Retour de scène*.

It was a year of considerable achievement, but the greatest was still to come. The long-planned production of *La Bayadère*, shelved when Nureyev embarked on the tour of *The King and I*, was further delayed by his urge to keep up the momentum of his professional activities, and complicated, as was becoming increasingly clear, by his failing health. He began to work on *La Bayadère* in 1992, but in September, when he returned to the Opéra after the summer break, he was clearly a very sick man. With superhuman devotion to his art, he appeared at rehearsal every day, even though there were times when he could give no more than an hour or two before his strength failed him. The production was finally completed, and at the première he was given a triumphant ovation. No one who was present that evening would forget his appearance from the wings to take his bow, in full evening dress and leaning on the arm of one of the dancers. It was the last that many of them would see of him. Less than two months later, he died.

The inauguration of the Opéra-Bastille opened a new era. When its teething problems were overcome, Paris found itself the possessor of two opera houses that, for all the difference in size, structure and design, complemented one another in a singularly happy relationship. Although, as events turned out, the Palais Garnier would not be exclusively a dance theatre, the dancers were not to be short-changed. Indeed, when the new strategy was in place, the ballet would find itself allotted a significant share in the offerings at the Bastille, while the Palais Garnier remained, as originally planned, its artistic and administrative headquarters, with facilities for studios and rehearsal rooms.

Dance had been featured at the Bastille from its inauguration, when the programme over which President Mitterand presided included a ballet by Andy Degroat, *Bacchanale*. When the new opera house opened, only opera was given there until July 1992, when the Bourmeister *Lac des cygnes* was given a three-week run. It was then abundantly clear that the Bastille provided the perfect arena for the full-length spectacular ballet, and in subsequent years nearly every work of this kind in the repertory was given its turn to draw packed houses in these new surroundings. The extent of Nureyev's extraordinary legacy of grandiose productions is reflected in the statistic that, taken together, they account for 60% of more than 300 ballet programmes presented at the Bastille in the last decade of the twentieth century.

A problem that might have complicated these rearrangements had fortunately been removed when, in 1987, the Opéra's School of Dance had been moved to purpose-built premises in Nanterre. As a result, its pupils were lodged and given their dance classes and general schooling on a single campus. The School had grown enormously since its modest beginnings when Louis XIV had founded it in 1713. In the course of time the technical level of the training had risen, as had the number of pupils; the introduction of a perfection class in 1806 had been a notable landmark. It had been housed in various localities conveniently close to the Opéra, but from 1875, when the Palais Garnier opened, dance classes had been held in the theatre itself. The School was established as an independent entity in 1958, and since 1973 had been directed with great flair by Claude Bessy, who masterminded its move to Nanterre. In 1977, on her initiative, the School gave its first public performance, now an annual event avidly followed by critics and public alike, its programme traditionally comprising an interesting revival – a recent choice was Lifar's *Le Chevalier et la Damoiselle*, happily resuscitated before memories of it vanished – and sometimes a piece specially composed by a distinguished choreographer.

The absence of the main body of the company on a tour of Asia, Spain and America did not interrupt the flow of activity in the first half of 1993, although the opportunity was taken of inviting a number of other companies to give short seasons at the Palais Garnier. For those of the Opéra's dancers who remained in Paris, productions of several proven classics by Balanchine, Robbins and Petit were introduced into the repertory, but the main event of the year was undoubtedly the alternative version of *Giselle* presented by the Swedish choreographer Mats Ek. Ek had dared to place the action in a modern setting, interpreting the plot freely without any suggestion of the traditional choreography, and concluding with a startling scene set not in the moonlit forest, but in an asylum.

There was, of course, no intention to replace the traditional version of *Giselle*, and when the company presented it on tour in Nîmes in July 1993, the unprecedented opportunity was taken to nominate three *étoiles* before a performance in which they were all to be featured: Fanny Gaïda as Giselle, Carole Arbo as Myrtha, and Nicolas Le Riche as Albrecht.

The new year of 1994 was ushered in with a revival of Nureyev's version of *Casse-Noisette*, featuring Patrick Dupond's brilliant portrayal of Drosselmeyer as a caricature of the ballet's original creator, Marius Petipa. Dupond was also featured in the title role of the next important offering, a recreation by Millicent Hodson and Kenneth Archer of *Till Eulenspiegel* to the Richard Strauss tone poem, based on documents and memories of the last ballet that Nijinsky staged before lapsing into madness.

There followed a Roland Petit programme, containing three creations: *Camera obscura*, a somewhat overlong ballet based on a tale by Vladimir Nabokov, to music by Schönberg; *Rythme de valses*, a witty concoction of Strauss waltzes; and *Passacaille No.1* to music by Webern. More to the public taste, however, was a new ballet by Angelin Preljocaj, *Le Parc*, an attractive full-length work to music by Mozart, evoking in an intriguingly graceful way the sensual dalliance associated with the court of Louis XV.

Inspired by the added prestige acquired through its foreign tours, the dancers of the Opéra were dancing at the top of their form. But they were now to face a long disruption. With the teething troubles of the Bastille cured, it was the turn of the Palais Garnier to be modernised, a transformation that required it to be vacated for eighteen months.

During this period, extending over the seasons of 1994–95 and 1996–97, ballet had to alternate with opera at the Bastille. Because of its size, the Bastille was particularly suitable to the spectacular full-length ballet, and *Le Lac des cygnes*, *Roméo et Juliette*, *Giselle*, *La Bayadère* and *Le Parc* accounted for over 60% of all ballet performances given in those two seasons. Only one novelty, and that a contemporary piece, was added to the repertory: Jean-Claude Gallotta's *Les Variations d'Ulysse*, a work that, through evocative lighting and fantastic, even surrealistic costumes, presented a glimpse into a strange world with undertones not only of Homer, but also of James Joyce.

By the time the ballet company returned to the Palais Garnier in the spring of 1996, there had been a development that promised great changes for the future. Hugues Gall, who had been secretary-general of the Opéra from 1968 to 1972, then assistant administrator under Liebermann, and after that director of the Grand Théâtre in Geneva, had in 1993 been appointed director of the Opéra, taking up his functions in 1995.

In his report to the Ministry of Culture setting out the elements of the policy he proposed to follow, he envisaged an increase in the number both of ballet performances and of tours. He terminated the existing arrangement with Patrick Dupond and appointed Brigitte Lefèvre to the post of director of dance.

The responsibility for the ballet was thus placed in her hands. Her training as dancer, choreographer, company director and administrator had prepared her well for the task that was thus confided in her. A graduate of the School of Dance, where she had been trained under Yvette Chauviré, Serge Peretti and Raymond Franchetti, she had been reared in the profession from childhood. Her interest had very soon turned to choreography and contemporary dance, and in 1972 she had left the Opéra to found, in collaboration with her friend Jacques Garnier, a contemporary company, the Théâtre du Silence.

In 1983 she was called to the Ministry of Culture, being appointed two years later as that Ministry's first delegate for the dance. On her return to the Palais Garnier as general administrator in 1992 and two years later becoming assistant director for the dance, Brigitte Lefèvre initiated a policy of relative autonomy for the ballet within the institution, increasing the number of performances to 170–190 a season and introducing a broad policy of programming that appealed to contemporary choreographers while also keeping a watchful eye on the classical repertory.

The Palais Garnier was now revealed, with its scenic capabilities vastly enhanced by state-of-the-art stage facilities and with the front of the house completely renovated. In this new setting, in the spring of 1996, the dancers responded appropriately to music that echoed the *'style Napoléon III'* of the surroundings: Verdi's *Les Quatre Saisons*, originally composed for his opera, *Les Vêpres siciliennes*, in 1855, and Delibes's effervescent *Coppélia* of 1870. The first of these scores had been re-used by Jerome Robbins for a classical divertissement conceived with an engaging touch of humour. As for *Coppélia*, it was given a 'new look', for it had been decided not to revive the Lacotte restoration, but instead to present an entirely new production by Patrice Bart, who had been appointed 'ballet-master attached to the direction of the dance'. In this, Coppélius was no longer the quaint old doll-maker, but a brooding romantic figure who sees in Swanilda (in this version the mechanical doll) an incarnation of his dead wife.

On a more profound level, 1996 saw the production of two major dance works, each conceived with the daunting aim of interpreting in movement a great musical masterpiece. Maurice Béjart's homage to Beethoven, *La Neuvième Symphonie*, had been constructed using his own company of dancers, the Ballet du XXe Siècle, and he had long been unwilling to allow it to be revived elsewhere. Hugues Gall's powers of persuasion overcame his reluctance, however, and in May 1996 it was given a triumphant ovation at the Bastille. A few weeks later, at the Palais Garnier, Angelin Preljocaj responded with his *Annonciation,* a work of limpid beauty to Vivaldi's *Magnificat*, with Elisabeth Maurin giving a portrayal of mystical radiance as the Virgin.

Along with regular presentations of new works, the Opéra was not neglecting its policy of preserving ballets that had gained acceptance both on its own stage and elsewhere. The opening programme of the 1997–98 season included three such twentieth-century classics: Lifar's *Suite en blanc*, still an impressive test of virtuosity; Frederick Ashton's *Rhapsody*; and Agnes de Mille's *Fall River Legend*, this last work being memorable for Elisabeth Maurin's dramatic interpretation as Lizzie Borden.

However, 1997 was to be particularly notable for John Neumeier's new staging of *Sylvia*, a revival of Pina Bausch's version of Stravinsky's *Sacre du printemps*, and – produced at the Bastille – a remarkable full-length contemporary work, *Signes*, a joint creation by the painter Olivier Debré and Carolyn Carlson. This year also saw the nomination of two *étoiles*: José Martinez and Agnès Letestu.

Ushering in 1998, Nureyev's *Raymonda* drew large houses to the Bastille over a seven-week run. At the Palais Garnier, as a counter to Ek's modernistic *Giselle*, Patrice Bart refurbished the traditional version of that ballet with great attention both to traditional detail and to the psychological motivations of the characters, particularly that of Hilarion, who was presented, not as a two-dimensional villain, but as a man of deep and complex feelings. One performance of this production was chosen to mark the eightieth birthday of one of the greatest Giselles, Yvette Chauviré, who had made her farewell in this ballet in 1972. Another affecting occasion during the year was a revival of *So Schnell* to music by Bach, the work of Dominique Bagouet, a talented young choreographer in the contemporary style who had died in his prime some years before. As for creations, the public was offered Odile Duboc's *Rhapsody in Blue* to the Gershwin score and Angelin Preljocaj's *Casanova*.

The last year of the century was marked by two farewells and the nomination of a new *étoile*. In the spring, Marie-Claude Pietragalla, recently appointed director of the ballet in Marseilles in succession to Roland Petit, made her last appearance at the Palais Garnier in *Don Quichotte*, and later in the year Elisabeth Platel – retiring, to universal regret, in accordance with the rigid retirement rule imposed by the Caisse des Retraites (female dancers at forty and male dancers at forty-five) – bowed out with a memorable rendering of *La Sylphide*. But on the last day of the year the regrets stirred by those farewells were partly assuaged by the nomination of a new *étoile*, Aurélie Dupont, after a sparkling performance as Kitri in *Don Quichotte*.

The three memorable highlights of 1999 could hardly have been more contrasted. The first was a programme of stimulating modernism devoted to the work of William Forsythe that included three works new to Paris: *The Vertiginous Thrill of Exactitude* (an unconcealed tribute to Balanchine's influence on his work) and two creations, *Woundwork 1* and *Pas/parts*.

The second highlight was the return to the repertory of Maurice Béjart's *Le Concours*, a choreographic detective story, which included in its cast two stars from an earlier generation, Claude Bessy and Michaël Denard.

The third of these highlights was a dramatic ballet from the hand of Roland Petit. Based on Goethe's drama recounting the real-life story of Beaumarchais's visit to Spain to settle accounts with the man who had seduced his sister, *Clavigo* was a powerful work heavy with Romanticism. Among its highlights were a dream scene showing a great spider descending on to the heroine's bed, a long lip-to-lip sequence in her love *pas de deux* with Clavigo, her funeral procession, and finally Clavigo's death. Nicolas Le Riche was the sole *étoile* among the principal characters, Petit having cast lesser-known dancers in the other roles as if to emphasise that it is largely on its younger blood that a company must rely to ensure its future.

And it can perhaps be seen as symbolic that the next chapter in the history of the ballet of the Opéra should open with the nomination of the last *étoile* of the twentieth century, Jean-Guillaume Bart.

The turn of the millennium offers a pause for reflection on the state at which the art of ballet has arrived. A century ago the Paris Opéra would have been judged almost exclusively on the merits of its opera productions and its singers; today the main yardstick is unquestionably that of its choreographic repertory and its dancers. There can be no doubt that one of the most notable artistic developments of the twentieth century has been the acceptance of ballet as a major theatrical form. In 1900 very few ballets survived for more than a decade, and the very idea that a dance work might be granted the status of a classic would have been rejected as absurd. How different is the position a century later! Now, buttressed by an impressive array of classics, ballet has become universally recognised as an equal partner of opera. To this development the Paris Opéra has made an outstanding contribution, and is today setting an example not only in providing the soil for the fruits of French choreography to flourish, but also by preserving acclaimed classics from the past, whatever their provenance. It has, in a true sense, become both an arena and a museum of dance, encouraging new creations and preserving the patrimony of an art that knows no frontiers.

List of Ballets produced at the Paris Opéra

The following list consists only of ballets in the modern sense of the term, and excludes opera-ballets and divertissements in operas. Ballets created elsewhere than at the Opéra are marked with an asterisk.

Date of first performance	Title	Choreography	Music	Scenery, Costumes (c), Staging (sc)
26/1/1776	* MÉDÉE ET JASON[1]	Noverre, arr. G. Vestris	Rodolphe, Berton	
1/10/1776	* APELLES ET CAMPASPE	Noverre	Rodolphe	
17/11/1776	* LES CAPRICES DE GALATHÉE	Noverre	Granier	
21/1/1777	* LES HORACES	Noverre	Starzer	
6/3/1777	* LES RUSES D'AMOUR	Noverre	Granier	
1/3/1778	LA CHERCHEUSE D'ESPRIT	M. Gardel		
11/6/1778	LES PETITS RIENS	Noverre	Mozart *et al.*	
9/7/1778	ANNETTE ET LUBIN	Noverre		
18/8/1778	NINETTE À LA COUR	M. Gardel	Ciampi, Duni, *et al.*	
27/8/1778	ALCIMADURE	Dauberval	Mondonville	
18/11/1779	MIRSA	M. Gardel	Gossec *et al.*	
15/2/1781	LA FÊTE DE MIRZA	M. Gardel	Gossec, Grétry	
29/7/1783	LA ROSIÈRE	M. Gardel	Gossec *et al.*	
11/1/1784	L'ORACLE	M. Gardel		
26/7/1785	LE PREMIER NAVIGATEUR	M. Gardel		
31/10/1786	LES SAUVAGES	M. & P. Gardel		
12/12/1786	LE NID D'OISEAU	M. Gardel		
18/2/1787	LE COQ AU VILLAGE	M. Gardel		
17/6/1787	LE PIED DE BŒUF	M. Gardel		
16/1/1788	LE DÉSERTEUR	M. Gardel		
23/2/1790	TÉLÉMAQUE	P. Gardel	Miller	
6/11/1790	L'ÎLE D'AMOUR	Hus	Haydn *et al.*	
14/12/1790	PSYCHÉ	P. Gardel	Miller	

1. Staged by Noverrre himself at the Opéra, 30 January 1780.

Date of first performance	Title	Choreography	Music	Scenery, Costumes (c), Staging (sc)
11/12/1791	BACCHUS ET ARIANE	Gallet	Rochefort	
6/3/1793	LE JUGEMENT DE PÂRIS	P. Gardel	Méhul, Haydn, Pleyel	
12/12/1793	LES MUSES	Hus	Ragué	Fontaine, Porfillien
4/12/1799	HÉRO ET LÉANDRE	Milon	Lefebvre	
14/6/1800	LA DANSOMANIE	P. Gardel	Méhul	Degotti
20/8/1800	* PYGMALION	Milon	Lefebvre	Degotti
18/1/1801	LES NOCES DE GAMACHE	Milon	Lefebvre	
3/3/1802	LE RETOUR DE ZÉPHIRE	P. Gardel	Steibelt	
14/1/1803	DAPHNIS ET PANDROSE	P. Gardel	Méhul	Degotti, Protain
2/6/1803	LUCAS ET LAURETTE	Milon	Lefebvre	
23/10/1804	UNE DEMI-HEURE DE CAPRICE	P. Gardel		
18/12/1804	ACHILLE À SCYROS	P. Gardel	Cherubini	
10/5/1805	ACIS ET GALATHÉE	Duport	Darondeau, Gianella	Degotti, Protain, Moench; Berthélémy (c)
29/10/1805	L'AMOUR À CYTHÈRE	Henry	Gaveaux	
30/5/1806	FIGARO	Duport, after J.B. Blache		
24/6/1806	PAUL ET VIRGINIE	P. Gardel	Kreutzer	
20/7/1806	LE VOLAGE FIXÉ	Duport		
27/2/1807	LE RETOUR D'ULYSSE	Milon	Persuis	
8/3/1808	LES AMOURS D'ANTOINE ET DE CLÉOPÂTRE	Aumer	Kreutzer	Isabey, Degotti
4/10/1808	VÉNUS ET ADONIS	P. Gardel	Lefebvre	
20/12/1808	ALEXANDRE CHEZ APELLES	P. Gardel	Catel	Degotti, Daguerre
26/12/1809	LA FÊTE DE MARS	P. Gardel	Kreutzer	Ciceri, Boquet
24/1/1810	VERTUMNE ET POMONE	P. Gardel	Lefebvre	
8/6/1810	PERSÉE ET ANDROMÈDE	P. Gardel	Méhul	Protain fils, Lebe-Gigun, Mathis, Desroches Ménageot (c)
25/6/1811	L'ENLÈVEMENT DES SABINES	Milon	Berton	Isabey; Ménageot (c)
28/4/1812	L'ENFANT PRODIGUE	P. Gardel	Berton	Isabey; Ménageot (c)
23/11/1813	NINA	Milon	Persuis, after Dalayrac	Ciceri, Daguerre
17/5/1814	LE RETOUR DES LYS	P. Gardel		
4/4/1815	L'ÉPREUVE VILLAGEOISE	Milon	Persuis, after Grétry	
25/7/1815	L'HEUREUX RETOUR	Milon, P. Gardel	arr. Persuis, Kreutzer, Berton	Daguerre et al.
12/12/1815	FLORE ET ZÉPHIRE	Didelot	Venua	Ciceri; Marches (c)
22/2/1816	LE CARNAVAL DE VENISE	Milon	Persuis, Kreutzer	Ciceri; Daguerre

Appendix

Date of first performance	Title	Choreography	Music	Scenery, Costumes (c), Staging (sc)
26/11/1816	LES SAUVAGES DE LA MER DU SUD	Milon	Lefebvre	Degotti
17/9/1817	LES FIANCÉS DE CASERTE	P. Gardel, Milon	Dugazon	Ciceri
18/2/1818	PROSERPINE	P. Gardel	Schneitzhoeffer	Ciceri
3/6/1818	LE SÉDUCTEUR AU VILLAGE	Albert	Schneitzhoeffer	Ciceri; Berthélémy (c)
30/9/1818	LA SERVANTE JUSTIFIÉE	P. Gardel	Kreutzer	Degotti
19/6/1820	CLARI	Milon	Kreutzer	Ciceri; Garneray (c)
18/10/1820	LES PAGES DU DUC DE VENDÔME	Aumer	Gyrowetz	Garneray (c)
15/6/1821	LA FÊTE HONGROISE	Aumer	Gyrowetz	
18/9/1822	* ALFRED LE GRAND	Aumer	Gallenberg, Dugazon	Ciceri; Garneray (c)
3/3/1823	CENDRILLON	Albert	Sor	Ciceri; Albert (c)
1/10/1823	* ALINE	Aumer	Dugazon	Ciceri
18/12/1823	* LE PAGE INCONSTANT	Aumer, after Dauberval	Habeneck	
20/10/1824	ZÉMIRE ET AZOR	Deshayes	Schneitzhoeffer	Ciceri; A.E. Fragonard (c)
29/5/1826	MARS ET VÉNUS	J.B. Blache	Schneitzhoeffer	Ciceri; Lecomte (c)
29/1/1827	ASTOLPHE ET JOCONDE	Aumer	Hérold	Ciceri; Lecomte (c)
11/6/1827	LE SICILIEN	Anatole	Sor, Schneitzhoeffer	Ciceri; Lecomte (c)
19/9/1827	LA SOMNAMBULE	Aumer	Hérold	
2/7/1828	* LYDIE	Aumer	Hérold	
17/11/1828	* LA FILLE MAL GARDÉE	Aumer, after Dauberval	Hérold	Ciceri
27/4/1829	LA BELLE AU BOIS DORMANT	Aumer	Hérold	Ciceri
3/5/1830	MANON LESCAUT	Aumer	Halévy	Ciceri ; Lecomte, Lami, Duponchel (c)
18/7/1831	L'ORGIE	Coralli	Carafa	Ciceri; Lami (c)
12/3/1832	LA SYLPHIDE	F. Taglioni	Schneitzhoeffer	Ciceri; Lami (c)
7/11/1832	*NATHALIE	F. Taglioni	Gyrowetz, Carafa	Ciceri
4/12/1833	LA RÉVOLTE AU SÉRAIL	F. Taglioni	Labarre	Ciceri, Léger, Feuchères, Despléchin; Lormier, Duponchel (c)
15/9/1834	LA TEMPÊTE	Coralli	Schneitzhoeffer	Ciceri, Séchan, Despléchin, Diéterle, Feuchères; Boulanger (c)
8/4/1835	BRÉZILIA	F. Taglioni	Gallenberg	Philastre, Cambon
12/8/1835	L'ÎLE DES PIRATES	Henry	Carlini, Gide	Feuchères, Despléchin, Séchan, Philastre, Cambon ; Lami (c)

Date of first performance	Title	Choreography	Music	Scenery, Costumes (c), Staging (sc)
1/6/1836	LE DIABLE BOITEUX	Coralli	Gide	Feuchères, Séchan, Diéterle, Philastre, Cambon
21/9/1836	LA FILLE DU DANUBE	F. Taglioni	Adam	Ciceri, Diéterle, Feuchères, Despléchin, Séchan
5/7/1837	LES MOHICANS	A. Guerra	Adam	Devoir, Pourchet
16/10/1837	LA CHATTE MÉTAMORPHOSÉE EN FEMME	Coralli	Montfort	Pourchet, Devoir, Philastre, Cambon
5/5/1838	LA VOLIÈRE	T. Elssler	Gide	Lormier (c)
28/1/1839	LA GIPSY	Mazilier	Benoist, Thomas, Marliani	Philastre, Cambon; Lormier (c)
24/6/1839	LA TARENTULE	Coralli	Gide	Feuchères, Séchan, Diéterle, Despléchin; Lormier (c)
23/9/1840	LE DIABLE AMOUREUX	Mazilier	Benoist, Reber	Philastre, Cambon; Lormier (c)
28/6/1841	GISELLE[1]	Coralli, Perrot	Adam, Burgmüller	Ciceri ; Lormier (c)
22/6/1842	LA JOLIE FILLE DE GAND	Albert	Adam	Ciceri, Philastre, Cambon ; Lormier (c)
17/7/1843	LA PÉRI	Coralli	Burgmüller	Séchan, Diéterle, Philastre, Cambon; Lormier, d'Orschwiller (c)
21/2/1844	LADY HENRIETTE	Mazilier	Flotow, Burgmuller, Deldevez	Ciceri, Rubé; Lormier
7/8/1844	EUCHARIS	Coralli	Deldevez	Ciceri, Séchan, Diéterle, Despléchin; Lormier (c)
11/8/1845	LE DIABLE À QUATRE	Mazilier	Adam	Ciceri, Séchan, Diéterle
1/4/1846	PAQUITA	Mazilier	Deldevez	Philastre, Cambon, Diéterle, Séchan, Despléchin ; Lormier, d'Orschwiller (c)
10/7/1846	BETTY	Mazilier	Thomas	Ciceri, Rubé, Despléchin, Diéterle, Séchan, Philastre, Cambon ; Lormier (c)

1. Restaged by E. Coralli in 1863, with scenery by Despléchin, Cambon and Thierry and costumes by Albert. Restaged by N. Sergueyev in 1924, with scenery and costumes by Benois. Production revised by Lifar in 1932. New costumes and scenery by Leyritz in 1939, and by Carzou in 1954. Restaged by A. Alonso in 1972 with scenery and costumes by Thierry Bosquet, then by Patrice Bart and Eugène Poliakov on 25 April 1991 with décor by Le Groumellec, and finally with a restoration of Benois's scenery and costumes in 1998.

Appendix

Date of first performance	Title	Choreography	Music	Scenery, Costumes (c), Staging (sc)
26/4/1847	OZAÏ	Coralli	Gide	Ciceri ; Lormier (c)
20/10/1847	*LA FILLE DE MARBRE	Saint-Léon	[Costa], Pugni	Cambon, Thierry; Lormier (c)
18/2/1848	GRISELDIS	Mazilier	Adam	Cambon, Thierry; Lormier (c)
11/8/1848	NISIDA	A. Mabille	Benoist	Philastre, Cambon, Thierry; Lormier (c)
20/10/1848	*LA VIVANDIÈRE	Saint-Léon	Pugni	Despléchin, Séchan, Diéterle; Lormier (c)
19/1/1849	*LE VIOLON DU DIABLE	Saint-Léon	Pugni	Despléchin, Thierry; Lormier (c)
8/10/1849	LA FILLEULE DES FÉES	Perrot	Adam, Saint-Julien	Cambon, Thierry, Despléchin; Lormier, d'Orschwiller (c)
22/2/1850	STELLA	Saint-Léon	Pugni	Cambon, Thierry; Lormier (c)
15/1/1851	PÂQUERETTE	Saint-Léon	Benoist	Despléchin, Cambon, Thierry; Lormier, Marchal (c)
24/11/1851	VERT-VERT	Mazilier, [Saint-Léon]	Deldevez, J.B. Tolbecque	Cambon, Thierry; Lormier (c)
29/12/1852	ORFA	Mazilier	Adam	Cambon, Thierry; Lormier (c)
21/9/1853	AELIA ET MYSIS	Mazilier	Potier	Cambon, Thierry, Despléchin, Lormier (c)
11/11/1853	JOVITA	Mazilier	Labarre	Despléchin, Cambon, Thierry; Lormier (c)
31/5/1854	GEMMA	Cerrito	Gabrielli	Rubé, Nolau; Lormier (c)
8/1/1855	LA FONTI	Mazilier	Labarre	Martin, Cambon, Thierry; Lormier (c)
23/1/1856	LE CORSAIRE[1]	Mazilier	Adam	Martin, Despléchin, Cambon, Thierry; Albert (c)
11/8/1856	LES ELFES	Mazilier	Gabrielli	Nolau, Rubé, Despléchin, Martin, Cambon, Thierry; Albert (c)
1/4/1857	MARCO SPADA	Mazilier	Auber	Cambon, Thierry, Despléchin, Nolau, Rubé; Albert, Lormier (c)
14/7/1858	SACOUNTALA	L. Petipa	Reyer	Martin, Nolau, Rubé; Albert (c)

1. Scenery for the 1867 revival by Cambon, Despléchin, Rubé, Chaperon, Lavastre.

Date of first performance	Title	Choreography	Music	Scenery, Costumes (c), Staging (sc)
26/11/1860	LE PAPILLON	M. Taglioni	Offenbach	Martin, Despléchin, Nolau, Rubé, Cambon, Thierry; Albert (c)
25/3/1861	GRAZIOSA	L. Petipa	Labarre	Cambon, Thierry; Albert (c)
29/5/1861	*LE MARCHÉ DES INNOCENTS	M. and L. Petipa	Pugni	Cambon, Thierry; Albert (c)
20/11/1861	L'ÉTOILE DE MESSINE	Borri	Gabrielli	Despléchin, Thierry, Martin, Cambon; Albert (c)
6/7/1863	DIAVOLINA	Saint-Léon	Pugni	Cambon, Thierry; Lormier, Albert (c)
19/2/1864	LA MASCHERA	Rota	Giorza	Cambon, Thierry, Despléchin; Albert (c)
11/7/1864	NÉMEA	Saint-Léon	Minkus	Despléchin, Lavastre; Lormier, Albert (c)
28/12/1865	LE ROI D'YVETOT	L. Petipa	Labarre	Cambon, Thierry; Albert (c)
12/11/1866	LA SOURCE	Saint-Léon	Delibes, Minkus	Despléchin, Lavastre, Rubé, Chaperon; Lormier, Albert (c)
25/5/1870	COPPÉLIA[1]	Saint-Léon	Delibes	Cambon, Despléchin, Lavastre; Albert (c)
5/5/1873	GRETNA-GREEN	Mérante	Guiraud	Rubé, Chaperon; Albert (c)
14/6/1876	SYLVIA[2]	Mérante	Delibes	Chéret, Rubé, Chaperon ; Lacoste (c)
26/11/1877	LE FANDANGO	Mérante	Salvayre	Daran; Lacoste (c)
17/1/1879	YEDDA	Mérante	Métra	Daran, Lavastre jeune, Lavastre, Carpezat; Lacoste (c)
1/12/1880	LA KORRIGANE	Mérante	Widor	Lavastre, Rubé, Chaperon; Lacoste (c)
6/3/1882	NAMOUNA	L. Petipa	Lalo	Rubé, Chaperon, Lavastre jeune; Lacoste (c)

1. New scenery by Daran in 1875. New production by Larthe in 1936. Revived by Lacotte in 1973, the last act being restaged with Lacotte's own choreography; the scenery and costumes were made from the original designs. New version by Patrice Bart (see 23/5/1996).
2. Revived by Staats in 1919, with scenery and costumes by Dethomas. Revived by Aveline in 1951, with scenery and costumes by Brianchon for Lifar's version of 1941 (see 5/2/1941). New version by Lycette Darsonval (see 16/11/1979), and version with new choreography by John Neumeier (see 30/6/1997).

Appendix

Date of first performance	Title	Choreography	Music	Scenery, Costumes (c), Staging (sc)
14/12/1883	LA FARANDOLE	Mérante	Dubois	Rubé, Chaperon, Lavastre ; Lacoste (c)
26/1/1886	LES JUMEAUX DE BERGAME	Mérante	Lajarte	Lepic (c)
18/10/1886	LES DEUX PIGEONS[1]	Mérante	Messager	Rubé, Chaperon, Lavastre; Bianchini (c)
26/6/1889	LA TEMPÊTE	Hansen	Thomas	Lavastre, Carpezat; Bianchini (c)
9/6/1890	LE RÊVE	Hansen	Gastinel	Lavastre, Carpezat Bianchini (c)
24/2/1893	LA MALADETTA	Hansen	Vidal	Jambon; Bianchini (c)
24/10/1893	FÊTE RUSSE	Hansen	arr. Vidal	
31/5/1897	L'ÉTOILE	Hansen	Wormser	Carpezat; Bianchini (c)
11/11/1900	* DANSES DE JADIS ET DE NAGUÈRE	Hansen		Amable
26/11/1902	BACCHUS	Hansen	Duvernoy	Amable, Moisson, Jambon, Brandt, Rabuteau; Bianchini (c)
22/12/1905	LA RONDE DES SAISONS	Hansen	Busser	Jambon, Bailly; Betout (c)
25/11/1907	LE LAC DES AULNES	Vanara	Maréchal	Jambon, Bailly; Betout (c)
30/3/1908	NAMOUNA	Staats	Lalo	Pinchon (c)
5/2/1909	JAVOTTE	Staats	Saint-Saëns	Amable ; Pinchon (c)
16/2/1910	LA FÊTE CHEZ THÉRÈSE	Stichel	Hahn	Rochette, Landrin; Pinchon (c)
3/5/1911	ESPAÑA	Staats, Mauri	Chabrier	Mouveau, Demoget; Pinchon (c)
8/12/1911	LA ROUSSALKA	Clustine	Lambert	Simas; Pinchon (c)
30/10/1912	LES BACCHANTES	Clustine	Bruneau	Mouveau; Pinchon (c)
23/6/1913	SUITE DE DANSES	Clustine	Chopin	Pinchon (c)
18/2/1914	PHILOTIS	Clustine	Gaubert	Mouveau, Anglas, Canu; Pinchon (c)
22/6/1914	HANSLI LE BOSSU	Clustine	N.& J. Gallon	Bailly; Pinchon (c)
10/1/1917	LES ABEILLES	Staats	Stravinsky	Dethomas
8/4/1917	ADÉLAÏDE	Ambrosiny	Ravel	
1/4/1919	LA TRAGÉDIE DE SALOME	N. Guerra	Schmitt	Piot
4/5/1920	TAGLIONI CHEZ MUSETTE	Staats	Auber, Boieldieu, Meyerbeer, Weckerlin	Dethomas
11/5/1921	LE RÊVE DE LA MARQUISE	Fokine	Mozart	
20/6/1921	* DAPHNIS ET CHLOÉ	Fokine	Ravel	Bakst
20/6/1921	* LA PÉRI	Clustine	Dukas	Piot

1. Restaged by Aveline in 1942, with scenery and costumes by Larthe.

Date of first performance	Title	Choreography	Music	Scenery, Costumes (c), Staging (sc)
24/3/1922	PETITE SUITE	Pasmanik, Howarth	Debussy	
1/5/1922	FRIVOLANT	Staats	Poueigh	Dufy (c)
15/1/1923	CYDALISE ET LE CHÈVRE-PIED	Staats	Pierné	Dethomas
9/5/1923	CONCERTO	de Montoliu	San Martini	
9/5/1923	FRESQUES	de Montoliu	Gaubert	
12/11/1923	LA NUIT ENSORCELÉE	Staats	Chopin	Bakst
19/3/1924	SIANG-SIN	Staats	Huë	Piot
10/7/1924	ISTAR	Staats	D'Indy	Bakst
30/6/1925	SOIR DE FÊTE[1]	Staats	Delibes	Barbey
23/11/1925	LES RENCONTRES	Nijinska	Ibert	Dethomas (c)
11/6/1926	ORPHÉE	Staats	Ducasse	Allegri, after Golovine
17/12/1926	LA PRÊTRESSE DE KORYDWEN	Staats	Ladmirault	Darlot
8/4/1927	IMPRESSIONS DE MUSIC-HALL[2]	Staats	Pierné	Dethomas
3/6/1927	LE DIABLE DANS LE BEFFROI	N. Guerra	Inghelbrecht	Per Krogh
16/12/1927	CYRCA	N. Guerra	Delmas	Rubé, Chaperon
7/12/1928	RAYON DE LUNE	Ari	Fauré	Ari
4/3/1929	L'ÉVENTAIL DE JEANNE	Franck, A. Bourgat	Ravel, Ferroud, Ibert, Poulenc, Roussel, Roland-Manuel, Delannoy, Milhaud, Auric, Schmitt	Legrain, Moulaert; Laurencin (c)
15/5/1929	L'ÉCRAN DES JEUNES FILLES	Staats	Roland-Manuel	Drésa
30/12/1929	LES CRÉATURES DE PROMÉTHÉE	Lifar	Beethoven	Quelvée
16/2/1931	PRÉLUDE DOMINICAL	Lifar	Ropartz	Colin
16/2/1931	L'ORCHESTRE EN LIBERTÉ	Lifar	Sauveplane	Colin
22/5/1931	BACCHUS ET ARIANE	Lifar	Roussel	Chirico
7/12/1931	LE RUSTRE IMPRUDENT	Staats	Fouret	C. Martin
31/12/1931	LE SPECTRE DE LA ROSE	Fokine	Weber	
8/6/1932	DIVERTISSEMENT[3]	Lifar, after M. Petipa	Tchaikovsky	Goncharova
16/12/1932	SUR LE BORYSTHÈNE	Lifar	Prokofiev	Goncharova, Larionov
27/4/1933	JEUNESSE	Lifar	Ferroud	Godebski
17/11/1933	ROSELINDE	Staats	Hirschmann	Charlemagne
22/6/1934	LA VIE DE POLICHINELLE	Lifar	Nabokov	Pruna

1. New production by Touchagues in 1941, and by Malclès in 1946.
2. New production by Wild in 1943.
3. New production by Bouchène in 1948.

Appendix

Date of first performance	Title	Choreography	Music	Scenery, Costumes (c), Staging (sc)
13/2/1935	SALADE	Lifar	Milhaud	Derain
18/3/1935	PRÉLUDE À L'APRÈS-MIDI D'UN FAUNE	Lifar	Debussy	
21/6/1935	IMAGES	Staats	Pierné	Hellé
21/6/1935	LA GRISI	Aveline	Tomasi on themes by Métra	Dignimont
28/6/1935	PANTÉA	Magito	Malipiero	
9/7/1935	ICARE	Lifar	Szyfer	Larthe
22/1/1936	*LE LAC DES CYGNES (FRAGMENTS)	Lifar, after Petipa and Ivanov	Tchaikovsky	
3/2/1936	LE ROUET D'ARMOR	Staats	Piriou	Ventrillo-Horber
27/4/1936	HARNASIE	Lifar	Szymanowski	Lorentowicz
20/5/1936	ILÉANA	Staats	Bertrand	Mouveau
15/6/1936	LE ROI NU	Lifar	Françaix	Pruna
15/6/1936	UN BAISER POUR RIEN	Aveline	Rosenthal	Larthe
14/12/1936	PROMENADES DANS ROME	Lifar	Samuel-Rousseau	Decarie; Zambaux (c)
8/2/1937	ELVIRE	Aveline	Scarlatti	Sigrist
26/5/1937	DAVID TRIOMPHANT	Lifar	Rieti	Léger
21/6/1937	ALEXANDRE LE GRAND	Lifar	Gaubert	Larthe
7/1/1938	ORIANE ET LE PRINCE D'AMOUR	Lifar	Schmitt	Pruna
2/2/1938	LE CANTIQUE DES CANTIQUES	Lifar	Honegger	Colin
4/4/1938	AENÉAS	Lifar	Roussel	Moulaert
18/11/1938	LES SANTONS	Aveline	Tomasi	Hellé
17/3/1939	LA NUIT VÉNITIENNE	Darsonval	Thiriet	S. Roland-Manuel
1/5/1939	LE FESTIN DE L'ARAIGNÉE	Aveline	Roussel	Leyritz
24/4/1940	ENTRE DEUX RONDES	Lifar	Samuel-Rousseau	Landowski
5/2/1941	SYLVIA	Lifar	Delibes	Brianchon
2/7/1941	LA PRINCESSE AU JARDIN	Lifar	Grovlez	Bony
2/7/1941	LE CHEVALIER ET LA DAMOISELLE	Lifar	Gaubert	Cassandre
16/7/1941	JEUX D'ENFANTS	Aveline	Bizet	Drésa
31/12/1941	BOLÉRO	Lifar	Ravel	Leyritz
31/12/1941	ISTAR	Lifar	D'Indy	Bakst
10/7/1942	JOAN DE ZARISSA	Lifar	Egk	Brayer
8/8/1942	LES ANIMAUX MODÈLES	Lifar	Poulenc	Brianchon
26/1/1943	L'AMOUR SORCIER	Lifar	de Falla	Brayer
23/6/1943	LE JOUR	Lifar	Jaubert	Ernotte

Date of first performance	Title	Choreography	Music	Scenery, Costumes (c), Staging (sc)
23/7/1943	SUITE EN BLANC	Lifar	Lalo	Dignimont
29/4/1944	GUIGNOL ET PANDORE	Lifar	Jolivet	Dignimont
7/7/1944	LA TRAGÉDIE DE SALOMÉ	Aveline	Schmitt	Brayer
9/7/1945	L'APPEL DE LA MONTAGNE	Peretti	Honegger	Wild
24/1/1947	DIANE DE POITIERS	Bergé	Ibert	
30/4/1947	* SÉRÉNADE	Balanchine	Tchaikovsky	Delfau
21/5/1947	* APOLLON MUSAGÈTE	Balanchine	Stravinsky	Delfau
2/7/1947	* LE BAISER DE LA FÉE	Balanchine	Stravinsky	Hali
28/7/1947	LE PALAIS DE CRISTAL (SYMPHONY IN C)	Balanchine	Bizet	Fini
15/12/1947	LES MIRAGES	Lifar	Sauguet	Cassandre
31/12/1947	PAVANE POUR UNE INFANTE DÉFUNTE	Lifar	Ravel	Leyritz (c)
25/2/1948	LES MALHEURS DE SOPHIE	Quinault	Françaix	Hugo
7/4/1948	* PÉTROUCHKA	Fokine, arr. Lifar and Zvereff	Stravinsky	Benois
9/7/1948	ZADIG	Lifar	P. Petit	Labisse
28/7/1948	ESCALES	Lifar	Ibert	de Bravura
10/12/1948	* LA MORT DU CYGNE	Lifar	Chopin	
15/12/1948	LUCIFER	Lifar	Delvincourt	Brayer
13/4/1949	* ROMÉO ET JULIETTE	Lifar	Tchaikovsky	Moulène
22/6/1949	LA NAISSANCE DES COULEURS	Lifar, Popard	Honegger	Klausz
22/6/1949	* DANSES POLOVTSIENNES DU PRINCE IGOR	Lifar and Zvereff, after Fokine	Borodin	Dobujinski; Karinska (c)
27/7/1949	ENDYMION	Lifar	Lequerney	Bouchène
25/1/1950	SEPTUOR	Lifar	Lutèce	Bonnat, Potron
1/3/1950	* PASSION	Lifar	Franck	Maillart (c)
19/4/1950	L'INCONNUE	Lifar	Jolivet	Blanc
26/4/1950	LE CHEVALIER ERRANT	Lifar	Ibert	Cassandre
14/6/1950	PHÈDRE	Lifar	Auric	Cocteau
28/6/1950	* DRAMMA PER MUSICA	Lifar	Bach	Moulène
12/7/1950	LA GRANDE JATTE	Aveline	Barlow	Dignimont
25/4/1951	L'ASTROLOGUE	Lifar	Barraud	S. Roland-Manuel
25/4/1951	* SCHÉHÉRAZADE	Fokine, arr. Lifar, Zvereff	Rimsky-Korsakov	Bakst
14/11/1951	BLANCHE-NEIGE	Lifar	Yvain	Bouchène
27/2/1952	* LES CAPRICES DE CUPIDON	Galeotti, arr. Lander	Lolle	Chapelain-Midy
27/2/1952	FOURBERIES	Lifar	Rossini, arr. Aubin	Oudot
19/11/1952	* ÉTUDES	Lander	Riisager	Moulène ; Fost (c)
5/3/1953	VARIATIONS	Lifar	Schubert	

Appendix

Date of first performance	Title	Choreography	Music	Scenery, Costumes (c), Staging (sc)
5/3/1953	CINÉMA	Lifar	Aubert	Touchagues
17/6/1953	GRAND PAS	Lifar	Brahms	
17/6/1953	HOP FROG	Lander	Loucheur	Untersteller
7/4/1954	L'OISEAU DE FEU	Lifar	Stravinsky	Wakhévitch
12/7/1954	* NAUTÉOS	Lifar	Leleu	Brayer
28/7/1954	PRINTEMPS À VIENNE	Lander	Schubert	Malclès
9/2/1955	LES NOCES FANTASTIQUES	Lifar	Delannoy	Chastel; Levasseur(c)
6/4/1955	LA BELLE HÉLÈNE	Cranko	Offenbach	Vertès
28/12/1955	ROMÉO ET JULIETTE	Lifar	Prokofiev	Wakhévitch
11/7/1956	CONCERTO AUX ÉTOILES	Lander	Bartok	Commère
15/7/1957	COMBATS	Darsonval	Banfield	
30/10/1957	CHEMIN DE LUMIÈRE	Lifar	Auric	Cassandre
24/1/1958	* LA VALSE	Lander	Ravel	Maillart
5/3/1958	* IDYLLE	Skibine	Serette	Gamble
5/3/1958	PAS ET LIGNES	Lifar	Debussy	
12/3/1958	* ANNABEL LEE	Skibine	Schiffmann	Delfau
19/3/1958	SYMPHONIE CLASSIQUE	Lifar	Prokofiev	
22/10/1958	* CONCERTO	Skibine	Jolivet	Delfau
28/1/1959	* LA DAME À LA LICORNE	Rosen	Chailley	Cocteau
4/3/1959	* SYMPHONIE	Balanchine	Gounod	Bouchène
3/6/1959	DAPHNIS ET CHLOÉ	Skibine	Ravel	Chagall
16/12/1959	CONTE CRUEL	Skibine	Delerue	Delfau
16/12/1959	* PAS DE QUATRE	Dolin	Pugni	after Chalon (c)
16/12/1959	* LES SYLPHIDES	Fokine	Chopin	Benois
3/2/1960	* LA DAME AUX CAMÉLIAS	Gsovsky	Sauguet	Dupont
3/2/1960	* QARRTSILUNI	Lander	Riisager	Daydé
6/7/1960	PAS DE DIEUX	Kelly	Gershwin	François
21/12/1960	* LE LAC DES CYGNES[1]	Bourmeister	Tchaikovsky	Bouchène
20/12/1961	* PASTORALE	Skibine	Couperin	Dupont
14/3/1962	SYMPHONIE CONCERTANTE	Descombey	Martin	Daydé
18/7/1962	SUR UN THÈME	Bourmeister	Bizet	
17/4/1963	BUT	Descombey	Castérède	Henry
18/12/1963	* CONCERTO BAROCCO	Balanchine	Bach	
18/12/1963	* SYMPHONIE ÉCOSSAISE	Balanchine	Mendelssohn	Francès
18/12/1963	* LES QUATRE TEMPÉRAMENTS	Balanchine	Hindemith	

1. New production in 1974, with scenery by Le Nestour and costumes by Escoffier.

Date of first performance	Title	Choreography	Music	Scenery, Costumes (c), Staging (sc)
18/12/1963	* BOURRÉE FANTASQUE	Balanchine	Chabrier	Francès
1/7/1964	SARRACENIA	Descombey	Bartok	Singier
9/12/1964	ARCADES	Labis	Berlioz	
23/4/1965	RENARD	Béjart	Stravinsky	Casado
23/4/1965	* LES NOCES	Béjart	Stravinsky	Roustan, Bernard
23/4/1965	* LE SACRE DU PRINTEMPS	Béjart	Stravinsky	Caille ; Roustan (c)
11/12/1965	NOTRE-DAME DE PARIS	Petit	M. Jarre	Allio ; Saint-Laurent (c)
11/12/1965	ADAGE ET VARIATIONS	Petit	Poulenc	
29/6/1966	COPPÉLIA	Descombey	Delibes	Clayette
14/12/1966	LA PÉRI	Skibine	Dukas	Cernovich, Mitchell
18/1/1967	ROMÉO ET JULIETTE	Labis	Prokofiev	Le Corre
29/4/1967	*WEBERN OPUS V	Béjart	Webern	
13/10/1967	*PARADIS PERDU	Petit	Constant	Raysse
7/12/1967	*BACCHUS ET ARIANE	Descombey	Roussel	Daydé
8/3/1968	ZYKLUS	Descombey	Stockhausen	
21/6/1968	TURANGALILA	Petit	Messiaen	Ernst
14/10/1968	EXTASE	Petit	Scriabin	Chirico
22/1/1969	CONSTELLATIONS	Lifar	Liszt	
22/1/1969	LE GRAND CIRQUE	Lifar	Khatchaturian	Buffet
23/10/1970	* BOLÉRO	Béjart	Ravel	
31/10/1970	L'OISEAU DE FEU	Béjart	Stravinsky	Roustan (c)
21/10/1971	AOR	Schmucki	I. Wakhévitch, J.-M. Jarre	Schmucki
30/12/1971	FORMES	Petit	Constant	
9/6/1972	*LA SYLPHIDE	Lacotte, after Tagliani	Schneitzhoeffer	Musson after Ciceri, Fresnay after Lami (c)
2/11/1972	CANTADAGIO	Lazzini	Mahler	
12/4/1973	JEUX	Flindt	Debussy	Daydé
12/4/1973	L'APPRENTI SORCIER	Schmucki	Dukas	Sardy
24/5/1973	OCTANDRE[1]	Blaska	Varèse	Daydé
24/5/1973	POÈME ÉLECTRONIQUE[1]	Blaska	Varèse	Daydé
24/5/1973	ARCANA[1]	Blaska	Varèse	Daydé
24/5/1973	INTÉGRALES[1]	Butler	Varèse	Daydé
24/5/1973	AMÉRIQUES[1]	Butler	Varèse	Daydé
24/5/1973	HYPERPRISMES[1]	Charrat	Varèse	Daydé
24/5/1973	OFFRANDES[1]	Charrat	Varèse	Daydé
24/5/1973	DENSITÉ 21.5[1]	Carlson	Varèse	Daydé

1. Given at a performance in honour of Edgar Varèse.

Appendix

Date of first performance	Title	Choreography	Music	Scenery, Costumes (c), Staging (sc)
24/5/1973	IONISATION[1]	Keuten	Varèse	Daydé
29/9/1973	* PAS DE QUATRE	Alonso	Pugni	after Chalon (c)
6/11/1973	UN JOUR OU DEUX	Cunningham	Cage	Johns
29/11/1973	*LE FILS PRODIGUE	Balanchine	Prokofiev	Rouault
28/2/1974	SCHÉHÉRAZADE	Petit	Ravel	Saint-Laurent (c)
13/3/1974	* AGON[2]	Balanchine	Stravinsky	
13/3/1974	* SCHERZO FANTASTIQUE[2]	Robbins	Stravinsky	
13/3/1974	* ORPHÉE[2]	Balanchine	Stravinsky	Noguchi
13/3/1974	* CIRCUS POLKA[2]	Robbins	Stravinsky	
13/3/1974	* CAPRICCIO[2]	Balanchine	Stravinsky	
30/4/1974	VARIATIONS ON A SIMPLE THEME	McDonald	Beethoven	
30/4/1974	IL Y A JUSTE UN INSTANT	Carlson	Phillips	Gatecloud de Bellecroix (c)
30/4/1974	SABLIER-PRISON	Carlson	Surman	
3/10/1974	* L'APRÈS-MIDI D'UN FAUNE	Robbins	Debussy	Rosenthal; Sharaff(c)
3/10/1974	* LA BAYADÈRE (THE SHADES)	M. Petipa, arr. Nureyev	Minkus	Kamer (c)
13/11/1974	TRISTAN	Tetley	Henze	Baylis
31/12/1974	* LA BELLE AU BOIS DORMANT	M. Petipa, arr. Alonso	Tchaikovsky	Varona
18/3/1975	* LE LOUP	Petit	Dutilleux	Carzou
18/3/1975	LA SYMPHONIE FANTASTIQUE	Petit	Berlioz	Svoboda; Skalicky (c)
?/7/1975	*L'OR DES FOUS	Carlson	Phillips	Davis (sc)
?/7/1975	*LES FOUS D'OR	Carlson	Wakhévitch	Davis (sc)
12/12/1975	* SONATINE[3]	Balanchine	Ravel	Daydé
12/12/1975	* LE TOMBEAU DE COUPERIN[3]	Balanchine	Ravel	Daydé
12/12/1975	* TZIGANE[3]	Balanchine	Ravel	Daydé
12/12/1975	* LA VALSE[3]	Balanchine	Ravel	Karinska
12/12/1975	* CONCERTO EN SOL[3]	Robbins	Ravel	Erté
4/2/1976	WIND, WATER, SAND	Carlson	Phillips, Surman	Davis (sc), Ramseyer (c)
3/3/1976	* LES NOCES	Nijinska	Stravinsky	Gontcharova
3/3/1976	* L'APRÈS-MIDI D'UN FAUNE	after Nijinski	Debussy	Bakst
6/5/1976	NANA	Petit	Constant	Frigerio
6/5/1976	MOUVANCES	Petit	Verdi	Squarciapino (c)
6/5/1976	LA NUIT TRANSFIGURÉE	Petit	Schoenberg	Delfau

1. Given at a performance in honour of Edgar Varèse.
2. Given at a performance dedicated to Stravinsky.
3. Given at a performance dedicated to Ravel.

Date of first performance	Title	Choreography	Music	Scenery, Costumes (c), Staging (sc)
10/6/1976	QUININE	Carlsan	[musical medley]	Davis
14/10/1976	* IVAN LE TERRIBLE	Grigorovich	Prokofiev	Virsaladze
23/12/1976	*LE PAPILLON PAS DE DEUX	Lacotte	Offenbach	
18/12/1977	*ADAGIETTO	Araiz	Mahler	Peter Maag
18/12/1977	MAHLERS LIEDER	Araiz	Mahler	
19/4/1977	THIS, THAT AND THE OTHER	Carlson	Wakhévitch	Davis (sc)
5/10/1977	THE BEGINNING, THIS, THAT, THE OTHER AND THE END	Carlson	Wakhévitch	Davis (sc)
22/2/1978	*ROMÉO ET JULIETTE	Grigorovich	Prokofiev	Virsaladze
31/3/1978	*DIVERTIMENTO N° 15	Balanchine	Mozart	Le Nestour, Bozin (c)
31/3/1978	*CHACONNE	Balanchine	Gluck	Le Nestour, Bozin (c)
28/4/1978	YEAR OF THE HORSE	Carlson	Schwarz	Kano (c)
23/11/1978	MÉTABOLES	MacMillan	Dutilleux	Kay
23/11/1978	*LES QUATRE SAISONS	MacMillan	Verdi	Kay
23/11/1978	*LE CHANT DE LA TERRE	MacMillan	Mahler	Georgiadis
28/3/1979	*AURÉOLE	Taylor	Handel	Tacet
9/6/1979	*BOLÉRO III	Béjart	Ravel	
9/6/1979	*LIFE	Béjart	Bach, Gualda	Crocker
9/6/1979	*SERAIT-CE LA MORT?	Béjart	R. Strauss	Burrett
16/11/1979	SYLVIA	Darsonval	Delibes	Daydé
2/2/1980	TRIO	Carlson	Phillips, Surman	
2/2/1980	SLOW, HEAVY AND BLUE	Carlson	Aubry	Squarciapino (c)
22/2/1980	LE FANTÔME DE L'OPÉRA	Petit	Landowski	Coltellacci, Squarciapino (c)
7/5/1980	THE ARCHITECTS	Carlson	Bach	Ionesco, Ashpool(c)
31/10/1980	*CONSERVATOIRE	Bournonville	Paulli	Le Nestour
31/10/1980	*VASLAW	Neumeier	Bach	Neumeier (c)
31/10/1980	*ÉTUDES	Lander	Riisager after Czerny	Daydé
31/10/1980	*TCHAIKOVSKY PAS DE DEUX	Balanchine	Tchaikovsky	after Karinska (c)
31/10/1980	*PAQUITA	Vinogradav	Minkus et al.	Le Nestour
6/11/1980	SOLSTICE D'ÉTÉ	Moreland	Field	Dunlop
18/11/1980	PULCINELLA	Dunn	Stravinsky	Schmucki (c)
18/12/1980	SCHÉMA	Nikolaïs	Darling, Nikolaïs	Nikolaïs (c)
6/3/1981	*DON QUICHOTTE	Nureyev, after M. Petipa	Minkus	Georgiadis
25/5/1981	*LA FILLE MAL GARDÉE	Spoërli	Hérold, Hertel	Balthès, Berner (c)

Appendix

Date of first performance	Title	Choreography	Music	Scenery, Costumes (c), Staging (sc)
7/12/1981	TROIS PRÉLUDES	Stevenson	Rachmaninov	
7/12/1981	ESPLANADE	Taylor	Bach	Rawlings
5/5/1982	*LE SONGE D'UNE NUIT D'ÉTÉ	Neumeier	Mendelssohn, Ligeti	Rose
4/7/1982	MASSACRE SUR MCDOUGAL STREET	Armitage	Chatam	
24/12/1982	*CASSE-NOISETTE	Hightower, after Ivanov	Tchaikovsky	Le Nestour, Binot (c)
8/4/1983	*VOLUNTARIES	Tetley	Poulenc	Ter-Arutunian
8/4/1983	NOUVELLE LUNE (C'EST À DIRE)	Degroat	Debussy	Degroat
8/4/1983	AU BORD DU PRÉCIPICE	Ailey	Metheny, Mays	Garner
30/4/1983	*ROMÉO ET JULIETTE	Cranko	Prokofiev	Rose
5/11/1983	*RAYMONDA	Nureyev, after Petipa	Glazunov	Georgiadis
9/3/1984	*LA TEMPÊTE	Nureyev	Tchaikovsky	Georgiadis
22/3/1984	*MARCO SPADA	Lacotte	Auber	Lacotte after original designs
6/6/1984	*CONCERTO POUR VIOLON	Balanchine	Stravinsky	
6/6/1984	*LE SACRE DU PRINTEMPS OU LA RÉPÉTITION	Taylor	Stravinsky	Rawling
6/6/1984	*DANSES CONCERTANTES	MacMillan	Stravinsky	Georgiadis
6/6/1984	SYMPHONIE EN TROIS MOUVEMENTS	Christe	Stravinsky	Dekker
9/7/1984	GV-10	Armitage	Stockhausen	Atlas
9/7/1984	GENUS	Grossman	Stockhausen	
9/7/1984	LE CHANT DES PETITS GOSSES	Van Dantzig	Stockhausen	Van Schayk, Stockvis (c)
29/8/1984	ARLEQUIN MAGICIEN PAR AMOUR[1]	Cramer	Du Puy	Gostini (c)
29/8/1984	*CARNAVAL[1]	Fokine	Schumann	Bakst
29/8/1984	*LE BOURGEOIS GENTILHOMME[1]	Balanchine	Strauss	Daydé
19/10/1984	*ROMÉO ET JULIETTE	Nureyev	Prokofiev	Frigerio, Pagano (c)
2/11/1984	PREMIER ORAGE	Childs	Shostakovitch	Platé
22/12/1984	LE LAC DES CYGNES	Nureyev, after Petipa and Ivanov	Tchaikovsky	Frigerio; Squarciapino (c)
6/3/1985	BEFORE NIGHTFALL	Christe	Martinu	Dekker
29/4/1985	QUELQUES PAS GRAVES DE BAPTISTE	Lancelot	Lully	Bigel
7/6/1985	WASHINGTON SQUARE	Nureyev	Ives	Taulé, Georgiadis (c)
7/6/1985	MOUVEMENT-RYTHME-ÉTUDE	Béjart	Henry	Corte-Real (c)
19/12/1985	*CASSE-NOISETTE	Nureyev, after Petipa	Tchaikovsky	Georgiadis

1. Performance given at Opéra-Comique.

Date of first performance	Title	Choreography	Music	Scenery, Costumes (c), Staging (sc)
24/3/1986	*SONATE À TROIS	Béjart	Bartok	Bert (c)
24/3/1986	AREPO	Béjart	Gounod, Le Bars	Corte-Real (c)
3/3/1986	MANFRED	Nureyev	Tchaikovsky	Georgiadis
16/4/1986	*SALOMÉ	Béjart	Drigo	Corte-Real (c)
5/5/1986	FANTASIA SEMPLICE	Bagouet	Monnet	Platé; Fabrègue (c)
24/10/1986	CENDRILLON	Nureyev	Prokofiev	Ionesco; Mori (c)
20/12/1986	TWO BROTHERS	Parsons/Ezralow	Stravinsky	Strave
20/12/1986	*IN MEMORY OF...	Robbins	Berg	Mitchell (sc), Marcus (c)
16/1/1987	*SYMPHONIE EN TROIS MOUVEMENTS	Balanchine	Stravinsky	
16/1/1987	SANS ARMES, CITOYENS	Van Dantzig	Berlioz	Van Schayk
28/4/1987	*LA FILLE MAL GARDÉE	Lazzini	Hertel	Balthès
28/4/1987	LEÇONS DE TÉNÈBRES	Marin	Couperin	Casanova
29/5/1987	LES ANGES TERNIS	Armitage	Mingus	Salle; Lacroix (c)
29/5/1987	SOON	Ezralow	U2	Mahurin (sc), Havane (c)
29/5/1987	THE ENVELOPE	Parsons	Rossini	Wirkula (c)
29/5/1987	IN THE MIDDLE, SOMEWHAT ELEVATED	Forsythe	Willems	Forsythe
29/5/1987	ARC-EN-CIEL	Nikolaïs	Nikolaïs	Nikolaïs
25/6/1987	*LA PAVANE DU MAURE	Limón	Purcell	
25/6/1987	QUATRE DERNIERS LIEDER	Van Dantzig	R. Strauss	Van Schayk
11/10/1987	MAGNIFICAT	Neumeier	Bach	Neumeier
17/2/1989	*LES PRÉSAGES	Massine	Tchaikovsky	Masson
17/2/1989	*AS TIME GOES BY	Tharp	Haydn	
17/2/1989	RULES OF THE GAME	Tharp	Bach, Colombier	Dufour
18/4/1989	*LA BELLE AU BOIS DORMANT	Nureyev, after Petipa	Tchaikovsky	Georgiadis
20/10/1989	*TANTZ-SCHUL	Kylián	Kagel	McFarlane
20/10/1989	*SINFONIETTA	Kylián	Janáček	Nobbe
26/11/1989	*IN THE NIGHT	Robbins	Chopin	Dowell (c)
5/4/1990	*LE JEUNE HOMME ET LA MORT	Petit, Cocteau	Bach	Wakhévitch
5/4/1990	DEBUSSY POUR SEPT DANSEURS	Petit	Debussy	
5/4/1990	*CARMEN	Petit	Bizet	Clavé
6/6/1990	*POINTS IN SPACE	Cunningham	Cage	Anastasi, Bradshaw (c)
6/6/1990	*SPEAKING IN TONGUES	Taylor	Patton	Loquasto
6/6/1990	EIN HERZ	Morris	Bach	Pakledinaz (c)
9/11/1990	*L'HISTOIRE DE MANON	MacMillan	Massenet	Georgiadis
6/12/1990	HAUTBOIS	Lubovitch	Mozart	

Appendix

Date of first performance	Title	Choreography	Music	Scenery, Costumes (c), Staging (sc)
6/12/1990	*AUNIS	Garnier	Pacher	
2/4/1991	*LES BICHES	Nijinska	Poulenc	Laurencin
2/4/1991	*LE SACRE DU PRINTEMPS	Hodson, after Nijinsky	Stravinsky	Roerich, Archer
20/6/1991	*PUSH COMES TO SHOVE	Tharp	Haydn	Loquasto (c)
17/10/1991	RHYTHM OF THE SAINTS	Tharp	Simon	
16/11/1991	*GLASS PIECES	Robbins	Glass	Bates, Benson
16/11/1991	*DANCES AT A GATHERING	Robbins	Chopin	Eula
11/3/1992	*LE TRAIN BLEU	Nijinska	Milhaud	Laurens, Picasso; Chanel (c)
11/3/1992	*LE RENDEZ-VOUS	Petit	Kosma	Brassaï, Picasso; Mayo (c)
11/3/1992	*LE TRICORNE	Massine	De Falla	Picasso
7/5/1992	ATTENTAT POÉTIQUE	Larrieu		
7/5/1992	RETOURS DE SCÈNE	Duboc		Fabregue (c)
8/11/1992	*LA BAYADÈRE	Nureyev, after M. Petipa	Minkus	Frigerio; Squarciapino (c)
11/12/1992	*THE CONCERT	Robbins	Chopin	Steinberg, Sharaff
12/5/1993	*LES FORAINS	Petit	Sauguet	Bérard
1/6/1993	*GISELLE	Ek	Adam	Ekman
24/6/1993	*THEME AND VARIATIONS	Balanchine	Tchaikovsky	Thompson
24/6/1993	*MOVES	Robbins		
17/12/1993	*CASSE-NOISETTE	Neumeier	Tchaikovsky	Rose
?/1/1994	*DON'T LOOK BACK	Carlson	Aubry	
9/2/1994	*TILL EULENSPIEGEL	Hodson, after Nijinsky	R. Strauss	Jones, Archer
9/3/1994	CAMERA OBSCURA	Petit	Schönberg	Léger (c), Michel (sc)
9/3/1994	RYTHME DE VALSES	Petit	J. Strauss, arr. Berg, Schönberg, Webern	Léger (c), Michel (sc)
9/3/1994	PASSACAILLE	Petit	Webern	Léger (c)
9/4/1994	LE PARC	Preljocaj	Mozart, Vesvoda	Leproust; Pierre (c)
17/6/1994	*JARDIN AUX LILAS	Tudor	Chausson	Lingwood; Stevenson (c)
10/1/1995	*TEMPTATIONS OF THE MOON (BASTILLE)	Graham	Bartók	Halston; Graham (c)
23/10/1995	LES VARIATIONS D'ULYSSE (BASTILLE)	Gallotta	Drouet	Langlais
13/2/1996	*ALLEGRO BRILLANTE	Balanchine	Tchaikovsky	After Karinska (c)
18/3/1996	*A SUITE OF DANCES	Robbins	Bach	Loquasto
18/3/1996	*LES QUATRE SAISONS	Robbins	Verdi	Loquasto
23/5/1996	COPPÉLIA	Bart	Delibes	Toffolutti

Date of first performance	Title	Choreography	Music	Scenery, Costumes (c), Staging (sc)
24/5/1996	*LA IXᵉ SYMPHONIE (BASTILLE)	Béjart	Beethoven	Bernard
9/10/1996	*ANNONCIATION	Preljocaj	Vivaldi, Roy	Sanson
24/10/1996	*FALL RIVER LEGEND	De Mille	Gould	Smith; White (c)
24/10/1996	*RHAPSODY	Ashton	Rachmaninov	Caulfield
31/1/1997	LA BELLE AU BOIS DORMANT (BASTILLE)	Nureyev, after M. Petipa	Tchaikovsky	Frigerio; Squarciapino (c)
17/2/1997	EJA MATER	Grand-Maître	Lemelin, Vivaldi	Lord (sc); Bertrand (c)
17/2/1997	*ANCIENT AIRS AND DANCES	Tanner	Respighi	
17/2/1997	*MUSINGS	Kudelka	Mozart	Janson (c)
27/5/1997	SIGNES (BASTILLE)	Carlson	Aubry	Debré
9/6/1997	*DARK ELEGIES	Tudor, Wilson	Mahler	Benois
9/6/1997	*LE SACRE DU PRINTEMPS	Bausch	Stravinsky	Borzik
30/6/1997	SYLVIA	Neumeier	Delibes	Kokkos
6/11/1997	*L'ARLÉSIENNE	Petit	Bizet	Allio, Laurent
3/3/1998	CASANOVA	Preljocaj	Vejvoda	Leproust; Preljocaj (c)
17/3/1998	*SO SCHNELL	Bagouet	Bach	Le Moigne; Fabrègue
21/11/1998	RHAPSODY IN BLUE	Duboc	Gershwin	Le Jeune; Fabrègue (c)
21/11/1998	*LAMENTATION	Graham	Kodaly	Graham
31/3/1999	*THE VERTIGINOUS THRILL OF EXACTITUDE	Forsythe	Schubert	Forsythe (sc), Galloway (c)
31/3/1999	WOUNDWORK I	Forsythe	Willems	Galloway
31/3/1999	PAS/PARTS	Forsythe	Willems	Galloway
20/5/1999	ORISON	Darde	Miereanu	Comar (sc), Chattoune (c)
20/5/1999	DOUX MENSONGES	Kylián	Gesualdo, Monteverdi	Simon (sc), Visser (c)
15/10/1999	CLAVIGO	Petit	Yared	Wilmotte (sc), Spinatelli (c)
27/11/1999	*LE CONCOURS	Béjart	Le Bars	Tissier (sc), Verneuil (c)
18/12/1999	REVERSIBILITÉ	Kelemenis	Ravel	Cassagne
18/12/1999	LE RIRE DE LA LYRE	Mantalvo		Bertaut (c)
27/5/2000	*PERPETUUM	Naharin	J. Strauss fils	A. Levy (sc), R. Levy (c)
27/5/2000	APPARTEMENT	Ek	Flesh Quartet	Freiij
21/10/2000	YAMM	Hoche	Fénelon	Pécheur

Appendix   135

Date of first performance	Title	Choreography	Music	Scenery, Costumes (c), Staging (sc)
15/12/2000	*JEWELS[1] (EMERALDS AND DIAMONDS)	Balanchine	Fauré, Tchaikovsky	Lacroix
25/1/2001	*PAQUITA	Lacotte	Deldevez	Spinatelli
15/2/2001	THE CAGE	Robbins	Stravinsky	Rosenthal; Sobotka (c)
15/2/2001	OTHER DANCES	Robbins	Chopin	Santo Loquasto (c)
23/3/2001	STEPPING STONES	Kylián	Cage, Webern	Michael Simon; Visser (c)
23/3/2001	BELLA FIGURA	Kylián	Foss, Pergolesi Marcello, Vivaldi Torelli	Kylián; Visser (c)
26/11/2001	LES SEPT PÉCHÉS CAPITAUX	Scozzi	Weill	Pelly (& c) Thomas (c)
19/12/2001	SHÉHÉRAZADE	Li	Rimsky-Korsakov	Leproust; Lacroix (c)
26/2/2002	WUTHERING HEIGHTS	Belarbi	Hersant	Pabst, Pavanel (c)
15/4/2002	*DON QUICHOTTE	Nureyev	Minkus	Beliaev; Rivkina (c)
15/11/2002	ANDRÉAURIA	Lock	Lang	Roy ; Vandal (c)
26/2/2003	AIR	Teshigawara	Cage	Teshigawara
25/4/2003	LA PETITE DANSEUSE DE DEGAS	Bart	Levaillant	Toffolutti; Skinazi (c)
17/12/2003	GLACIAL DECOY	Brown		Rauschenberg
17/12/2003	*LIEBESLIEDER WALZER	Balanchine	Brahms	Spinatelli
17/12/2003	UN TRAIT D'UNION	Preljocaj	J.S. Bach	Preljocaj (c)
16/4/2004	LA SEPTIÈME LUNE	Bombana	Prodromidès	Paolini; Yoshiki Hishinuma (c)

1. For *Rubies* see *Capriccio*, 13/3/1974.

Principal dancers (étoiles) of the Opéra

The dates given are those of their employment at the Opéra. A number of dancers, including Jean-Pierre Bonnefous, Attilio Labis, Eric Vu An, Jacqueline Rayet, Sylvie Guillem, Marie-Claude Pietragalla and Elisabeth Platel have returned as guest artists.

Danseuses
La Fontaine (also de Lafontaine), 1681-93
Subligny, Marie-Thérèse de, 1688-1707
Prévost, Françoise, 1699-1730
Dangeville, Michelle, 1699-1706
Guyot, Marie-Catherine, c. 1705-25
Sallé, Marie, 1721,1727-32,1735-40
Thybert, Jeanne-Éléanore, 1722-37
Petit, Marie-Antoinette, 1722-40, 1742-46
Camargo, Marie-Anne de Cupis de, 1726-35,1742-51
Barbarina [Campanini], 1739-40
Puvignée (daughter), 1743-60
Lyonnois, Marie-Françoise, 1744-67
Lany, Louise-Madeleine (Mme Gélin), 1748-67
La Batte, 1750-54
Rey, Louise (Mme Pitrot), 1751-57, 1765-71
Vestris, Teresa, 1751-66
Allard, Marie, 1761-74, 1777-81
Peslin, Marguerite-Angélique, 1761-84
Guimard, Marie-Madeleine, 1762-89
Asselin, 1759-64, 1768-79
Dorival, Anne-Marguerite, 1774-87
Théodore (originally Marie-Madeline Crépé), 1777-82
Cécile [Dumesnil], 1777-82
Pérignon, Marie-Ève, née Gervais, 1779-1802
Rose, (Marie-Rose Pole), 1786-93
Saulnier, Victoire[1], 1784-94
Langlois, Louise, 1784-88
Miller, Marie-Anne (Mme Gardel), 1786-1816
Chevigny, Geneviève-Sophie, 1790-1804, 1806-14
Collomb, Émilie, 1791-1808
Clotilde [Mafleuret], 1793-1818
Chameroy, Adrienne, 1791-92, 1796-1802
Saulnier, Marie-Jeanne, 1796-1814
Bigottini, Emilie, 1801-23
Bias, Fanny, 1807-25
Gosselin, Geneviève, 1809-16
Gosselin, Constance (Mme Anatole), 1813-29
Noblet, Lise, 1818-41
Montessu, Pauline (née Paul), 1820-36
Legallois, Amélie, 1822-37
Julia [de Varennes], 1823-37
Leroux, Pauline, 1826-37,1840-44
Taglioni, Marie, 1827-37,1840, 1844
Duvernay, Pauline, 1831-36
Elssler, Fanny, 1834-40
Maria [Jacob], 1837-49
Dumilâtre, Adèle, 1840-48
Grisi, Carlotta, 1841-49
Plunkett, Adeline, 1845-52, 1855-57
Fabbri, Flora, 1845-51
Fuoco, Sofia, 1846-50
Cerrito, Fanny, 1847-55
Taglioni, Louise, 1848-57
Bogdanova, Nadezhda, 1851-55, 1865

1. Not to be confused with the dancer of the same name but lesser renown, who danced at the Opéra from 1804 to 1820.

Appendix

Rosati, Carolina, 1853-59
Couqui [Cucchi], Claudina, 1855-58
Beretta, Caterina, 1855-57
Ferraris, Amalia, 1856-63
Mérante (née Richard), Zina, 1857-63
Livry, Emma, 1858-62
Petipa, Marie S., 1861-62
Beaugrand, Léontine, 1861-80
Fioretti, Angelina, 1863-70
Muravieva, Marfa, 1863-64
Boschetti, Amina, 1864
Salvioni, Guglielmina, 1864-67
Grantzow, Adèle, 1866-68
Dor, Henriette, 1867
Bozzacchi, Giuseppina, 1870
Sangalli, Rita, 1872-84
Mauri, Rosita, 1878-98
Subra, Julia, 1881-98
Sandrini, Emma, 1888-1907
Zambelli, Carlotta, 1894-1930
Urban, Marthe, 1903-15
Johnsson, Anna, 1907-27
Boni, Aïda, 1908-22
Bos, Camille, 1907-35
Schwarz, Jeanne, 1908-28
Lorcia, Suzanne, 1919-50
Daunt, Yvonne, 1918-22
Spessivtseva, Olga, 1924-26, 1928-29, 1931-32
Schwarz, Solange[1], 1937-44, 1948-57
Toumanova, Tamara, 1929,1947,1950
Darsonval, Lycette, 1930,1935-60
Chauviré, Yvette, 1934-45,1947-49,1954-63
Bardin, Micheline, 1936-57
Vaussard, Christiane, 1936-57
Lafon, Madeleine, 1941-60
Bessy, Claude, 1945-72
Rayet, Jacqueline, 1946-74
Talechief, Maria, 1947
Daydé, Liane, 1948-59
Vyroubova, Nina, 1950-57
Motte, Claire, 1951-77
Vlassi [Bassi], Christiane, 1952-78
Amiel, Josette, 1952-71
Tallchief, Marjorie, 1957-61
Thibon, Nanon, 1958-83
Piollet, Wilfride, 1960-83
Pontois, Noëlla, 1961-83
Scouarnec, Claudette, 1972-80
Thesmar, Ghislaine, 1972-83
Loudières, Monique, 1972-96
Legrée, Françoise, 1973-97
Carlson, Carolyn, 1974-80
Khalfouni, Dominique, 1976-80
Platel, Élisabeth, 1976-99
Clerc, Florence, 1977-92
Vulpian, Claude de, 1978-93
Guérin, Isabelle, 1978-2001
Gaïda, Fanny, 1978-2001
Arbo, Carole, 1979-2001
Maurin, Élisabeth, 1979-
Pietragalla, Marie-Claude, 1979-99
Guillem, Sylvie, 1981-89
Letestu, Agnès, 1987-
Dupont, Aurélie, 1989-
Pujol, Laëtitia, 1993-
Osta, Clairemarie, 1988-
Gillot, Marie-Agnès, 1990-

---

1. The title of *étoile* only became official in 1938. Solange Schwarz was the first ballerina to be so nominated (in 1938), and Serge Peretti the first male dancer (1941).

Danseurs
Beauchamp, Pierre, 1673-87
Lestang, Louis, 1673-89
Pécour, Louis, 1674-1721
Blondy, Michel, 1691-1728
Balon, Claude, 1691-1710
Dangeville, Antoine-François, 1699-1748
Dumoulin, David, 1705-51
Bandieri de Laval, Antoine, 1706-48
Dupré, Louis, 1714-22,1730-51
Lany, Jean-Barthélémy, 1741-43,1748-69
Sodi, Pietro, 1744-46,1748-52
Lyonnois, 1746-68
Vestris, Gaétan, 1748-81
Gardel, Maximilien, 1759-82
Dauberval, Jean, 1761-82
Gardel, Pierre, 1772-96
Vestris, Auguste, 1772, 1775-1816
Nivelon, Louis, 1777-99
Milon, Louis, 1783-93, 1798-1826
Laborie, Louis, 1786-89, 1791-94
Beaupré, Charles, 1789-1819
Didelot, Charles, 1791-94
Saint-Amand, Charles, 1794-1808
Deshayes, André-Jean-Jacques, 1792-98, 1800-02
Aumer, Jean, 1798-1809
Vestris, Armand, 1800-03
Duport, Louis, 1800-08
Taglioni, Filippo, 1800-02
Henry, Louis, 1803-07
Taglioni, Salvatore, 1806
Albert, 1808-31, 1842-43
Paul, Antoine, 1813-31
Coulon, Antoine, 1816-32
Blasis, Carlo, 1817
Ferdinand, 1818-33
Gosselin, Louis, 1820-26
Bournonville, Auguste, 1826-28,1834
Taglioni, Paul, 1827,1831, 1844
Perrot, Jules, 1830-35,1849
Mazilier, Joseph, 1830-48
Coralli, Eugène, 1834-70

Mabille, Auguste, 1835-45
Guerra, Antonio, 1836-38
Petipa, Lucien, 1839-62
Saint-Léon, Arthur, 1847-52
Mérante, Louis, 1848-87
Segarelli, Domenico, 1856-58
Vasquez, Miguel, 1874-1900
Staats, Léo, 1898-1909
Ricaux, Gustave, 1901-11, 1919-31
Aveline, Albert, 1905-34
Peretti, Serge, 1922-46
Lifar, Serge, 1929-44,1949-56
Ritz, Roger, 1930-51
Bozzoni, Max, 1936-63
Fenonjois, Roger, 1936-49
Renault, Michel, 1940-59
Andréani, Jean-Paul, 1945-67
Kalioujny, Alexandre, 1947-60
Babilée, Jean, 1949,1953
Algaroff, Youly, 1952-64
Labis, Attilio, 1954-72
Van Dijk, Peter, 1955-58
Skibine, George, 1957-61
Atanassoff, Cyril, 1957-86
Franchetti, Jean-Pierre, 1959-89
Bonnefous, Jean-Pierre, 1959-69
Bart, Patrice, 1959-89
Flindt, Flemming, 1961-64
Piletta, Georges, 1963-89
Guizerix, Jean, 1964-90
Denard, Michaël, 1967-89
Lormeau, Jean-Yves, 1971-96
Jude, Charles, 1972-98
Dupond, Patrick, 1975-88, 1990-97
Hilaire, Laurent, 1979-
Wilfri Romoli, Wilfid, 1979-
Legris, Manuel, 1980-
Belarbi, Kader, 1980-
Le Riche, Nicolas, 1988-
Martinez, José, 1988-
Bart, Jean-Guillaume, 1988-
Pech, Benjamin, 1992-
Ganio, Mathieu, 2001-

Principal Ballet-Masters of the Opéra

Several of the ballet-masters named in this list had previously been assistant ballet-masters. Among the most celebrated ballet-masters who were never first ballet-masters were Louis Milon (1800-26), Albert (1822-32, 1843-45) Filippo Taglioni (1831-36), Albert Aveline (1927-55) and Harald Lander (1952-63). From 1971 additional responsibilities were laid on the principal ballet-master and his title was changed to "Director of the Dance".

Des Brosses, 1669
Pierre Beauchamp, 1669-87
Louis Pécour, 1687-1729
Michel Blondy, 1729-39
Antoine Bandieri de Laval, 1739-48
Jean-Barthélémy Lany, 1748-69
Gaétan Vestris, 1770-75
Jean-Georges Noverre, 1776-81
Maximilien Gardel and Jean Dauberval, 1781-83
Maximilien Gardel, 1783-87
Pierre Gardel, 1787-1827
Jean Aumer, 1827-31
Jean Coralli, 1831-50
Arthur Saint-Léon, 1850-53
Joseph Mazilier, 1853-59
Lucien Petipa, 1860-68
Henri Justament, 1868-69
Louis Mérante, 1869-87
Joseph Hansen, 1887-1907
Léo Staats, 1908-09
Mme Stichel, 1909-10
Ivan Clustine, 1911-14
Léo Staats, 1919-26
Nicola Guerra, 1927-29
Serge Lifar, 1930-45, 1947-58
George Skibine, 1958-61
Michel Descombey, 1962-69
John Taras, 1969-70
Claude Bessy, 1970-71
Raymond Franchetti, 1971-78
Violette Verdy, 1978-80
Rosella Hightower, 1980-83
Rudolf Nureyev, 1983-89
Patrice Bart and Eugène Poliakov, interim, 1989-90
Patrick Dupond, 1990-95
Brigitte Lefèvre, 1995-

Guest Artistes with the Ballet of the Opéra

This list does not include *étoiles* of the Opéra who returned to dance with the company after their retirement.

Female artists
Baccelli, Giovanna, 1782
Nielson, Augusta, 1842
Fjeldsted, Caroline, 1843
Smirnova, Tatiana, 1844
Andreanova, Elena, 1845
Dell'Era, Antonietta, 1889 *(Coppélia)*
Zucchi, Virginia, 1895 *(Tannhäuser)*
Trouhanova, Natalia, 1907 *(Samson et Dalila, Le Lac des aulnes)*
Kshessinska, Matilda, 1908, 1909 *(La Korrigane, Coppélia)*
Rubinstein, Ida, 1919, 1924 *(La Tragédie de Salomé, Le Martyre de Saint-Sébastien, Istar)*
Pavlova, Anna, 1921 *(La Péri)*
Fokina, Vera, 1921 *(Daphnis et Chloé, Le Rêve de la marquise)*
Ari, Carina, 1928, 1929, 1934, 1938 *(Rayon de lune, Le Cantique des Cantiques)*
Semyonova, Marina, 1935, 1936 *(Giselle, Le Lac des cygnes, Divertissement)*
Cortez, Espanita, 1947, 1948 *(Le Chevalier errant)*
Charrat, Janine, 1947 *(Roméo et Juliette)*
Tcherina, Ludmilla, 1957, 1958, 1969 *(Le Martyre de Saint-Sébastien)*
Plissetskaya, Maya, 1961, 1964, 1976 *(Le Lac des cygnes, Bolero)*
Fonteyn, Margot, 1967 *(Le Paradis perdu)*
Maximova, Ekaterina, 1969, 1973 *(Giselle, Le Lac des cygnes)*
Thesmar, Ghislaine, 1972 *(La Sylphide)*
Alonso, Alicia, 1972 *(Giselle)*
Mendez, Josefina, 1972, 1973 *(Giselle, Pas de quatre)*
Verdy, Violette, 1972, 1975 *(Giselle, Sonatine)*
Makarova, Natalia, 1973 [Cour Carrée du Louvre], 1978, 1979, 1981
  (*Le Lac des cygnes, Giselle*)
McBride, Patricia, 1974 *(Capriccio)*
Jeanmaire, Zizi, 1975 *(La Symphonie fantastique)*
Kirkland, Gelsey, 1975 *(La Bayadère, Don Quichotte)*
Farrell, Suzanne, 1975 *(Tzigane, Concerto en sol)*
Kain, Karen, 1976 *(Nana)*
Bessmertnova, Natalia, 1976, 1977, 1978 *(Ivan le Terrible, Giselle, Roméo et Juliette)*
Losano, Sandra, 1978 *(Les Quatre Saisons)*

Evdokimova, Eva, 1982 *(Pas de quatre, Paquita, Grand Pas classique)*
Morishita, Yoko, 1982 *(Pas de quatre, Le Cygne noir)*
Keil, Birgit, 1982 *(Pas de quatre, Casse-Noisette* pas de deux)
Desutter, Evelyne, 1982, 1989 *(Roméo et Juliette, La Belle au bois dormant)*
Haydée, Marcia, 1983 *(Roméo et Juliette)*
Guillem, Sylvie, 1990, 1991, 1994,1998, 2000, 2001, 2003 *(L'Histoire de Manon, Giselle, Don Quichotte, Roméo et Juliette, La Bayadère, La Belle au Bois Dormant, Hommage à Rudolf Noureev)*
Hart, Evelyn, 1991 *(Roméo et Juliette* pas de deux)
Hyatt, Gigi, 1991 *(Spring and fall)*
Bussell, Darcey, 1991 *(Tchaikovsky pas de deux)*
Semenyaka, Ludmilla, 1991 *(Le Cygne, Don Quichotte* pas de deux)
Ferri, Alessandra, 1992, 1996, 2000 *(Carmen, Notre-Dame de Paris)*
Asylmuratova, Altynai, 1994 *(La Bayadère, Le Lac des cygnes)*
Pietragalla, Marie-Claude, 2000 *(Signes, Cendrillon)*
Zakharova, Svetlana, 2001, 2002, 2004 *(La Bayadère, Le Lac des Cygnes, Giselle)*
Vishneva, Diana, 2002, 2003 *(Don Quichotte, L'Histoire de Manon)*
Cojocaru, Alina, 2004 *(Giselle)*

Male artists
Legat, Nicolai, 1908, 1909 *(La Korrigane, Coppélia)*
Fokine, Michel, 1921 *(Daphnis et Chloé, Le Rêve de la marquise)*
Fadeyechev, Nicolai, 1961, 1964 *(Le Lac des cygnes)*
Bruhn, Erik, 1964 *(Giselle, Daphnis et Chloé)*
Petit, Roland, 1965 (*Notre-dame de Paris)*
Nureyev, Rudolf, 1967, 1968, 1969, 1974, 1975, 1978, 1979, 1981, 1983 *(Le Paradis perdu, Giselle, Agon, Pétrouchka, L'Après-midi d'un faune, Apollon Musagète, Tristan, La Bayadère* acte III, *Le Lac des cygnes, La Sylphide, Don Quichotte, Raymonda)*
Vassiliev, Vladimir, 1969, 1973 *(Giselle)*
Bonnefous, Jean-Pierre, 1972, 1974, 1975 *(Giselle, Orphée, Sonatine)*
Lacotte, Pierre, 1974 *(Coppélia)*, 1976 *(Le Papillon)*
Clifford, John, 1974 *(Capriccio)*
Kehlet, Niels, 1975 *(La Belle au bois dormant)*
Baryshnikov, Mikhail, 1975, 1977, 1978 *(La Bayadère, Don Quichotte* pas de deux, *Giselle)*
Martins, Peter, 1975 *(Tzigane, Concerto en sol)*
Ganio, Denys, 1976 *(La Nuit transfigurée)*
Golovine, Serge, 1976 *(Petrouchka)*
Vladimirov, Yuri, 1976 *(Ivan le Terrible)*
Tomasson, Helgi, 1977 *(Giselle)*
Bogatyriev, Alexandre, 1978 *(Roméo et Juliette, Giselle)*
Lüders, Adam, 1978 *(Chaconne)*
Williams, David, 1978 *(Les Quatre Saisons)*

Babilée, Jean, 1979, 1990 *(Life, Bonjour Mr Satie, Carte blanche à Jean Guizerix)*
Donn, Jorge, 1979 *(Boléro, Serait-ce la mort?)*
Schaufuss, Peter, 1980 *(Le Fantôme de l'Opéra)*
Murray, Louis, 1980, 1981 *(Schéma)*
Bujones, Fernando, 1981 *(Don Quichotte)*
Gil, Jean-Charles, 1985 *(Roméo et Juliette)*
Vu-An, Éric, 1986, 1987, 1988, 1989, 1990, 1991 *(Kabuki, Le Lac des cygnes, Études, In the Middle, Somewhat Elevated, L'Après-midi d'un faune, Le Jeune Homme et la mort, Les Mirages, Capriccio, Le Songe d'une nuit d'été, Roméo et Juliette)*
Greves, Kenneth, 1989 *(Le Lac des cygnes)*
Mukhamedov, Irek, 1989, 1991 *(La Belle au bois dormant, Don Quichotte* pas de deux)
Liepa, Andris, 1990 *(Le Lac des cygnes)*
Malakhov, Vladimir, 1990 *(Suite en blanc)*
Bocca, Julio, 1991 *(Diane et Actéon)*
Liska, Ivan, 1991 *(La Dame aux camélias)*
Solymosi, Zoltan, 1991 *(Tchaikovsky* pas de deux)
Tsiskaridze, Nicolaï, 2001 *(La Bayadère)*
Murru, Massimo, 2001 *(Notre-Dame de Paris)*
Vu-An, Éric, 2003 *(Hommage à Rudolf Noureev)*
Dowell, Anthony, 2003 *(Hommage à Rudolf Noureev)*
Saunders, Christopher, 2003 *(Hommage à Rudolf Noureev)*

Ballets performed at the Opéra more than 100 times

The number of performances, taken to 31 December 2004, is based on counts made by the author down to 1900, and thereafter on the records of the Paris Opéra Ballet.

Title of ballet	Duration in repertory	Number of performances
COPPÉLIA	1870-1991	826
(original version and Lacotte revival)		
GISELLE	1841-1998	718
PSYCHÉ	1790-1829	560
TÉLÉMAQUE	1790-1829	413
SUITE EN BLANC	1943-1996	375
LA SYLPHIDE	1832-1999	353
(original version and Lacotte revival)		
SUITE DE DANSES	1913-1974	325
SOIR DE FÊTE	1925-1997	269
LE LAC DES CYGNES	1960-1992	256
(Bourmeister, full-length version only)		
ÉTUDES	1952-1995	253
LA DANSOMANIE	1800-1826	245
LE PALAIS DE CRISTAL	1947-1994	244
LE SPECTRE DE LA ROSE	1931-1997	212
LES DEUX PIGEONS	1886-1949	196
LES MIRAGES	1947-1990	192
NINA	1813-1840	190
LA CHERCHEUSE D'ESPRIT	1778-1816	189
LE JUGEMENT DE PÂRIS	1793-1825	188
SYLVIA	1876-1980	186
(original version and Darsonval revival)		
LE LAC DES CYGNES (Nureyev version)	1984-1999	183
LE SACRE DU PRINTEMPS	1965-1986	180
(Béjart version)		
LA MALADET''TA	1893-1927	176
LE DÉSERTEUR	1788-1816	175
FLORE ET ZÉPHIRE	1815-1831	173
DIVERTISSEMENT	1932-1959	170
LA BELLE AU BOIS DORMANT	1974-1982	169
(Alonso and Hightower versions)		
DAPHNIS ET CHLOÉ	1959-1970	168
LE CARNAVAL DE VENISE	1816-1838	166

Title of ballet	Duration in repertory	Number of performances
LES NOCES DE GAMACHE	1801-1841	160
LA KORRIGANE	1880-1935	160
PÉTROUCHKA	1948-1997	157
MIRSA	1779-1808	155
L'OISEAU DE FEU	1970-1982	155
LA PÉRI (Clustine version)	1921-1992	148
DON QUICHOTTE (Nureyev version)	1981-1998	148
LA BAYADÈRE	1992-1999	141
ELVIRE	1937-1952	139
MARS ET VÉNUS	1826-1837	138
LES PAGES DU DUC DE VENDÔME	1820-1833	126
LA SOMNAMBULE	1827-1859	120
ENTRE DEUX RONDES	1940-1959	118
APOLLON MUSAGÈTE	1947-1999	117
LA ROSIÈRE	1783-1808	115
LES QUATRE TEMPÉRAMENTS	1963-1995	113
CENDRILLON (Albert version)	1823-1831	111
PAUL ET VIRGINIE	1806-1828	111
ISTAR (Lifar version)	1941-1997	111
IN THE MIDDLE, SOMEWHAT ELEVATED	1987-1999	111
DANSES POLOVTSIENNES	1949-1959	109
LE RETOUR DE ZÉPHIRE	1802-1822	108
AURÉOLE	1974-1996	108
AGON	1974-1997	107
LA GRISI	1935-1959	106
LE DIABLE À QUATRE	1845-1863	105
SIANG-SIN	1924-1944	105
L'APRÈS-MIDI D'UN FAUNE (Lifar version)	1935-1962	103

Index

Adam, Adolphe, 48, 50, 51, 55, 71
Albert (François Decombe), 39, 42
Alexander II, Emperor of Russia, 57
Algaroff, Yuli, 91-93
Allard, Marie, 27
Alonso, Alicia, 98, 99
Ambrosiny, François, 73
Amiel, Josette, 95
Andréani, Jean-Paul, 92, 95
Angiolini, Gasparo, 25
Appia, Adolphe, 73
Araiz, Oscar, 100
Arbo, Carole, 112,
Archer, Kenneth, 110, 112
Ari, Carina, 79, 87
Argentina, La, 74
Ashton, Frederick, 108, 114
Atanassoff, Cyril, 97-99, 102
Auber, Daniel, 55, 56, 64
Aubry, Julie, 35
Aumer, Jean, 38, 42, 44
Auric, Georges, 91, 92
Aveline, Albert, 71, 73, 74, 76-79, 82-84, 87, 89, 92

Babilée, Jean, 82, 89, 92, 109
Bach, Johann Sebastian, 109, 115
Bagouet, Dominique, 115
Bakst, Leon, 70, 77, 78
Balanchine, George, 81-83, 89, 90, 95-97, 99, 106, 110, 112, 115
Balfe, Michael William, 48
Balon, Claude, 11, 18, 24
Balzac, Honoré de, 41
Bandieri de Laval, Antoine, 15
Bardin, Micheline, 90-92
Barlow, Fred, 92
Barre, Jean-Auguste, 48, 56
Bart, Jean-Guillaume, 115
Bart, Patrice, 99, 107, 109, 110, 114
Bartók, Béla, 107
Baryshnikov, Mikhail, 110
Bausch, Pina, 114
Beauchamp, Louis, 6
Beauchamp, Pierre, 6-12
Beaugrand, Léontine, 59, 61-63

Beaumarchais, Pierre Caron de, 42, 115
Beethoven, Ludwig van, 81, 114
Béjart, Maurice, 96-98, 106, 107, 115
Belarbi, Kader, 108-110
Bellini, Vincenzo, 43
Benois, Alexandre, 76
Benserade, Isaac de, 6
Bérard, Christian, 93
Bergé, Marcel, 89
Berlioz, Hector, 89, 93, 96, 100
Berry, Duc de, 41
Bessy, Claude, 95, 96, 98, 112
Bias, Fanny, 42
Bigottini, Emilie, 37, 42, 48
Bizet, Georges, 90
Blasis, Carlo, 54, 55
Blondy, Nicolas, 11, 12, 15, 17
Bolm, Adolphe, 70
Boni, Aïda, 69, 71, 73, 74, 77
Bonnefous, Jean-Pierre, 97
Börlin, Jean, 74
Borri, Pasquale, 56
Bos, Camille, 78, 79, 84-86
Boschetti, Amina, 57
Bourgat, Alice, 75, 77
Bourmeister, Vladimir, 96, 106, 107, 111
Bournonville, Auguste, 45, 75, 92
Bozzacchi, Giuseppina, 58, 59
Bozzoni, Max, 90, 92
Brahms, Johannes, 92
Brayer, Yves, 88
Brillant, Maurice, 76
Broussan, L., 69, 72
Brugnoli, Amalia, 43
Bruhn, Erik, 97
Busser, Henri, 68
Byron, Lord George, 55

Cahusac, Louis de, 19, 21
Camargo, Marie-Anne Cupis de, 16-20, 55
Cambert, Robert, 7
Campanini, Barbarina, 20
Campra, André, 10
Carlson, Carolyn, 99, 101, 114
Carzou, Jean, 98, 100

Casanova, Giacomo, 15, 18
Cassandre, A.-M., 88
Castil-Blaze, 9
Catherine de Medici, 5
Cecchetti, Enrico, 81
Cerrito, Fanny, 53, 54
Chagall, Marc, 95
Chaliapin, Fyodor, 69
Chardin, Jean-Baptiste, 65
Chasles, Jeanne, 73
Charles-Eugene, Duke of Württemberg, 25
Chauviré, Yvette, 87-90, 93, 105, 110, 113, 115
Cherubini, Luigi, 36
Childs, Lucinda, 106
Chirico, Giorgio de, 83
Choiseul, Maréchal de, 11
Chopin, Frédéric, 72, 111
Christe, Nils, 106
Ciceri, Pierre, 41, 44, 46
Clerc, Florence, 101, 108
Clotilde, Mlle, 35, 36, 38
Clustine, Ivan, 71-73, 77
Cocteau, Jean, 91
Collé, Charles, 25
Colombier, 109
Coppée, François, 64
Coralli, Jean, 44, 45, 47, 48, 50, 79
Cornalba, Elena, 63
Corneille, Pierre, 24, 28
Cortez, Españita, 91
Coulon, Jean-François, 40, 43
Couperin, François, 108
Craig, Edward Gordon, 73
Cranko, John, 93, 103
Cuevas, Marquis Georges de, 102
Cunningham, Merce, 109
Czerny, Karl, 92

Darsonval, Lycette, 86-88, 91, 92, 95
Dauberval, Jean, 26, 29, 31, 32, 34, 38, 40, 42
Daunt, Yvonne, 75, 78
David, Jacques-Louis, 29
Daydé, Liane, 91, 92
Debussy, Claude, 75
Debré, Olivier, 114
Degas, Edgar, 65, 66
Degroat, Andy, 111
De Hesse, Jean-Baptiste, 25
Delacroix, Eugène, 41

Delannoy, Marcel, 91
Delavigne, Casimir, 44
Delibes, Léo, 57, 58, 62, 78, 114
De Mille, Agnes, 114
Denard, Michaël, 98-100
Derain, André, 85
Des Brosses, 7
Descombey, Michel, 96, 97
Deshayes, Jean-François, 40
Dethomas, Maxime, 73, 76
Diaghilev, Serge, 54, 69, 71, 72, 78-81, 83, 91, 110
Didelot, Charles, 38, 39
Diderot, Denis, 24
Didion, Marie-Louise, 85, 86
Dolin, Anton, 95
Dominique, Mme, 55, 57-59, 63
Dorat, Claude-Joseph, 15
Drésa, Jacques, 73, 74, 76
Duboc, Odile, 111, 115
Dufy, Raoul, 76
Dukas, Paul, 77
Dumoulin, David, 17
Duponchel, Henri, 48
Dupond, Patrick, 101-103, 107, 108, 110, 112, 113
Dupont, Aurélie, 115
Duport, Louis, 37-40
Dupré, Louis, 15-17, 21, 24, 27
Dutilleux, Henri, 100
Dynalix, Paulette, 86, 88, 90

Egorova, Lubov, 82
Egk, Werner, 88
Ek, Mats, 112, 114
Elssler, Fanny, 47-51, 54-56
Elssler, Therese, 48
Ernst, Max, 97
Euripides, 91

Fadeyechev, Nicolai, 97
Fauré, Gabriel, 79
Fernon, Mlle, 9
Ferraris, Amalia, 54, 55, 57
Feuillet, Raoul, 9, 11
Fiocre, Eugénie, 57-59
Flindt, Flemming, 96, 99
Fokina, Vera, 77
Fokine, Michel, 70, 77, 82, 83, 85, 86
Fonta, Laure, 59
Fonteyn, Margot, 102
Forsythe, William, 108, 115

Index 147

Fouquet, Nicolas, 7
Franchetti, Jean-Pierre, 98, 100
Franchetti, Rémond, 98, 100, 113
Francine, Nicolas de, 10
Franck, Yvonne, 79
François, André, 96
Fratellini, 79

Gaïda, Fanny 109, 110, 112
Gailhard, Pedro, 66, 69
Galeotti, Vincenzo, 92
Gall, Hugues, 113, 114
Gallotta, Jean-Claude, 113
Garbo, Greta, 91
Gardel, Marie, 34, 36, 37
Gardel, Maximilien, 26-29, 31-33, 35
Gardel, Pierre, 26-28, 32-39, 42, 45, 82, 93, 95
Garnier, Charles, 59
Garnier, Jacques, 101, 113
Garrick, David, 25
Gaubert, Philippe, 75, 87, 88
Gautier, Théophile, 41, 48-50, 54, 55, 59, 62
Géricault, Théodore, 41
Gershwin, George, 96
Goija, Gaetano, 34
Glazunov, Alexandre, 105
Gluck, Christoph Willibald, 25, 79, 99
Goethe, Johann Wolfgang von, 115
Gosselin, Geneviève, 37, 40, 43
Gounod, Charles, 63, 64, 95
Goya, Francisco, 102
Grahn, Lucile, 49
Grantzow, Adèle, 57, 58
Grigorovich, Yuri, 100
Grimm brothers, 27
Grisi, Carlotta, 49-51, 53, 84
Gsovsky, Tatiana, 95
Gsovsky, Victor, 89
Guérin, Isabelle, 107, 108
Guerra, Nicola, 74, 75, 79, 82
Guillem, Sylvie, 106-108, 110
Guimard, Madeleine, 26, 27, 29, 32, 33, 35, 39, 40
Guiraud, Ernest, 59
Guizerix, Jean, 99, 100, 105, 106, 108, 110
Gyrowetz, Adalbert, 42

Habeneck, François Antoine, 42
Hahn, Reynaldo, 71

Halanzier, Olivier, 59, 61
Halévy, Jacques, 43
Handel, George Friderik, 19
Hansen, Joseph, 66-68
Haydn, Franz Joseph, 34, 109
Heine, Heinrich, 49
Heinel, Anne, 26-28
Henry, Louis, 38
Henry, Pierre, 107
Henze, Hans Werner, 99
Herold, Ferdinand, 42, 43
Hightower, Rosella, 102, 103, 105
Hilaire, Laurent, 107
Hilferding, Franz, 25
Hirsch, Georges, 89, 90
Hodson, Millicent, 110, 112
Homer, 113
Honegger, Arthur, 85, 86, 89
Howarth, Jessminn, 75
Hue, Georges, 78
Hugard, Jeanne, 73
Hugo, Victor, 41, 49

Ibert, Jacques, 79, 91
Indy, Vincent d', 75
Ives, Charles, 106

James, Henry, 106
Janáček, Leoš, 110
Jaques-Dalcroze, Emile, 75
Jeanmaire, Renée [Zizi], 89, 100
Johnsson, Anna, 74, 78
Jolivet, André, 89, 95
Joyce, James, 113
Jude, Charles, 100, 105, 108
Julia [de Varennes], 44

Kalidasa, 55
Kalioujny, Alexandre, 90, 92
Karsavina, Tamara, 70, 71, 81, 84
Kelly, Gene, 96
Kennedy, Jacqueline, 95
Khalfouni, Dominique, 100, 101
Kreutzer, Rodolphe, 37, 38
Kshessinskaya, Matilda, 69, 71, 82
Kylián, Jirí, 110

Labis, Attilio, 96
La Borde, 25
Lacotte, Pierre, 98, 99, 106
Lafon, Madeleine, 90, 92
La Fontaine, Jean de, 90, 92

La Fontaine, Mlle de, 9, 11, 79
Lalande, Michel Richard de, 73
Lalo, Édouard, 64
Lami, Eugène, 47
Lamartine, Alphonse de, 41
Lamballe, Lucienne, 84
Lambranzi, Gregorio, 110
Lancelot, Francine, 106
Lander, Harald, 92, 96
Landowski, Marcel, 101
Lany, Jean-Barthélémy, 20, 21, 25
Lany, Louise Madeleine, 20, 21
Larrieu, Daniel, 111
Laurencin, Marie, 76
La Valette, Marquis de, 48
Lazzini, Joseph, 108
Lefèvre, Brigitte, 101, 113
Legallois, Amélie, 44
Legat, Nicolai, 69, 71
Legnani, Pierina, 67
Legrée, Françoise, 108
Legris, Manuel, 107
Leleu, Jeanne, 91
L'Enclos, Ninon de, 11
Lenoir, 31
Lepeintre, Mlle, 9
Leroux, Gaston, 101
Leroux, Pauline, 49
Le Riche, Nicolas, 112, 115
Lesage, Alain-René, 47
Leskova, Tatiana, 109
L'Étang, Louis, 10
Letestu, Agnès, 114
Levinson, André, 74, 76, 78, 79, 82-84
Lifar, Serge, 80-93, 95, 96, 98, 106, 110, 112, 114
Ligeti, György, 103
Limón, José, 100, 108
Livry, Emma, 55, 56
Longfellow, Mrs, 46
Lorcia, Suzanne, 84, 87, 88
Lormeau, Jean-Yves, 102, 103, 108
Lormier, Paul, 44
Loucheur, Raymond, 92
Loudières, Monique, 108, 110
Louis XIV, King, 5-7, 9, 12, 13, 112
Louis XV, King, 13, 20
Louis XVI, King, 34
Louis XVIII, King 39
Louis-Philippe, King, 44
Lully, Jean-Baptiste, 6-10, 73, 78, 106
Lyonnois, Marie-Françoise, 20

MacMillan, Kenneth, 100, 106, 110
Mafleuret, Clotilde, 35
Mahler, Gustav, 100
Maillard, Marie-Thérèse, 35
Maine, Duchesse du, 24
Manet, Édouard, 65
Manzotti, Luigi, 64
Marie-Antoinette, Queen, 28, 31
Marie-Thérèse, Empress of Austria, 28
Marin, Maguy, 108
Mariquita, 70
Markévitch, Igor, 85
Martin, Frank, 97
Martinez, José, 114
Martinu, Bohuslav, 106
Massenet, Jules, 59, 65
Massine, Leonide, 72, 82, 83, 86, 93, 99, 109, 111
Mauri, Rosita, 64, 65, 67, 75
Maurin, Elisabeth, 108, 114
Maywood, Augusta, 49
Mazilier, Joseph, 45, 48-51, 53-56, 59, 65, 106
Méhul, Étienne, 34, 36
Mendelssohn, Felix, 103
Messager, André, 69, 71, 72
Mérante, Annette, 59
Mérante, Louis, 59, 62-66, 76, 79
Mérante, Zina, 59
Messiaen, Olivier, 97
Métra, Olivier, 85
Meyerbeer, Giacomo, 46
Milhaud, Darius, 85
Miller, Ernest, 34
Miller, Marie, see Gardel, Marie
Milon, Louis, 37-39, 42, 45
Minkus, Ludwig, 57, 99
Mitterand, President, 111
Molière, 7, 73, 91
Monplaisir, Hippolyte, 59
Montessu, Pauline, 43, 45
Monteverdi, Claudio, 73
Montoliu, Placido de, 75
Moreau, Jacqueline, 90
Morris, Mark, 109
Motte, Claire, 96, 97
Mozart, Wolfgang Amadeus, 113
Muravieva, Marfa, 57
Musset, Alfred de, 73
Mussorgsky, Modest, 69
Mustel, 64

Index

Nabokov, Nicolas, 84
Nabokov, Vladimir, 112
Napoleon I, 37, 38
Napoleon, III, 56
Nemchinova, Vera, 81
Neumeier, John, 102, 114
Nicolas II, Emperor of Russia, 54
Nijinska, Bronislava, 79, 81, 82, 110, 111
Nijinsky, Vaslav, 70-72, 79, 81, 84, 99, 105, 110, 112
Nikolais, Alwin, 101
Noblet, Lise, 42, 44, 45
Nourrit, Adolphe, 46
Noverre, Jean-Georges, 8, 14, 19, 21, 22, 31, 32, 35, 36, 93
Nuitter, Charles, 58, 62
Nureyev, Rudolf, 97, 99, 101, 102, 105-112, 114

Offenbach, Jacques, 56, 93
Orléans, Duc d', 13

Parmain, Martine, 97
Parsons, David, 108
Pasmanik, Rachel, 75
Patu, 15
Paul, 39, 42
Pavlova, Anna, 70, 74, 77, 78
Pécour, Louis, 10-12, 15, 17
Peretti, Serge, 78, 79, 82, 85, 87-90, 113
Perrin, Émile, 57
Perrin, Pierre, 7
Perrot, Jules, 45, 47, 49-51, 53, 56, 59, 65
Pertoldi, Erminia, 59
Petipa, Lucien, 49-51, 55-57, 65, 79
Petipa, Maria, 57
Petipa, Marius, 56, 57, 68, 84, 102, 105, 112
Petit, Roland, 89, 90, 97, 100, 101, 109, 111, 112, 115
Pierné, Gabriel, 76
Pietragalla, Marie-Claude, 108-110, 115
Piletta, Georges, 97, 100
Piollet, Wilfride, 97, 106
Piot, René, 73, 76
Platel, Elisabeth, 102, 105, 115
Pleyel, Ignaz, 34
Plisetskaya, Maya, 97
Pluque, Édouard, 65
Polyakov, Evgeni, 109, 110
Pontois, Noëlla, 97-100, 102, 103

Poulenc, Francis, 88
Poussin, Nicolas, 9
Preljocaj, Angelin, 113-115
Preobrajenska, Olga, 69, 71, 78, 79, 82
Prévost, Abbé, 29, 110
Prévost, Françoise, 12, 16, 17, 21, 24
Prokofiev, Sergei, 85, 91, 100, 103, 106, 107
Proust, Antonin, 66
Pruna, Pedro, 84, 86
Pugni, Cesare, 54
Purcell, Henry, 108
Pure, abbé de, 8
Pushkin, Alexandré, 72
Puvignée, Mlle, 20

Quinault, Robert, 89

Rameau, Jean-Philippe, 13, 14, 19, 20, 73, 74, 92
Raphael, 9
Ravel, Maurice, 73, 77, 95
Rayet, Jacqueline, 96
Rayne, Michel, 98
Rebel, Jean-Ferry, 16
Reichstadt, Duc de, 47
Renault, Michel, 82, 90-93
Reyer, Ernest, 55
Ricaux, Gustave, 82, 83
Riccoboni, François, 24
Rich, John, 18
Riisager, Knudåge, 92
Rimsky-Korsakov, Nicolai, 69
Ritz, Roger, 90
Robbins, Jerome, 99, 108, 110, 111, 114
Roland, Mlle, 9
Roland-Manuel, 79
Romanoff, Boris, 74
Roqueplan, Nestor, 45
Rosati, Carolina, 54, 55, 57
Rossini, Gioacchino, 91
Rota, Giuseppe, 56
Rouché, Jacques, 70, 74-83, 85, 87-89
Rousseau, Jean-Jacques, 29
Roussel, Albert, 87
Royer, Alphonse, 56
Rubinstein, Ida, 74, 75, 85

Saint-Georges, Jules Henri Vernoy de, 49-51
Saint-Léon, Arthur, 9, 53, 54, 56-59, 62, 65, 66, 79

Saint-Pierre, Bernardin de, 37
Saint-Saëns, Camille, 70
Sallé, Marie, 16, 18-20, 24, 55
Salvioni, Guglielmina, 57
Samuel-Rousseau, Marcel, 86
Sangalli, Rita, 59, 61-65
Sartre, Jean-Paul, 107
Sauguet, Henri, 90, 96
Saulnier, Victoire, 34
Scarlatti, Alessandro, 87
Schaufuss, Peter, 101
Schmitt, Florent, 75, 86
Schmucki, Norbert, 99
Schneitzhoeffer, Jean, 46, 98
Schönberg, Arnold, 112

Schwarz, Jeanne, 77-78
Schwarz, Solange, 79, 84, 86-89
Schubert, Franz, 92
Scribe, Eugène, 42, 43
Second, Albéric, 46
Semyonova, Marina, 86
Sergeyev, Nicolai, 78
Shakespeare, William, 41, 102, 203
Shaw, George Bernard, 73
Skibine, George, 95, 96
Smithson, Harriet, 48
Spessivtseva, Olga, 78, 79, 81, 83, 84, 86
Spoerli, Heinz, 102
Staats, Leo, 69-71, 73, 74, 76-79, 82, 85
Stanislavsky, Konstantin, 73
Stepanov, Vladimir, 78
Stichel, Thérèse, 71
Stowitts, Hubert, 77
Strauss, Johann, 112
Strauss, Richard, 112
Stravinsky, Igor, 71, 90, 91, 99, 106, 114
Subligny, Marie-Thérèse, 11
Subra, Julia, 63, 67
Svoboda, Josef, 100
Szyfer, J.-E., 86

Taglioni, Filippo, 45-48, 98
Taglioni, Marie, 40, 43-51, 53, 55, 56, 59, 76, 98
Tallchief, Maria, 89, 90
Tallchief, Marjorie, 95
Taras, John, 97
Taylor, Paul, 106, 109
Tchaikovsky, Pyotr Illyich, 62, 64, 90, 99, 109
Tetley, Glen, 99

Tharp, Twyla, 109, 110
Théodore, Mlle, 31, 32
Thesmar, Ghislaine, 98
Tomasi, Henri, 87
Torelli, Giocomo, 6
Toumanova, Tamara, 79, 89-91
Trefilova, Vera, 69, 82
Trouhanova, Natalia, 73, 77

Valéry, Paul, 74
Vanara, 68
Van Dantzig, Rudi, 108
Van Dyk, Peter, 91, 92
Vaussard, Christiane, 90, 91, 93
Vasquez, Michel, 66, 67
Vaucorbeil, Auguste Emmanuel, 64
Verdi, Giuseppe, 114
Verdy, Violette, 100
Véron, Louis, 44, 46-48
Veronese, Paolo, 9
Vestris, Auguste, 26, 27, 31, 34, 36-38, 45, 47, 75
Vestris, Gaétan, 21, 22, 25-29, 32
Vidal, Paul, 67, 72
Viganò, Salvatore, 34
Vigarani, Carlo, 6
Vismes, de 31
Vivaldi, Antonio, 114
Vladimirov, Pierre, 83
Vlassi, Christiane, 97
Volinine, Alexander, 82
Voltaire (François-Marie-Arouët), 18, 29
Vu An, Éric, 107, 109
Vulpian, Claude de, 101, 102, 108, 110
Vyroubova, Nina, 91, 92, 95

Wagner, Richard, 66, 71,
Washington, George, 31
Weaver, John, 18, 24
Webern, Anton, 112
Widor, Charles, 64

Zambelli, Carlotta, 63, 67, 68, 70-72, 74-79, 82, 90, 92
Zucchi, Virginia, 63, 67